Learning Responsive Web Design

A Beginner's Guide

Clarissa Peterson

D1053465

O'REILLY®   Beijing · Cambridge · Farnham · Köln · Sebastopol · Tokyo

Learning Responsive Web Design
by Clarissa Peterson

Printed in the United States of America.

Published by O'Reilly Media, Inc.,
1005 Gravenstein Highway North, Sebastopol, CA 95472.

O'Reilly books may be purchased for educational, business, or sales
promotional use. Online editions are also available for most titles (*safari.
oreilly.com*). For more information, contact our corporate/institutional
sales department: (800) 998-9938 or *corporate@oreilly.com*.

Editor: Mary Treseler
Production Editor: Kara Ebrahim
Copyeditor: Jasmine Kwityn
Proofreader: Rachel Head
Indexer: Angela Howard

Cover Designer: Randy Comer
Interior Designers: Ron Bilodeau and
Monica Kamsvaag
Illustrator: Rebecca Demarest
Compositor: Kara Ebrahim

June 2014: First Edition.

Revision History for the First Edition:

2014-05-30	First release
2014-07-14	Second release

See *http://www.oreilly.com/catalog/errata.csp?isbn=0636920029199*
for release details.

ISBN: 978-1-4493-6294-2

[LSI]

[Contents]

[*Preface*]

When the iPhone was introduced in 2007, it was a turning point for web design. All of a sudden web designers lost control of the canvas on which we designed websites. Previously, websites only had to work on monitor screens, which varied in size, but not all that much. How were we supposed to make our websites work on these tiny little screens?

For a while we made mobile websites, optimized for the size of an iPhone screen, that were separate from our "regular" websites. Two sites to maintain wasn't that bad, but soon there were many phones of varying sizes, and then tablets, and smaller tablets, and eventually we realized we couldn't make separate sites for each of the possible screens that our websites could be viewed on.

We needed a solution that would work on all screen sizes, a way to design websites that could adapt to the screens they were being displayed on.

It took a while, and a lot of different ideas, before one stuck. *Responsive web design* is a method of designing websites that are flexible, that don't rely on a fixed screen size, and that are also able to detect the size of the screen and adjust the design to provide an optimal viewing experience for that device. Ethan Marcotte first wrote about responsive web design (*http://alistapart.com/article/responsive-web-design*) in *A List Apart* in 2010.

Like any other new technique, responsive web design had a rocky start. Many people continued to argue—and some still do—that we needed to create separate websites for mobile phones. But with the proliferation of devices on the market today, it's clear that we can't rely on one model of mobile phone to be our design target; we have to be able to accommodate all of these devices, with screens at pretty much every measurement you can imagine.

And responsive design has grown, too. It's no longer just about adapting to screen sizes, but also adapting to the capabilities of different devices, such as touchscreens, retina displays, and slow connections.

As of 2014, 58% of American adults own a smartphone—a phone with an operating system like iOS, Android, or Windows Phone that is feature-rich and allows the user full access to the Web.[1] And 35% of American adults own a tablet.[2] We have amazing devices, and responsive design helps us take full advantage of the Web.

However, although the majority of American adults have smartphones, 32% of those polled have a mobile phone that's *not* a smartphone. Many of those people use their phones to access the Web using browsers with limited capabilities that may not be able to display all websites as intended. Responsive web design is a solution for that too.

A responsive website *starts* with a simple, content-focused design that doesn't rely on advanced Cascading Style Sheets (CSS) or JavaScript and can be displayed on essentially any web-connected device. Using *progressive enhancement*, the responsive website builds on that, creating a design that is optimized for the size of the screen it's displayed on and for the capabilities of the device. So the *feature phones*—the older phones with limited capabilities—get only what they can use, while newer devices get a rich design and interface that fits nicely on the screen and that takes advantage of the features of these devices.

Responsive web design allows us to present the best website possible to all users, regardless of the devices they use. The Web needs to be available to everybody, and responsive design is how we can do that.

Creating a responsive website isn't just a matter of learning some new bits of code. It's about reexamining the way we think about websites, focusing on the experience of the user, and making sure that the content and functionality are not afterthoughts to the design.

---

1 For the full report, see Susannah Fox and Lee Rainie, "The Web at 25 in the U.S.," Pew Research Internet Project, February 27, 2014 (*http://www.pewinternet.org/2014/02/27/the-web-at-25-in-the-u-s/*).

2 For more information, see Lee Rainie and Aaron Smith, "Tablet and E-reader Ownership Update," Pew Research Internet Project, October 18, 2013 (*http://www.pewinternet.org/2013/10/18/tablet-and-e-reader-ownership-update/*).

We also have to change the way we work on websites, moving to a more collaborative process involving designers, developers, and other team members.

There *are* some new bits of code to learn—but responsive design is not a new programming language. Creating a responsive website requires only HTML, CSS, and sometimes a little bit of JavaScript. If you already know how to make websites, much of what you read in this book will be familiar to you. You'll need to keep in mind that when creating a responsive website, 90% of what you do is the same as what you do when creating a nonresponsive website. But besides adding on a few new techniques, you need to get the basics right, using properly structured, standards-compliant markup (HTML and CSS). Without that strong foundation, you can't have confidence that your site will work correctly and display properly across devices.

If you work on websites—whether you're a web designer, developer, content strategist, UX designer, website manager, IT director, or any of the other myriad of jobs that are involved in creating and maintaining websites—this book will show you how responsive design works, how you can adapt your work processes for responsive design, and how to create responsive websites that will provide an optimal design and user experience for any device.

How This Book Is Organized

The book is divided into four parts.

We start with Part I, "Foundations of Responsive Design," which explains what responsive design is and how it differs from other approaches to web design. We'll also look at creating flexible content that will work well on responsive sites.

Then Part II, "Creating Responsive Websites," outlines the basics of putting together a responsive site. We'll look at a few parts of HTML and CSS that are essential to making your site work correctly. Then we'll dive into media queries, the heart of responsive design, and finally we'll take a look at how to handle images on responsive websites.

Next, Part III, "Working Responsively," looks at responsive workflow, the step-by-step process for creating a responsive site, starting from the project kickoff meeting and continuing all the way to the site launch. We'll then go into a little more depth and look at responsive design from a user experience perspective, examining how to make sure your site works with various input methods, such as touch, and how to make sure it functions well for all users, including those using assistive technology.

Finally, Part IV, "Designing Responsive Websites," delves into some of the design elements that need special consideration for responsive websites. We'll start with typography, which is key to making sure your content is readable across screen sizes. Then we'll look at how to code responsive navigation and page headers. Finally, we'll talk about performance, a big issue with responsive design, as we try to make sites with reasonable load times even for users on slow connections.

Who Should Read This Book

This book is for anyone who works with websites. The material is presented in a way that is accessible to everyone, regardless of experience level.

If you're a developer who is already very familiar with HTML and CSS, some of this material will already be familiar to you—remember that much of responsive design is the same as nonresponsive web design. But there are also things that are different in responsive design. If you don't have any experience with this approach, this book will get you started with the basics, and also give you an overview of the design aspects of responsive design.

If you've never worked with HTML and CSS, you'll get to see all of the code necessary for putting together a responsive site, and an explanation of how it works. However, this book is not meant to be an introduction to HTML or CSS, so each concept is covered fairly quickly without a lot of detail. If you want to learn HTML and CSS, you should refer to other books and resources that cover them in more depth. But if you don't actually write code for your job and just want to understand how responsive design works, this book will tell you what you need to know.

If you're somewhere in the middle, the book will remind you of everything that goes together to make a website, and show you what's different in responsive design. You'll see not only the code, but also the design considerations and the theory behind how responsive design works.

How to Contact Us

Please address comments and questions concerning this book to the publisher:

O'Reilly Media, Inc.
1005 Gravenstein Highway North
Sebastopol, CA 95472
800-998-9938 (in the United States or Canada)
707-829-0515 (international or local)
707-829-0104 (fax)

We have a web page for this book, where we list errata, examples, and any additional information. You can access this page at:

http://oreil.ly/learn-rwd

There is also a companion website to this book (*http://www.learning rwd.com*) where you can download all of the code samples used.

To comment or ask technical questions about this book, send email to:

bookquestions@oreilly.com

For more information about our books, courses, conferences, and news, see our website at *http://www.oreilly.com*.

Find us on Facebook: *http://facebook.com/oreilly*

Follow us on Twitter: *http://twitter.com/oreillymedia*

Watch us on YouTube: *http://www.youtube.com/oreillymedia*

Acknowledgments

A ton of thanks to Scott Berkun. His talk at An Event Apart Seattle in 2012 inspired me to quit my cubicle job so I could move on to better things. Reading Scott's book *Confessions of a Public Speaker* (O'Reilly) got me started giving talks on responsive design, which opened up a lot of opportunities for me. And Scott also got me going down the book-writing path by offering encouragement and advice, and then by introducing me to his editor at O'Reilly, who became my editor for this book. Without Scott, I would almost certainly still be unhappily sitting in a cubicle somewhere, and you would not be reading this book.

Thanks to Mary Treseler and everybody else at O'Reilly who was involved along the way.

While I was writing this book, I got married and also moved to a new country. My husband, A.J. Kandy, has been incredibly patient with me as I muddled through trying to write a book in the middle of these major life changes. I am so lucky to have married the most wonderful man in the world.

Of course a huge thank you to Ethan Marcotte, without whom there would not be responsive design for me to write a book about.

Thanks to Matt Bradley for teaching me HTML a long time ago.

A few people went out of their way to help get me moving in the right direction in my career, and I'm extremely grateful for their help: Dan Brown, Jeffrey Zeldman, Vera Rhoads, and Cory Lebson.

And thanks to the many other people who helped me out with encouragement and/or advice along the way: Theresa Amato, Melissa Ballowe, Chuck Borowicz, Erica Ciesielski Chaikin, Glennette Clark, Sibyl Edwards, Veronica Erb, Brad Frost, Robert Hoekman, Jr., Tim Kadlec, Dave Mankoff, Karen McGrane, Jeff Popovich, Chris Schmitt, Jared Spool, Anna Storkson, Sandy Tetreault, Estelle Weyl, and of course, my parents.

Thanks to all the Meetups and other groups that let me come talk to them about responsive design. I had a great time driving around the Northeast and Midwest and meeting so many wonderful people. Hopefully there will be many more trips in my future, as I have a lot more people to meet.

Part I

Foundations of Responsive Design

[1]

What Is Responsive Design?

By now pretty much everybody in the web world has heard of responsive web design (often referred to as *RWD*), but a surprising number don't have a good understanding of what it is.

In this chapter, you'll learn the basics of what it means for a website to be responsive. After that, we'll go through a little of the history of web design, so you can understand where the idea of responsive design came from and how it compares to the old way of doing things.

We'll also look at why responsive design is usually the best choice for making websites that will work well across different devices and screen sizes, and how it means less work in the long run. We'll also look at a less obvious effect of choosing responsive design: how it impacts your search engine rankings.

Just the Basics

If you picked up this book because you've heard of responsive design, but you're not quite sure what it is, this section will help you understand the basics.

Even if you're somewhat experienced with responsive design, you've probably found that it can be difficult to explain it to others without using overly technical language. This section will give you a better idea of how to explain responsive design to users, to clients, to less technical team members, or to your mom, who wonders what it is you get paid to do all day.

Responsive design, overall, is a way to make websites that can be easily viewed and used on any type of device and size of screen, all the way from the smallest mobile phones up to the widest desktop monitors.

The easiest way to explain it is to compare responsive websites to sites that are not responsive, and look at how each type of site is viewed on smartphones.

Imagine you're using your smartphone to view a fixed-width website—that is, a site that is designed to always display at a set width, such as 960 pixels. You'll see the entire website just as it appears on your desktop monitor, but it will initially be displayed at a tiny size to fit on the screen. You'll have to continually zoom in and out to read text and navigate through the site, as you can see in Figure 1-1. It's a lot of extra work.

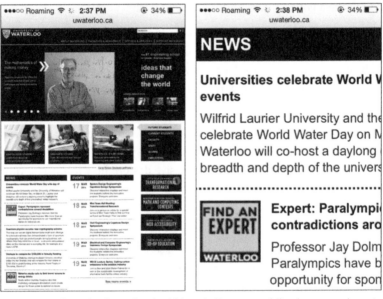

Figure 1-1. When viewing a fixed-width website on a mobile phone, you have to zoom in to see the text at a readable size.

And then for some websites, there is a mobile website that is separate from the regular desktop site. This type of site displays at full size when you load it on your smartphone (no zooming necessary), but you'll notice that it's often very different from the same website when you view it on your desktop monitor—there's often a lot of content missing, so the site owner can cut down on the work involved in maintaining multiple versions of the site.

And because mobile sites are usually made for one specific device size, like an iPhone, if you have a different device, the website may not fit on the screen so well.

Separate mobile websites are generally optimized to work on one size of device, but there are many different devices on the market, and building a mobile site to work on one device can mean leaving behind all the users who have different devices.

As an example, Ikea has a separate mobile website optimized to fit on phones of a certain size. In Figure 1-2, the navigation for the Ikea desktop site is at the top. On the bottom left is the site on an iPad, and the bottom right shows the site on an iPhone.

Figure 1-2. The Ikea desktop site (at the top) is the same as what you see on an iPad (bottom left), while the iPhone gets a special mobile website (bottom right).

The three screenshots are to scale, so you can compare the sizes of everything you see on the screen. Viewing the mobile site on the iPhone, you only have a few navigation links, but they're a similar size to the links on the desktop site. But on the iPad you don't get the mobile site, you get the desktop site, and everything is really tiny to fit on that small screen. You'll have to do a lot of zooming to use the site.

Ikea put a lot of work into creating a good mobile site, but if your device is a tablet, you don't get to use it, and you get a suboptimal experience. If Ikea had a responsive site, it could make sure that people using any size device would get an appropriate interface.

With responsive design, there is only one version of the website, so you get all the content, but the design *rearranges* itself so that it fits perfectly on any size screen, with full-size text so you don't have to zoom in and out, as you can see in Figure 1-3.

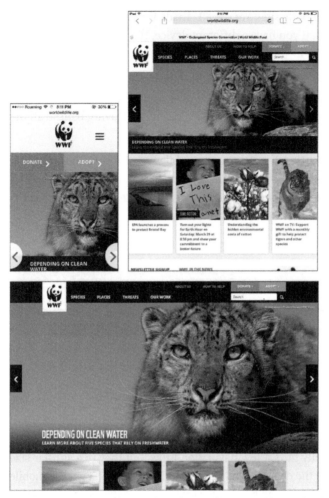

Figure 1-3. A responsive site viewed on a phone, a tablet, and a desktop monitor.

There are a lot more technical details (which we'll cover later in the book), but from the user's perspective, the key to describing a responsive site is that things can change size and move around to fit on the screen.

A Short History

Before learning where responsive design came from, it's helpful to know a little of the history of web design.

FIXED-WIDTH DESIGN

Up until the last few years, websites were designed so they would fit well on the most common sizes of desktop and laptop screens. In 2000, that meant designing for a screen width of 800 pixels (a *pixel* is a tiny dot of colored light on the screen); by the mid-2000s, most displays were 1,024 pixels wide.

Although most monitors were one of only a few fixed sizes, there were some much wider monitors on the market, and also some older, narrower monitors still in use. Web designers wanted their designs to look exactly the same no matter what monitor was being used, so they would usually create designs of a fixed width to fit on the most common monitor size, such as 960-pixel-wide sites to fit easily on 1,024-pixel-wide screens. Wider screens would simply display the sites with empty space (called *whitespace* in design terms) filling the extra space on either side of the design, as you see in Figure 1-4.

Figure 1-4. The fixed-width MSN site is the same width on any size screen, leaving whitespace on each side when the screen is wider than the site.

These fixed-width designs are actually still fairly common.

The ideas of *fluid design* and *liquid layout* gained some traction in the early 2000s. These techniques used percentage-based widths to allow a web page's design to flow to fit the width of the screen, so it could take advantage of the available space on wider screens. Although this sounded good in theory, giving up control of the design meant you could end up with super-long line lengths and weird column divisions on wide screens, leading most web designers to stick to easier-to-handle fixed-width designs.

MOBILE WEB BROWSING

When mobile phones with Internet access first became available in the mid-1990s, they generally didn't even have the capability to display actual websites, and instead provided only data that could be displayed in text, such as weather forecasts, stock reports, and sports scores. The first mobile browsers could only display basic HTML, often in grayscale rather than color. It wasn't until the mid-2000s that mobile browsers were able to display "real" web pages using technologies like CSS2 and JavaScript, on more advanced devices referred to as *smartphones*, such as the iPhone in Figure 1-5.

Figure 1-5. The iPhone 4S.

The iPhone, which came out in 2007, was a game changer. It had a beautiful interface that could take advantage of all the current web technologies to display web pages as they'd be seen on a full-size monitor.

Although touchscreen devices had been around for years, the iPhone was one of the first mobile devices with *multi-touch*, a technology that allows the device to recognize more than one simultaneous point of contact with the screen—necessary for browsing behavior we now take for granted, such as pinch-to-zoom.

All of this led the iPhone to be continually referred to as one of the most innovative products of that year—but there was a problem. Web pages were designed to be viewed on full-size monitors, not on tiny phones, so pretty much every web page was 960 pixels or wider. The iPhone's screen, on the other hand, was only 320 pixels wide. Apple's solution was to automatically shrink web pages to fit inside the viewing area of the screen (the *viewport*), and then allow the user to tap or pinch to zoom in on any area of the page.

But viewing little pieces of a page does not make for a good user experience.

Web designers knew that this was not an optimal way for people to use the Web, and that they would need to find a way to make web pages that were easier to view on the iPhone's small screen.

MOBILE WEBSITES

Because designers were accustomed to making web pages with fixed widths, the easiest and most obvious solution was to simply make separate mobile websites with a fixed page width that would fit on a 320-pixel-wide screen, instead of the common 1,024-pixel-wide monitor, as in Figure 1-6.

Users were often automatically redirected to the mobile version of the site if they were using a mobile phone. Otherwise, they could choose to go to the mobile website by clicking a link, or by visiting the site via a different URL, commonly using an *m* subdomain (such as *http://m. sprint.com*). This practice led these separate mobile sites to be referred to as *m-dot websites*.

Of course, this meant extra work for the web team, but they usually made the job easier by making the mobile site a stripped-down version of the regular website with only a small portion of the content, as in Figure 1-6.

Figure 1-6. The desktop version and the mobile version of *The Washington Post* website.

Their justification—that mobile phones were only used "on the go" or for certain basic activities—was probably true for most users at that point. But as mobile phones became more ubiquitous, people started to use these devices for more and more tasks that they had previously done only on their desktop or laptop computers.

MORE DEVICES

Having an "iPhone website," as they were often called, worked out okay in the early days, as for a while the iPhone was the only major player in the smartphone market. But that didn't last long. Other mobile phone companies soon jumped on the bandwagon and came out with their responses to the iPhone.

But these new smartphones were not all the same size. Compared to the iPhone's 320-pixel width, many had screens that were narrower (240 pixels or less), and others had screens wider than the iPhone's—especially those designed to be used with the screen held horizontally instead of vertically. A 320-pixel-wide iPhone website didn't fit perfectly on all those screens.

So web designers started trying to find a solution: how can we make websites that work on any size screen? There wasn't an easy answer.

Then, in 2010, Apple released the iPad. Again, this was a game changer. Mobile websites were too small to take advantage of the iPad's much larger screen, but desktop-sized fixed-width sites were too big to be easily viewed in portrait mode on an iPad.

Although some designers reacted by creating separate iPad websites (so now they had three separate websites), most realized that as more and more device sizes arrived on the market, it was no longer sustainable to create separate websites for every possible screen size.

MEDIA QUERIES

The web design community again came back to the concept of fluid layouts, using percentage-based widths, and tried to figure out how to make that into a solution for smaller, mobile devices.

Using percentages instead of pixels allows a web page and sections of the page to change width to fit in any screen size, so accounting for differences among similar-sized devices is easy.

But once you look at the entire range of devices, you have a problem. Narrowing a three-column design into a smartphone width makes the columns of text too narrow to be readable. Likewise, a one-column layout that looks good on a smartphone screen would be too wide to easily read when viewed on a desktop monitor.

Essentially, the problem was this: without having to create separate sites, how can a website be displayed in one column on narrow screens and multiple columns on wider screens? How can you ask the browser to make changes to the design, based on qualities of the device the site is being viewed on?

Enter media queries.

The CSS @*media* rule, which allows you to display different CSS styles based on device qualities, was actually part of CSS2 more than a decade ago, but back then it only supported queries of media *types*, such as screen or print. This was commonly used for creating a print version of a website's design (which may include changes as basic as removing background colors that will waste printer ink), but its utility stopped there.

It wasn't until CSS3 that the *specification* (i.e., a formal and detailed description of how something is required to work) for media queries allowed more precise queries based on media (device) features, such as width, height, and color capability. Media queries don't affect the HTML (the actual content and structure of the underlying page)—they only affect the styles that are applied to the page using CSS. Browsers started to support CSS3 media queries around 2009.

So what do these media queries do?

As a basic example, let's say we have a website with two separate sections of content. We might create a single-column design that fits well on smartphones, displaying the two sections stacked vertically. On wider screens, we may want to display the two sections of content as two separate columns, next to each other.

Using a media query, we can ask the device how wide its screen is. Then we can tell it to display the content in two columns only if its screen is wide enough for the columns to fit nicely.

To code this, we simply start out with CSS that will display the contents in one column. Then we add a CSS media query that asks if the screen is 40 ems or wider (you'll learn about ems in Chapter 4; 40 ems is slightly narrower than the width of a typical tablet, but you could specify any width in the media query).

Inside the media query, we add the CSS that will display the content in two columns instead of one. The browser will only use this CSS if the media query is true (i.e., if the screen is 40 ems or wider). If the screen is narrower, it ignores this CSS and the content remains in one column.

Thus, we can give our website a different layout for different screen sizes, without having to create separate websites.

By using media queries, we can change any aspect of the website's style, not just the number of columns. Media queries can be used to move things around, change the text size, hide or display pieces of content, adjust margins and spacing, and adjust any other style that can be applied with CSS.

FLEXIBILITY

Media queries can rearrange your layout, but responsive design wouldn't work without a foundation of flexibility.

For starters, pretty much every horizontal measurement on your site needs to be in flexible units rather than inflexible pixels. This means the width of columns and other layout elements will be in percentages, and the text will be measured in a relative unit called an *em*.

Sizing images on the page works a little bit differently, because you don't necessarily want them to change size depending on the width of the screen—you want photos large enough to see ample detail, as long as there's room on the screen. The problem is that depending on the size of the device's screen, there may not always be room to display an image at full size. You'll need to make sure that the image won't be cut off if it doesn't fit. In Chapter 6 we'll look at a CSS trick that will make sure images always fit in the space where we put them.

RESPONSIVE WEB DESIGN

Neither of these ideas—media queries or flexibility—was new or groundbreaking by itself. But in 2010, web designer Ethan Marcotte figured out a way to use these concepts together to make websites that would respond to different screen sizes.

Marcotte coined the term *responsive web design* and first wrote about it in an article for *A List Apart* (*http://alistapart.com/article/responsive-web-design*) in in 2010, and followed that with the book *Responsive Web Design* (*http://www.abookapart.com/products/responsive-web-design*) in 2011.

Why Responsive Design

The concept of responsive web design has been hotly debated since it was first introduced. Like any new technology idea, some people embraced it and others dismissed it.

GETTING THE RIGHT DESIGN ON EVERY DEVICE

The most compelling reason for using responsive design is that you will be creating a website that not only will look good and work correctly on the devices that are on the market now, but is likely to look good and work correctly on any new devices that will be available in the future.

In addition, with responsive design you don't run the risk that users will be viewing the mobile version of a site on their desktop monitors, or vice versa.

If you have separate websites, this can definitely be an issue, whether you use *device detection* to send the correct version of the site to each device or you use a separate set of URLs (such as an m-dot subdomain) to serve a mobile site.

Sites that have a separate mobile version commonly use device detection (which happens on the website's server before the page is displayed) to determine which version of a web page (mobile or desktop) should be sent to any particular device. That way, each page on the site will only have one URL, although there are actually two separate versions with different HTML. However, this process is not 100% accurate, and sometimes the incorrect version of the page will be sent. Additionally, the device detection process can increase the load time of the page.

Using a different URL for your separate mobile site (i.e., an m-dot site) is easier to implement, but it relies on the user to get to the correct version of the site. With links being passed back and forth between users via social media or email, getting to the correct version of a page will often add an extra burden on the users—or sometimes they won't have the option at all.

For example, if a desktop user emails a link from *The New York Times* to a mobile user, the mobile user will get a message at the top of the screen letting her know that there's a mobile version of the site, as in Figure 1-7. Nice, but it requires extra work by the user, and extra time for the user to click and then load a totally separate page.

Figure 1-7. Visiting a link from the desktop version of *The New York Times* gets you the desktop site with a message that a mobile site is available.

On the other hand, if I'm visiting *The New York Times* mobile site on my phone and I email a link to an article to someone who opens that link on a desktop computer, they get what you see in Figure 1-8: a mobile-optimized page, with no clear way to go to the full desktop website. The user can read the article, but he'll have to click to see full-size versions of any images, and he won't see a lot of the supplemental links and recommended articles that are on the desktop version of the site.

Figure 1-8. Clicking a link from the mobile version of *The New York Times* gets you the mobile version of the page, even if you're on a desktop computer.

With responsive design, you only have one web page, so you'll never get the "wrong version." The site will be displayed correctly no matter what device it's being viewed on.

LESS WORK

The most obvious advantage to using responsive design is that you only have to create one website, one design, one set of code, and one set of content.

If you have a separate mobile-only version of your site, you will have to create and maintain two (or more) entirely separate sets of HTML. Changes will need to be made on each site, and even if you're trying to keep them the same, there will almost certainly be issues and something will end up not matching. Although using a content management system (CMS) or templating system may make the work easier, there is more code and content to maintain, and more things that can potentially break.

With a responsive site, you only have one set of content, and it will be displayed appropriately no matter what the screen size is. Future design adjustments can be made by making changes to the stylesheet.

For someone who is inexperienced with responsive design, the initial task of creating a responsive website (as you learn how everything works) may take more effort than creating a fixed-width site, but in the long term you will have less work to do maintaining the website.

OPTIMIZED FOR SEARCH

A separate mobile site, with a separate set of URLs, can create issues with your site's placement in search results.

If you have two separate versions of a page with the same or similar content but different URLs (i.e., *http://www.example.com* and *http://m.example.com*), search engines need to know that they are considered to be the same page so that the page can be indexed correctly and displayed as one entry in the search results listing.

Although this is possible using JavaScript or code on your server, it's a bit complicated, and if you fail to do it correctly you may end up with both versions of a page appearing in search results, confusing users. It can also negatively affect your search ranking.

Google has recommended responsive design for smartphone-optimized websites since 2012, not only because it creates a better experience for users but also because it allows Google's site crawler to retrieve your content more efficiently, which means changes to your site will likely be updated in search results more quickly.

Bing recommends using a method that results in only one set of URLs, but hasn't specifically endorsed responsive design as a way to do that.

Summary

Until responsive design was introduced, websites were generally *fixed-width*, which meant the website's design was the same width no matter what size screen it was displayed on. When smartphones came along, that really didn't work, because websites appeared tiny on the small screens and users had to continually zoom in and out to read anything.

Mobile websites followed soon after, and many companies built these second websites separately from their main, or desktop, websites. Mobile websites often contained only a fraction of the content and functionality available on regular websites, so mobile users missed out.

As more devices came along, designers soon realized that it was impractical, if not impossible, to create multiple websites to fit each of the different screen sizes. The concept of responsive design was introduced as a way to make websites that could respond to the width of a device's screen and display the site's content in a way that was appropriate for that screen size.

Responsive web design consists of two main components: flexibility, which means that horizontal measurements need to use relative units like percentages so they can respond to the size of the screen, and media queries, which allow you to use CSS to change the design of the website depending on the width of the device's screen.

Responsive design allows you to provide an appropriate design for any screen size using only one set of code. Not having to maintain separate sets of code means less work. And implementing a responsive design means that your site will be optimized for search.

Next, in Chapter 2, we'll talk about why content is important and how to make sure you're designing content that works well on responsive websites.

[2]

Responsive Content

If you think that HTML and CSS are the most important parts of a website, it's worth looking at it from a different perspective. Users are coming to your website for the content (and functionality), not to admire the designer's talent or the developer's coding skills.

Your website's users don't care if your site is responsive, and most of them probably don't even know what "responsive web design" means. They aren't thinking about whether they're using the appropriate device for the site, or whether their screen is going to be the right size. They often don't even care what your website looks like. They just want to easily get to the information or functionality they need, on whatever device that they happen to have.

That's why, when you're designing a website, you should think about your content first.

If you do it the other way around—create a design and try to fit your content in around it—your content will always be stuck in second-class status, and you are less likely to give your users what they need.

With responsive websites, you need to think about content first, so you can make sure your content will work well on small screens. If you're using existing content from a fixed-width website, you're going to have a difficult time trying to shoehorn it into a layout for a smaller screen. If you're starting from scratch with new content, you need to make sure it is optimized for any screen size, not just one screen size.

Content Strategy

The phrase "content strategy" has been getting a lot of attention in the last few years, especially after Kristina Halvorson's book *Content Strategy for the Web* (New Riders) was published in 2009.

Before that, it was uncommon for companies to talk about having content strategies for their websites. When we talked about content for the Web, it was in the context of creating it, to fill all the spaces on our websites that needed to be filled with content.

And really, we often created sites without thinking about strategy at all. If our company or project needed a website, we would first design a site that looked nice and matched our branding. Next, we made a list of all the stuff we had that we wanted to put on the site (content), and then we tried to fit all of our stuff into the newly designed site.

If we were lucky, we had an *information architect* who created a nice structure to organize all of our content. If not, it just all got stuck in there somehow. Whatever content we had ended up on the website somewhere. After all, it costs very little to make a website bigger (more content and more pages) from a technical standpoint, so why not just put everything on the site, so it will always be available in case somebody needs it, forever and ever?

But then at some point we realized that it *matters* what's on our websites.

The content strategy refers to everything that goes into both planning and managing your content. This includes the text, as well as other forms of communication like pictures, video, and audio. And it's not just about what goes on your site, but also about how the site functions.

Start by looking at the big picture. What should the website accomplish? What do you want users to do when they visit the website? What's a successful user interaction? How does the website support your business or project goals? How will user needs be satisfied?

Developing a content strategy takes work, but your finished website will be much better if you're talking about the content *before* you create the visual design, rather than *after*.

For more information on content strategy, consult the following resources:

- *Content Strategy for the Web, Second Edition* (http://contentstrategy.com/) by Kristina Halvorson and Melissa Rach (New Riders)

- *Content Strategy for Mobile* (http://www.abookapart.com/products/content-strategy-for-mobile) by Karen McGrane (A Book Apart)

- Brad Shorr's *Smashing Magazine* article, "Content Strategy Within the Design Process" (*http://uxdesign.smashingmagazine.com/2011/12/02/content-strategy-within-design-process/*)

[NOTE]

Not sure of the differences between "content strategy," "content marketing," "content governance," and all the other content-related buzzwords? Check out Melissa Rach's *UX Magazine* article, "Content Strategy and Its Cousins" (*http://uxmag.com/articles/content-strategy-and-its-cousins*).

MOBILE CONTENT STRATEGY?

Recently, because everybody's been focusing on how to make websites that work on mobile devices, the term "mobile content strategy" has come into vogue. Content strategy is definitely important, so mobile content strategy must be super-important, right?

Not quite so fast.

Remember, there's no longer a hard-and-fast line between mobile and nonmobile devices. And as you've learned so far in this book, our goal is to create websites that works across all devices, regardless of whether they're mobile devices or not.

So you don't need a separate mobile content strategy. In fact, a mobile content strategy is often the same thing as a regular web content strategy, except you *stop ignoring mobile.*

You need to continue everything you've been doing as part of a solid content strategy, but keep in mind that users will be accessing your content from a wide range of devices and in a wide range of contexts— you need to make sure your strategy is not leaving them out.

Producing content that works as well on mobile as it does on desktop-sized computers gives you a new set of challenges that you may not have previously considered. Make sure you're considering them now.

Managing Content

As you're designing a responsive website, you're probably starting out with a pile of potential content: either what was on your old website, pieces of offline content, or just ideas of what should go on the site.

The first thing you need to do is think about what to do with all this content.

USE ONLY WHAT YOU NEED

First: you need far less content than you think you do.

Stay away from the idea that you should put *everything* on your website, just in case somebody might need any particular piece of content. Sure, online storage is so incredibly inexpensive these days that we pretty much think of it as free, but there are definite costs to all of the content you put on your site.

The first cost is to the user. The more content that's on your website, the more content the user needs to sort through and pass by to get to the content she is looking for.

Sure, some of it may be of interest if she happens to encounter it on your site, but much of it is not. Really, does anyone need to see the past 10 years' worth of press releases your company has issued?

Unnecessary pages on your website will clutter up the navigation and search results. Unnecessary content on a page will force the user to scroll more. The more unnecessary things there are in the way, the harder it is for the user to find what he needs, and the more likely he will give up before he finds it.

The second cost is to the website owner, who needs to devote additional resources to keeping track of all the content, organizing and reorganizing it, keeping it updated, and continually checking for broken links. The more content that's on your site, the more likely it is that some of it will be outdated or incorrect—a potential liability if you're giving out wrong information. You can't just add content to your site and leave it there: it does need to be maintained.

The best time to pare down your content is before you start designing a new site, or before you start redesigning your existing site. The design process will be easier with less content, and you'll have to do less work while building the site.

HOW TO PARE DOWN

When determining what to keep, think about both your business goals and user needs.

For example, "Post all our press releases on the website" is not a business goal. Instead, a goal should be more like "Ensure media contacts can get the information they need to write articles about our business."

Perhaps you currently post links to the 10 most recent press releases on your website's front page, because you're proud of your accomplishments. But that takes up a lot of real estate on the front page. The vast majority of your users are *not* members of the press, and the rest of the world just isn't interested in reading your press releases. Having press releases available on a dedicated media page will make sure members of the media can still find them—they know to look for that page—and you're not forcing everybody else to look at links that they'll never click on. If you really want to share information about recent accomplishments, write them in a different format for the general public: short blurbs using straightforward and simple language, not business-speak.

Think too about the length of each individual piece of content. If your About Us page is 1,000 words long, you're saying far too much. It doesn't need to be a long and rambling story of how your company was founded, including the names of every board member for the past 30 years. Most users coming to that page want to know, very succinctly, what your website or company does. If that information isn't provided in the first couple of sentences, users likely won't read any further to look for it. If you absolutely must list all those board members, put them on a separate page.

Look also for content that is redundant. Even if your CMS makes it easy to put pieces of content in multiple places, don't do it unless it's really necessary. Not only does it take up space on the website, but it can be confusing to users. It will also mean that the same content will be showing up multiple times in search engines, which is confusing to users and can decrease your search rankings if the search engine perceives those pages to be duplicate content.

Later in this book we'll talk about a small-screen-first approach to design, where you design a layout for small-screen devices before moving on to layouts for wider devices. Designing this way is a really great help to your efforts to pare down. When you're trying to fit your content in a design that will fit on a small screen, it forces you to consider what's really important and gives you a clarity that's harder to find when you're designing your content for a desktop-sized site first.

CONTENT AUDIT/INVENTORY

When redesigning an existing site, it's a good first step to do a *content audit*, which is an inventory of all the content you currently have. If it's a large site, there are probably things in there that will surprise you.

Go through the list and decide what you want to keep and what to get rid of, what new content needs to be created, and who is responsible for editing and developing each piece of content.

Once you get everything in a list, it's easier to look at it and decide what to do with it all.

Your list doesn't need to include every piece of content, but should have at least the categories and major pieces. If it's a new site, you should come up with a list of the content that you plan to have on the site, and a timeline for producing it.

You can learn more about content audits by reading Donna Spencer's *UXmastery* article, "How to Conduct a Content Audit (*http://uxmastery.com/how-to-conduct-a-content-audit/*).

Developing Content

Once you've figured out what you need and where it goes, you also need to think about what the content looks like.

HOW USERS READ

Have you ever wondered how users read on a website? As much as we'd like to think they go to every page on our site and read it top to bottom, they won't.

"If you build it, they will come" is not the motto of web content creators—or, at least, it shouldn't be. But you could be easily fooled by the sites that are filled with lengthy press releases, self-promoting company information, and other nearly useless content that nobody actually reads.

Just because you think your product/idea/event is the most wonderful thing in the world, it doesn't mean that anybody wants to read thousands of words about it—not even the people who have already displayed an interest by visiting your website.

Users will browse through your site trying to find the information that they want or need. You need to make sure that everything else isn't getting in their way.

Scanning

Users scan when they read a web page. Website content isn't nearly as compelling to the rest of the world as it is to the website's owner, even if it's great content.

Users read in dribs and drabs. A little here, a little there. They'll skim through a page, their eyes briefly focusing on links, headings, images, and bits of text.

There are millions of web pages competing with yours for each user's attention, so don't waste users' time. Make it as easy as possible for them to get the information they need.

Inverted pyramid

One of the main keys to doing this well is to use a journalism technique called the *inverted pyramid*.

Back when newspapers were only issued on actual paper instead of on websites, editors had to deal with the problem of having to plan for a set amount of physical space that they had to fill with words and pictures each day. They had to produce the exact amount of content to fill that space, not more and not less. But it was pretty much impossible to plan everything out ahead of time, since the news hadn't happened yet.

So when reporters wrote articles for the newspaper, they had a target word count to provide, but they also understood that if more important news happened, their stories might have to be shortened to provide space for the more important articles.

To make this easier, reporters would put the most important details of their stories in the first few paragraphs, and fill the following paragraphs with progressively less important details as well as background information. That way, if the editor needed to shorten a story to fit in a smaller space, any number of ending paragraphs could be lopped off without removing the key points. Figure 2-1 will give you a better idea of how this works.

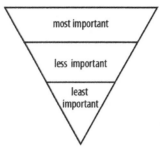

Figure 2-1. Use the inverted pyramid approach to make sure users are seeing the most important parts of your content.

You can use the same idea when writing content for the Web—not because an editor will cut off the end of your story, but because the user is likely to do so, by not reading all the way to the end. Make sure the most important details come first, and then follow those with the less important details, which the user may or may not get to.

Headings

If your page content is more than a couple paragraphs long, it could almost certainly benefit from being split up into sections.

For your users, the benefits of using headings include:

- Users can more easily understand the page structure, and get a better idea of what type of content is on the page, before they start reading.

- They can jump ahead to the parts of content that are relevant to them.

- People who are using assistive technology (e.g., blind users using screen-reading software) can navigate through the page content rather than having to read it all straight through.

- Users can find their place more easily while scrolling.

Benefits of headings for the website owner include the following:

- The page's search engine placement will be improved by letting the search engines know what the key topics of the page are.

- Content authors will be able to produce content that works better on the Web.

To write good headings, first divide your content into sections that address different main points.

Headings should be as short as possible to get the point across, and contain relevant key words. Ideally, each heading should *start* with the key words, to make skimming easier.

Headings should give a descriptive preview of the content that follows. They shouldn't be teasers.

Short and sweet

As users are scanning the page, they also tend to consume content in small pieces. Dense text will turn off users, and often keep them from reading the content at all.

Paragraphs should be short, generally no more than 100 words long.

Use bullet points when appropriate, if the content would make sense as a list. Bullets are much easier to scan and digest than the same content in paragraph form.

PLAIN LANGUAGE

The words you use in your content matter, as they provide the tone. But they also determine whether or not the user can understand your content.

The average reading level of US adults is generally accepted to be around the eighth- or ninth-grade level, according to studies like the 2003 National Assessment of Adult Literacy, sponsored by the National Center for Education Statistics (NCES) (*http://nces.ed.gov/NAAL/*). Nearly 50% of adults read below the sixth-grade level.

Those of us who are writing and editing content for the Web tend to be relatively well educated, and our reading level generally reflects that. But we need to remember that our audience is not us.

It's easy to make the incorrect assumption that your websites' users must be smarter or better educated than everyone else. After all, they were smart enough to choose your sites, right? But by not having accessible language, you're losing potential customers or missing out on giving information to people who might really need it.

In recent years, a *plain language* movement has emerged, where content creators make an effort to produce content that is easy to understand, as well as being arranged in a logical structure that makes it easier for users to find what they need.

A side benefit of using plain language is that it actually helps *all* users. Most people want to get their information in a hurry—they have the entire rest of the Internet to read, after all. Even for high-literacy users, plain language will help them consume and navigate content more quickly.

You're also assisting users who don't speak English as their first language. This doesn't just mean immigrants. It means foreign tourists who want to visit your restaurant, and residents of other countries who want to order your products. If your website provides information, it may not only be residents of your own country who are interested in reading that information.

A good starting point for plain language is to use simpler words, shorter sentences, and shorter paragraphs when possible. By paring down your content as discussed previously, you make sure low-literacy users don't have to spend a lot of extra time slowly reading through content that isn't relevant to them.

Here are some resources to help you get started with plain language:

- The Center for Plain Language's Plain Language Checklist (*http:// centerforplainlanguage.org/5-steps-to-plain-language/*)

- Jakob Nielsen, "Lower-Literacy Users: Writing for a Broad Consumer Audience," Nielsen Norman Group, March 14, 2005 (*http://www. nngroup.com/articles/writing-for-lower-literacy-users/*)

- United States Federal Plain Language Guidelines (*http://www. plainlanguage.gov/howto/guidelines/FederalPLGuidelines/TOC. cfm*)

Content Parity

When thinking of what you know about your audience, the first thing you need to consider is that most of what you "know" about them is based on assumptions, which may or may not be correct.

It's a common mistake to assume that users need or don't need certain content based on what device they're using.

For example, it's a frequent assumption that mobile phone users are "on the go," so they only need location-based information, such as the address of the restaurant they're going to, or whether or not their flight is on time.

But now that mobile phones have become ubiquitous, we use them pretty much anywhere, including when we're right next to our laptop or desktop computers.

Phones now feel like just another computer, and people expect the websites they view on their phones to have all the information that they would get on a desktop or laptop computer.

Everybody should have access to every part of a website, regardless of the device they're using. This concept is called *content parity*.

One of the advantages of responsive design is that we can provide the same content for all users regardless of device, but at the same time provide that content in a way that is optimized for the device in use.

As you'll learn in Chapter 5, there are lots of things you can do to present content differently based on the screen size of the device.

Content Governance

If your website has content, and they all do, you need to have a plan for *content governance*. This simply means taking care of the content once it's on your website.

You can't just post content and forget about it. Information becomes obsolete or incorrect, links become broken, and so on. You need to have a good plan for content governance before the content is posted on your site, or else you'll likely never get around to it.

CREATING TIMELESS CONTENT

One thing you can do to make your content easier to maintain is to make it as timeless as possible.

Not everything can be timeless, but a good way to go about this with each piece of content is to look at the content and imagine you happen to come across it in a year's time. Does it still stand on its own?

Include years in dates whenever possible. Have you ever heard about a great annual event you wanted to attend, went to the website to see it prominently described as happening on "October 15," and had no idea if that content described this year's event that's coming up, or last year's that has already happened?

If you know information is only valid for a certain amount of time, make a note of that in the content. If you forget to go back and change it or take it down, at least someone coming across it will know it's no longer valid.

Adaptive Content

Not only will your content be viewed at different screen widths as part of a responsive website, but it could also be viewed in different contexts entirely.

For example, Figure 2-2 shows an article by Rachel Nabors as it is displayed on the *A List Apart* website.

Figure 2-2. Viewing an *A List Apart* article on a desktop monitor.

But some people read posts and articles in an RSS reader, which relies only on the HTML and strips out any of the site's design, as you see in Figure 2-3.

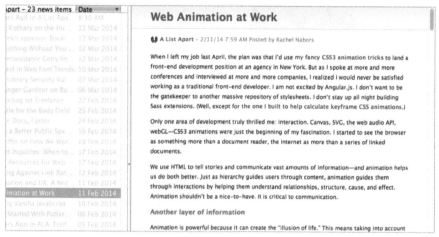

Figure 2-3. Viewing an article in an RSS reader application.

It's also common to use services like Instapaper (*http://www.instapaper.com/*) to view the main content of web pages without all the extra fluff such as ads and navigation, or to save articles to be viewed later. You can see what this looks like on a desktop computer in Figure 2-4, or on a mobile device in Figure 2-5.

Figure 2-4. Viewing an article in Instapaper on a desktop computer.

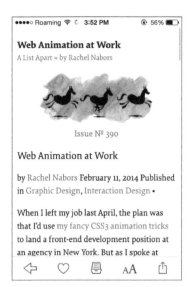

Figure 2-5. Viewing an article in Instapaper on an iPhone.

We can no longer think of our content just in terms of how it's laid out on our websites. Instead, we need to think of it as a series of chunks, such as the title, author name, and body content. These different chunks are called *metadata*, which essentially means "data about data."

If you use a CMS, you may have been doing this all along. There are probably separate fields for title, article date, and author name. In responsive design, we adapt the layout depending on how much screen real estate is available. On a small screen, the title, date, author, and body text may appear vertically one after another. On a wider screen, perhaps the date and author are off in a box on the side. These layout changes are only possible if the pieces are separated out into individual chunks.

If the article is reproduced in another application, the chunks allow the content to be displayed in a way that makes sense.

What about other types of content? For example, consider an ecommerce site. Instead of a description field that has *all* the details about the item for sale, use separate fields for color, size, material, use category, and so on. Not only will this allow you to easily change the layout of the page depending on screen width, but it will also allow you to create more powerful search and navigation, to give users a faster path to what they're looking for.

By giving your content structure and attaching metadata to it, you give it more power to adapt to different screen sizes and to be easily displayed outside of your website.

Summary

Until recently, content has always been thought of as an afterthought to the design, but in recent years the content strategy has gained increasing importance.

Starting with the content before the design will help you create a website that meets your business goals as well as the users' needs.

To manage your website's content when moving to a new site, start with a content audit to see what you have. Go through it and pare it down, using only what needs to be on the site. Unnecessary content just makes the site more difficult for both the users and the site owner.

Make sure that content is concise and written in plain language so that it's easy for users to consume. Users read web pages by scanning, so create short paragraphs and use headings to separate the content into sections. Make sure the most important information is at the top of the page, in case the user doesn't read all the way to the bottom.

Don't make assumptions about what content users will want based on the devices they are using to access the site. All users to your site should have access to all the content.

In addition to adding content to the newly designed site, put thought into how the content will be managed after the site launches. Have a plan for keeping things updated. Create timeless content where you can.

Divide your content into chunks that can be rearranged on the page, or easily moved to other media.

In the next chapter, Chapter 3, we'll start to look at the nitty-gritty of the code behind responsive sites.

[Part II]

Creating Responsive Websites

[3]

HTML for Responsive Sites

To create a responsive website, you'll be using both HTML and CSS (with an occasional smattering of JavaScript as well).

Even if your job doesn't involve creating the code for websites, you should know a bit about what's going on "under the hood" of responsive sites, so don't skip the next few chapters.

This chapter assumes you have at least some basic familiarity with HTML. If you're not a coder, you don't have to understand exactly how everything works, just get a general idea.

Even if you have a lot of experience with HTML, there will be concepts addressed in this chapter that you may not be familiar with, like the `viewport` attribute and creating a web page using the structural elements that are new in HTML5.

Other concepts, like `doctype` and `charset`, might not be new to you, but they're addressed here because they're necessary to understanding how to properly set up an HTML page for a responsive website.

In this chapter, we'll also look at versions of HTML, and what it means that you'll be using HTML5 to create websites. Then we'll set up an example web page, using HTML5 structural elements to put it together.

We'll finish up by talking about how to write good code, using semantic HTML and separating content and presentation, along with best practices for using HTML to properly mark up your content to make it accessible to all users.

Working with HTML

HTML is not set in stone: it is revised over time to accommodate new technologies and add new features. HTML was meant to be a living organism, which would change over time as the needs of the Web and the technology behind it changed.

Every several years, a new version of HTML comes out. As this book is published, browsers are still in the process of switching from one version to another (HTML 4 to HTML5).

For the examples in this book, we'll be using the most recent version of HTML, which is HTML5. But because HTML5 is a work in progress, not every part of HTML5 is available to use right now. In this section, you'll learn how versioning works and how to find out which new HTML5 elements you can safely use on your website.

VERSIONS OF HTML

A lot of HTML stays the same from one version to the next, so it's not like you need to start over learning HTML from scratch each time a new version comes along.

A good comparison is if you were to read something by Shakespeare, written 500 years ago. It's in English, the same language we speak today. But it's different. There are some words in Shakespeare's work that we no longer use in English. Other words are still around, but are spelled differently or have slightly different meanings. Likewise, if Shakespeare were suddenly transported to modern times, there would be many words that he wouldn't recognize.

But even with those differences, it's still the same language and you would be able to understand nearly all of it.

The same is true when comparing different versions of HTML. HTML is made of *elements*, which are the components that are used to describe the web page's content. For example, there's a paragraph element that is used to signify paragraphs, and an image element that is used to add images to a web page.

In each new version of HTML there will be new elements, some existing elements will have slightly different meanings, and some elements will go away. The paragraph element, <p>, has stayed consistent since the first version of HTML, but elements like <key> have disappeared, and new elements like <canvas> have only recently been added.

Browsers will understand any version of HTML for the most part, but older browsers may have trouble with some of the new pieces, so you'll have to do a little extra to make sure they can display everything correctly.

And as with human language, it takes a while for HTML to change; it doesn't happen all at once. A new version of HTML is proposed, and then the web community spends a lot of time (years) discussing it piece by piece. The browsers then start implementing it, piece by piece. As some parts of the new HTML specification are being implemented by the browsers, other parts are still being discussed and tested.

There's a lot of overlap between the versions. Work on HTML5 started in 2004, and the specification is scheduled to be "finished" in late 2014 (right now it's just a "draft"). But that won't mean the changes are done: there will be a version 5.1, then 5.2, and so on, with minor changes. HTML6 is already being discussed, and older versions of HTML are still being used.

Besides newer web pages created in HTML5, you will likely encounter websites that were created in HTML 4, as well as in XHMTL, which came between HTML 4 and HTML5.

WEB STANDARDS

The World Wide Web Consortium (W3C) is a voluntary standards organization that decides what's in the "official" version of HTML. (*Voluntary* means that although the industry has agreed to use the W3C's rules, it is not required to do so.)

Before the W3C came along, the browsers made up their own rules as to how they would interpret HTML. As a result, a web page could look very different from one browser to the next, and HTML that worked in one browser might not even be recognized by another.

Because the W3C is voluntary, the browsers aren't actually *required* to follow the rules. But for the most part, they do, because if a browser displays web pages very differently than the other browsers, nobody will want to use that browser. There are some differences, though, so as we go along you'll learn what you need to do in your code to make sure everything is displayed correctly in the situations where some browsers *aren't* playing by the rules.

And as web designers, *we* need to follow the rules. That's what will ensure our websites will work across different browsers and devices. Following the standards also makes sure your website is future-friendly, and much more likely to be compatible with devices and technologies that haven't even been invented yet.

USING HTML5

When someone talks about an "HTML5 element," he generally means an element that's new in HTML5 (i.e., that wasn't part of HTML 4).

If an element is new to HTML5, you need to know whether browsers are supporting that element yet. And even if they are, you need to be aware that some users still have older browsers on their computers that don't support some of the new elements.

When I reference new HTML5 elements in this book, I will let you know whether they are currently well supported, and what you need to do to accommodate older browsers.

And as I mentioned earlier, much of HTML stays the same from version to version.

There are more than 100 different elements in HTML5. In this book, we'll only talk about the elements you are likely to use with any frequency. There are many others. If you ever encounter an HTML element you don't recognize, look it up to determine what it does and if it is valid in HTML5.

Basic Page Structure

The first thing to do when creating a web page from scratch is to start out the page with basic HTML.

DOCUMENT TYPE DECLARATION (DOCTYPE)

The first thing that goes at the top of the HTML file is the *document type declaration* (doctype). The doctype tells the browser what version of HTML the page is using.

For HTML5, the doctype is:

```
<!DOCTYPE html>
```

If you work with existing websites that use an older version of HTML, you will encounter a few other doctypes.

Even after a new version of HTML comes out, pages using older versions of HTML continue to work—but they must have the correct doctype to match the version of HTML that's being used, or else the browser may have trouble displaying the page.

If the doctype doesn't match the HTML being used in the page, the browser will make some guesses and probably get everything to work correctly. But not always, so don't count on it. If things really aren't looking like you think they should on your web page, check and make sure your page has the correct doctype to match the version of HTML you are using.

[NOTE]

You can learn about the differences between the older doctypes in the "HTML <!DOCTYPE> Declaration" (*http://www.w3schools.com/tags/tag_ doctype.asp*) from W3Schools.

DOCUMENT STRUCTURE

Everything after the doctype in your HTML file comprises the HTML of the page, which is further separated into exactly two sections, the <head> and <body>:

```
<!DOCTYPE html>
<html>
<head>
...
</head>
<body>
...
</body>
</html>
```

Note that when you see "..." in a code example, it signifies that other code or content will go in that space—the "..." is not a part of the code.

You'll see that we're using a few elements here that come in matched sets, like <head> and </head>. Most HTML elements, but not all, have opening and closing *tags* that surround the content they're describing. Everything between those opening and closing tags comprises the <head>.

The <html> element should always have a lang attribute to tell the browser the language of the page's content—in this case, en for English. Although this attribute is optional, it's important because it tells screen readers what language to read in, and it helps the browser decide how to hyphenate words.

The <head> contains information about the page (often called *meta-data*, using the <meta> element). It also can contain links to external files containing CSS or JavaScript, and sometimes embedded styles or scripts. What's in the <head> is not part of what's displayed on the page as content.

The <body> contains all of your page content.

THE PAGE TITLE

The page's <title> doesn't appear anywhere on your web page, and can in fact be totally different from the title you see on the page.

However, the words you use in the <title> element need to be well thought out because they are used as the page title in a lot of other locations, such as:

- The top of the browser window, or in the page tab when using a browser with tabbed browsing

- The page name that will display in a user's bookmarks after the page has been bookmarked

- The link for the page in search engine results

The page title is often a combination of the site name and the page title, separated by a dash, colon, or pipe character.

A few examples:

```
<title>Metro - The Boston Globe</title>
<title>Flickr: Groups</title>
<title>Ways to Help | American Red Cross</title>
```

Although the `<title>` can be different from what appears on the page as its title, they should be fairly similar, otherwise users may get confused.

Long titles will show up truncated in search engine results, so don't make your title excessively long. A general guideline is 64 characters, although each search engine has a different maximum length.

CHARSET

The `charset` specifies the character encoding ("character set") of the characters in your HTML document (i.e., all of the HTML and content you are typing in your HTML file).

`charset` is not an HTML element; it's an attribute to the `<meta>` element. You can have one or more `<meta>` elements in the `<head>` of your HTML document, each one of them providing information about the page.

The character encoding is essentially the code that translates letters, numbers, and symbols into the binary language that the computer can recognize.

Even though you may not be aware of it, whatever application you're using to create your HTML file (such as a text editor) has a default encoding. Each browser also has a default encoding. If they don't use the same one, sometimes things get lost in translation. So you need to tell the browser which one to use, or it might have trouble displaying the page.

The charset you are going to use for your HTML5 page is *UTF-8*, which is the most widely used and flexible character encoding for web pages. It supports the characters found in most international languages:

```
<meta charset="utf-8">
```

Older versions of HTML declare the character encoding differently. If you're working with an existing website that uses an older version of HTML, you can learn more on the "Declaring character encodings in HTML" (*http://www.w3.org/International/questions/qa-html-encoding-declarations*) page of the W3C website.

Viewport

The `viewport` meta element is something that generally wasn't used for most nonresponsive websites in the past, but is key to making your responsive site work.

The *viewport* is the area on the computer or device screen where you are viewing a web page. In Chapter 1, you learned that responsive design media queries are based on the viewport width.

On a desktop computer, if you start with the browser window, and subtract the menus, toolbars, scrollbar, and everything else that's part of the browser itself, what's left inside it is the viewport, as you see in Figure 3-1.

On a mobile device, the viewport width is the same as the screen width.

The `viewport` meta attribute gives instructions to the browser as to what size the web page should be displayed at so it fits properly in the viewport.

Web pages without a `viewport` setting are rendered, or displayed, at full size on desktop monitors, the way you're accustomed to seeing them.

Figure 3-1. The space inside the dotted line is the viewport area.

A mobile phone browser, by default, will render a web page without `viewport` as it would look on a desktop-sized browser, but scale it down so that it fits inside the phone's viewport, as in Figure 3-2. If there are media queries based on viewport width, they won't work, because the browser will act as if the viewport is desktop-sized.

Most mobile phone browsers will render a web page using a default viewport width of 980 pixels. Just imagine you have a desktop monitor that's 980 pixels wide, and what you see on that screen will be scaled down to fit on the phone's screen. If the web page is wider than 980 pixels, it may be scaled down even further to fit on the screen.

For a responsive site, we don't want the mobile browser to render the page as it would appear on a 980-pixel-wide monitor; we want it to render the page at actual size for the mobile device's screen (which could be any width), because we've designed the page to fit the small screen's width without zooming.

Figure 3-2. The University of Wisconsin's full website renders at desktop size, forcing the user to zoom in to read the text.

In Figure 3-3, you see *The Boston Globe*'s front page rendered on an iPhone screen, and in Figure 3-4 you see the same site rendered on an iPad screen. The site is full size on both screens, although they are different physical widths.

Figure 3-3. *The Boston Globe* site rendered in full size on an iPhone.

Generally, you should set the viewport for a responsive site as follows:

```
<meta name="viewport" content="width=device-width,
initial-scale=1">
```

WIDTH

The `width` attribute tells the browser how to scale the web page.

For a responsive site, the value `width=device-width` tells the browser to render the page at full size, whatever the size may be. The browser is rendering the page so that the viewport width is the actual width of the device (i.e., at 100%).

Figure 3-4. *The Boston Globe* site rendered in full size on an iPad.

If device width is not specified in the `viewport` meta attribute, the device will use its own default viewport setting to render the page. For example, the default width for iPhones is 980 pixels. So in Figure 3-2, the browser is rendering the page *as if* the browser window was 980 pixels wide, but then shrinking it down to ⅓ of the size so that it fits on a screen that's only 320 pixels wide.

If you use `width=device-width`, the width used to render the page will automatically adjust if the user changes the orientation of the device. So, if the user turns her iPhone from vertical to horizontal, the web page that rendered as 320 pixels will automatically re-render for 480 pixels, the width of the screen as you hold the phone horizontally.

INITIAL-SCALE

The `initial-scale` attribute tells the browser how to scale the web page when it's first loaded on the screen (i.e., the zoom factor).

Using the value `initial-scale=1` means that the page will be rendered at the size determined by the `width` attribute, and will not be zoomed in or out.

If you use a number larger or smaller than 1, then the page will be zoomed to that level. For example, an `initial-scale=2` value would mean that the page would be zoomed to be twice as large as actual size, so you would only see half of the page on the screen.

[NOTE]

If you are working on a nonresponsive website, don't include the `initial-scale` attribute at all, as it will cause your site to render on mobile devices at a large size but zoomed in so that the user can't see the whole page at once.

USER-SCALABLE

The `initial-scale` value only determines the size of the web page when it's first loaded on the screen. Remember that your mobile device also gives users the ability to zoom in and out.

There's a value for `viewport` that will turn off the user's ability to zoom: `user-scalable=no`.

However, for most websites, you should avoid using this value—let users zoom if they want to. Although a responsive site will load at full size no matter the width of the screen, there may still be circumstances in which users may wish to zoom in, such as if they have difficulty reading small text.

You would only want to turn off zooming in very limited circumstances, such as for games built with HTML/CSS, and certain other web apps.

If you don't include this value, the default is yes, which allows users to zoom.

MAXIMUM-SCALE

You can also use the width attribute to set the maximum-scale value for the page. For example, maximum-scale=2 would mean your users could only scale the page to twice as big as full size, and then it would not let them zoom any further.

Setting maximum-scale=1 would mean that the user could not zoom in at all, having the same effect as using user-scalable=1.

Again, you should avoid using this value except in very limited circumstances.

[NOTE]

You may have noticed that I've been writing element names and attribute names in lowercase. In HTML5, these are case insensitive. That is, you can use lowercase, uppercase, or any combination. Most developers use lowercase because words in lowercase are easier to read than those in uppercase.

Structural Elements

The <body> element contains all the content for the page.

First, we'll use HTML5 structural elements to divide the page into major sections, such as <header>, <nav>, and <footer> (they're called structural elements because they give the page structure). This makes it easier for us to apply styles to different parts of the page.

The elements for each section of the page have descriptive names, such as <header>, <footer>, <nav> (navigation), <section>, and <aside>.

These elements are new in HTML5. Previously, web designers used generic elements such as <div> (division) to divide the page into sections, and then identified each one using an id or class as a way to target specific sections when applying CSS.

Using structural elements is an example of what's called *semantic markup*, which refers to using elements that accurately describe the meaning of page content, rather than generic elements like <div>.

> **[NOTE]**
>
> Although I'm showing you how to use particular elements as a preferred way to set up your HTML pages, they are not required. In fact, there are no elements that you *must* include inside the <body> element of a web page.

SCREEN READERS

Additionally, structural elements make it easier for users to navigate the page using assistive technology such as a screen reader, which reads the page content out loud for blind users, or voice command software, which allows users to speak to the computer if they can't use a keyboard or mouse (i.e., the user might speak, "go to *nav*").

> **[NOTE]**
>
> When creating a website, you need to make sure it's accessible for people with disabilities. We will discuss accessibility in depth in Chapter 8. Web accessibility is closely related to usability. You can learn more in "Web Accessibility and Usability Working Together" (*http://www.w3.org/WAI/intro/usable*) from the W3C.

However, not all older browsers and screen readers can recognize these new elements, so we need to do a little something extra to accommodate them.

Before these new elements came about, a separate specification had already been created to help make websites fully accessible. WAI-ARIA (Web Accessibility Initiative - Accessible Rich Internet Applications) comes from the W3C, the same organization that gives us standards for HTML. This is a set of attributes that can be added on to HTML to provide additional information and functionality.

Part of WAI-ARIA are *roles*, which are attributes set on HTML elements to provide more information about what they're used for, including roles that correspond to many of the new HTML5 structural elements.

The new structural elements are great, because they're built right into the HTML, but because not all browsers and screen readers will be able to take advantage of these elements, we need to also include the corresponding WAI-ARIA role attributes on our structural elements.

Newer browsers will look at the HTML elements, while older browsers will look at the WAI-ARIA roles.

I'll include the WAI-ARIA roles as I explain each page element. Although these aren't required, it's a best practice to include them in your code to make your websites as accessible as possible.

<HEADER>

Generally the first thing at the top of your page, inside the <body> element, is the <header>. (Keep in mind that <head> and <header> are different elements—it's easy to get them confused.)

According to the HTML specification, the <header> contains introductory and navigational aids. This may include the logo, site title, search functionality, and main navigation.

Besides having a header for the entire page, you can also have additional <header>s elsewhere on the page, which would contain introductory and navigational aids for a particular page section.

The corresponding WAI-ARIA attribute is banner, so you would just add that as an attribute to the <header>:

```
<header role="banner">
...
</header>
```

<NAV>

The page navigation is contained in a <nav> element, as are any subnavigations in the page. You will often have a <nav> inside the <header>, but not always.

Navigation can be either links to other pages on the site, or links to sections on the same page, such as in a table of contents.

You can have more than one <nav> on a page. The corresponding WAI-ARIA attribute is navigation:

```
<nav role="navigation">
...
</nav>
```

<FOOTER>

A <footer> is a section on the page, not necessarily at the end, which contains information about the content of the page.

For example, a footer may contain a copyright notice, information about the page, and links to related materials such as a privacy policy or contact page.

Besides having a footer for the entire page, you can also have footers elsewhere in the page, performing the same function for sections of content rather than the whole page.

You can have more than one <footer> on a page. The corresponding WAI-ARIA attribute is contentinfo:

```
<footer role="contentinfo">
...
</footer>
```

<ARTICLE>

An <article> is a self-contained piece of content within the web page. For example, it might be a newspaper article, a blog entry, or a post in a forum. Because it's self-contained, this type of content could be distributed in syndication, such as through an RSS feed.

You can have more than one <article> on a page. There is no WAI-ARIA attribute to coincide with <article>:

```
<article>
...
</article>
```

<ASIDE>

An <aside> is used for secondary content, either related to the site or page as a whole (e.g., a blogroll) or, if it's nested inside an <article>, related to that article (e.g., a glossary).

You can have more than one <aside> on a page. The corresponding WAI-ARIA attribute is complementary:

```
<aside role="complementary">
...
</aside>
```

IE SUPPORT

There's one little issue with these new HTML5 structural elements: some older browsers won't recognize these elements.

For most browsers, this is no big deal. They treat unrecognized elements like <span>s, which are generic elements.

However, while older versions of Internet Explorer (8 and earlier) will display these elements like <span>s, they will also refuse to apply any CSS to the elements, which could really mess up the design of a page.

If you want your site to look the way it's supposed to in these older versions of IE, you need to add a little JavaScript that will effectively make the browser recognize the elements.

There are two ways to go about this. Don't worry, you don't need to understand JavaScript to use them!

The first workaround is to use what's called a *polyfill* or a *shiv*, which is a bit of code that can be used to make an older browser act like a newer browser.

The HTML5 Shiv (*https://github.com/aFarkas/html5shiv*) is a piece of code created and improved by several developers (see the GitHub page for a list of all the people who were involved). All you need to do is follow the instructions on that page to download a JavaScript file and add it to your website, then link to it from the <head> of the site (use the Manual Installation instructions if you don't know what Bower is).

The instructions tell us to use this code to add the shiv to our site:

```
<!--[if lt IE 9]>
    <script src="files/html5shiv.js"></script>
<![endif]-->
```

The first part of that tells the browser to only run the script if the browser is Internet Explorer, in a version earlier than IE 9.

There are other resources, such as Modernizr (*http://modernizr.com/*), that do the same thing as the HTML5 Shiv.

Creating a Page

For our example page, we're going to start out with some common elements.

We're going to create a website about pandas, with the title "Pandas Forever." To make this simple, we'll only use some basic content sections.

On most websites, you'll be using a CMS (which includes blog software like WordPress), so your HTML might be distributed into separate files for editing purposes, instead of being all on one page. But for the purposes of this example, we'll be looking at a single page of HTML code.

If you're new to working with web pages, go ahead and open up a text editor on your computer, such as TextEdit on Mac OS or Notepad on Microsoft Windows. Save a file containing your HTML using the *.html* extension, not *.txt*. You'll then be able to open that from your browser and view it as a web page.

STRUCTURAL ELEMENTS

The <body> will start with a <header> that will contain the page title along with a <nav> that will contain our navigation.

After that, we'll have a blog post, which will use <article>, and then a related links section, which will use <aside>, because it's supplemental information to the page.

The page will end with a <footer> that will have some supplemental information like our copyright:

```
<body>
    <header role="banner">
        <nav role="navigation">...</nav>
    </header>
    <article>...</article>
    <aside role="complementary">...</aside>
    <footer role="contentinfo">...</footer>
</body>
```

[NOTE]

You'll often see in HTML that elements are indented to different levels, like in the preceding example. This isn't necessary—and the browser just ignores the extra spaces—but it helps the developer see what's going on with the structure of the page, and more easily match up opening and closing tags.

ADDING CONTENT

Keep in mind we're coding the page so that it can be viewed without any CSS if necessary. All the content should be coded in the order we would want it to appear on the page if there was no layout, just one piece of content after another.

Putting all the pieces together, and adding content, we get this:

```html
<!DOCTYPE html>
<html lang="en">
<head>
    <title>Pandas Forever</title>
    <meta charset="utf-8">
    <meta name="viewport" content="width=device-width,
    initial-scale=1">
    <!--[if lt IE 9]>
        <script src="files/html5shiv.js"></script>
    <![endif]-->
</head>
<body>
    <header role="banner">
        <h1>Pandas Forever</h1>
        <nav role="navigation">
        <ul>
        <li><a href="/">Home</a></li>
        <li><a href="/about/">About</a></li>
        <li><a href="/links/">Links</a></li>
        <li><a href="/contact/">Contact</a></li>
        </nav>
    </header>
    <article>
        <h2>Pandas in Wolong</h2>
        <p>The Wolong National Nature Preserve, in the
        Sichuan Province of China, is home to more than
        150 giant pandas. It's one of the key sites for
        panda breeding research, and 66 cubs have been
        born at Wolong since it was established in 1980.
        Pandas are an endangered species, with between
        1500 and 3000 living in the wild, and less than
        300 in captivity (research centers and zoos).</p>
    </article>
    <aside role="complementary">
        <h2>Related Links</h2>
        <ul>
        <li><a href="http://www.flickr.com/groups/
        pandasunlimited/">Pandas Unlimited</a></li>
        <li><a href="http://nationalzoo.si.edu/animals/
        webcams/giant-panda.cfm">National Zoo Panda
        Cams</a></li>
        <li><a href="http://worldwildlife.org/species/
        giant-panda">Panda Facts at WWF</a></li>
        </ul>
    </aside>
```

```
    <footer role="contentinfo">
        <p>&copy; 2014 Pandas Forever</p>
    </footer>
</body>
</html>
```

We have all the <header> elements previously described. This includes the HTML5 Shiv, which we've uploaded to the *files* directory on our site and linked to per the installation instructions, so that IE 8 and earlier browsers will recognize the new HTML5 structural elements.

The site title uses an <h1> heading, and the page title an <h2>. The convention for styling navigation is usually to put it in an unordered list with a <ul> as we've done, although it's not required—you can use <span>s or <div>s for each navigation item if you prefer.

Inside the <body>, we'll add all the content. This is a fairly basic page like what you might see as an article or a blog entry.

Following that, the <footer> contains our copyright notice.

UNSTYLED PAGE

You're starting off with unstyled content, so Figure 3-5 is what you'd see in a desktop browser without any CSS being applied, while Figure 3-6 is what you'd see on an iPhone.

Pandas Forever

- Home
- About
- Links
- Contact

Pandas in Wolong

The Wolong National Nature Preserve, in the Sichuan Province of China, is home to more than 150 giant pandas. It's one of the key sites for panda breeding research, and 66 cubs have been born at Wolong since it was established in 1980. Pandas are an endangered species, with between 1500 and 3000 living in the wild, and less than 300 in captivity (research centers and zoos).

Related Links

- Pandas Unlimited
- National Zoo Panda Cams
- Panda Facts at WWF

© 2014 Pandas Forever

Figure 3-5. This is our website on a desktop monitor with no CSS applied.

Figure 3-6. This is our website on an iPhone with no CSS applied.

We haven't added any CSS yet, and the site is already responsive! HTML is responsive by default.

Clean and Semantic HTML

A key to having a website that works well is to keep your code as simple as possible. I don't mean that you need to keep your design overly simple—I just mean that as you're creating the code to display your design, you should keep the code straightforward.

This will make the code for your site much easier to write and maintain.

Use the HTML elements correctly, and make sure you're familiar with all the elements so you know what's available to you.

Just to start, make sure you're doing the basics right, like using heading elements for headings (and in the correct numerical order), and list elements for lists. But also take advantage of new elements like <nav> and <section>, which we looked at earlier in this chapter, to properly label the sections of the page.

<div>s and <span>s are container elements that don't have any semantic meaning. You can use them when there is no semantic HTML element that conveys the meaning you need, but use them sparingly, only when necessary.

SEPARATING CONTENT AND PRESENTATION

HTML and CSS are separate languages that have different purposes. HTML is used to display the content and provide information about the content, not to provide any style or decoration. CSS is used to determine the visual appearance of everything on your site, such as layout, typeface, sizes, and colors.

Your content may not always be displayed using the styles you intended, so make sure not to use CSS to convey meaning.

For example, using the heading levels appropriately (<h1> through <h6>) will ensure that all devices and browsers displaying the content know which parts are most important, even if the browser can't apply the CSS. For example, for a blind user with a screen reader, if the software knows the page is divided into sections with headings, it will let the user jump from section to section instead of having to read the whole page straight through.

On the other hand, if instead you use CSS to give your headings a large, bold font, but you don't use the appropriate HTML heading elements, the browser won't actually know that those phrases are headings that describe the content on the page.

Even beyond users with disabilities, there will be plenty of people accessing your website's content from somewhere other than a page on your site—so they won't see your design, only your content.

These users might be using RSS readers or read-later apps, as we saw in Chapter 2. For them to be able to view your content correctly, the content needs to be structured in a way that this software can display it.

Also, some of the most important visitors to your site are search engines, and they will not be able to see the site's design. When search engine software, called a *robot*, looks at your website, it only sees the HTML, not the design. It uses the information provided by the HTML to determine how your page should be categorized and appear in search results.

Using HTML to structure your content lets the search engines know what the different pieces of content on the page are for, rather than just giving them a jumble of text. If your page does not use semantic code, it can definitely have a negative effect on where your site appears in search engine results.

Designing the page structure first is the best start toward making sure your content can be understood and displayed properly anywhere.

COMMENTS

Comments are an important part of your HTML (and CSS) files, even though the user will never see them. With comments, you can add notes to the source code, which the browser will then simply ignore when it is rendering the page. For example:

```
<!-- this is an HTML comment -->

<!-- this
is another comment,
on multiple lines -->
```

Comments are useful to the developer, or anyone who will be working on the code for the page. Often, multiple people will work on a website over time, and comments can be used to explain why things are set up in a certain way, or as reminders as to which things do what.

This is especially important in responsive sites, because there's so much going on. Adding comments to your code will make it much easier to keep track of what each part of your code does.

Of course, don't go overboard; as with any code, adding comments does add to the size of your page, which can increase the download time.

You might notice that comments use similar syntax to the code we just used to add the HTML5 Shiv to our example website:

```
<!--[if lt IE 9]>
    <script src="files/html5shiv.js"></script>
<![endif]-->
```

That code is actually called a *conditional comment*, which can only be read by IE browsers (the other browsers just see it as a regular comment and ignore it), and it can be used to give special instructions to IE.

Summary

Every web page is created using HTML, a markup language that uses elements to give meaning and context to each piece of content.

The current version of HTML is HTML5. The doctype at the top of your HTML document lets the browser know which version of HTML your page is written in. Not all elements in HTML5 are supported yet, so you need to be aware of which elements you can safely use, and which elements require additional code to make them work in older browsers.

You need to follow web standards, set by the W3C, so that browsers will display your website the way you expect it to be displayed.

Your HTML document starts with a doctype. That's followed by the <head>, which supplies information about the page, such as the <title>, as well as information that tells the browser how the page should be displayed, such as the charset and the viewport. For responsive websites, the viewport is key to making sure the page is displayed correctly.

The <head> is followed by the <body>, which contains all of the page content. Use semantic HTML to properly convey the meaning of each page element so that it's displayed properly regardless of the device or method of viewing the content.

The page structure can be set up using several HTML5 structural elements, such as <header>, <footer>, <nav>, <section>, and <aside>. To make your site accessible, you need to also use WAI-ARIA attributes on these elements to provide navigational help for older screen readers that don't recognize the HTML5 elements.

It's especially important on responsive sites—because there are so many complex things going on—that you write simple, semantic HTML, separating content from presentation. You should also include comments in your code to document information that might be helpful to anyone working on the website in the future.

In Chapter 4, we'll learn how to apply styles to a web page using CSS, and add some style to our example website.

[4]

CSS for Responsive Sites

While HTML gives structure to all the content on your site, CSS will tell the browser how to style it.

Like Chapter 3, this chapter will be a review for anyone who is already experienced with the technology. However, we're going to go into more detail on the basic concepts of CSS than we did with HTML, simply because CSS is the code that responsive design is made of. It's impossible to have a real comprehension of how a responsive website is put together without understanding concepts like the cascade and the box model.

We'll first look at how versioning of CSS works, and how browser prefixes are used to make sure that new style properties can be rendered appropriately in different browsers, even while these properties are still in the testing period.

Then we'll look at the different ways to include styles in your website, either by embedding the styles in web pages, by using stylesheets to apply styles to multiple pages or an entire website at once, or by using inline styles to apply styles to individual elements.

Next, you'll learn the concept of the *cascade*, which gives Cascading Style Sheets its name. The cascade determines the order in which styles are applied and how the browser chooses among conflicting style rules. We'll also look at the best way to use the cascade to implement styles on your site with minimal confusion.

After that, we'll go over the concept of the *box model*, which determines how elements are displayed on the web page: each element is represented as a box, having values (sometimes zero) for width, height, margins, padding, and borders. We'll also look at `display` and positioning, which affect where elements are placed on the page.

Finally, we'll go back to our example page and add some basic typography and layout styles to give some visual definition to the page.

How CSS Works

For anyone who isn't already familiar with CSS, here's a quick overview of how the code in a stylesheet is put together. This doesn't cover all the variations on what you can do with CSS, but it's enough that you'll be able to look at CSS and know what's happening.

To start, each time you apply a style to an HTML element, it's called a *rule*:

```
p { color: red; }
```

Each rule contains two separate sections. The *selector* corresponds to the HTML element that the style is applied to, just without the brackets. In this case, the p corresponds to the HTML element <p>, and this rule is telling the browser how to display the paragraphs on the page.

To go along with the selector, you have one or more *declarations*. This is everything inside the brackets, and it defines the style that's being applied to the element.

In a declaration, the *property* is the quality of the element that you're changing, such as the color or the width. The *value* is what you're setting it to, such as orange or 50%. Each property is followed by a colon and then a value, such as **color: red** in the earlier example, which specifies that paragraph text should be red.

If there are one or more declarations in the same rule, they are separated by semicolons:

```
p { color: red; font-size: 1.5em; }
```

The semicolon is optional after the last declaration (or if you have only one declaration), but many developers include it for consistency. All the declarations together are called the *declaration group*, which is surrounded by curly braces.

Styles can also be applied to a subset of an element, using a class or ID:

```
.classname { color: blue; }
#idname { color: green; }
```

This code will affect elements with the class **classname** (i.e., <p class= "classname">) or the ID idname (i.e., <div id="idname">).

Classes and IDs work similarly, by allowing you to target any element on the page, but you can only apply an ID to one element on a page, whereas you can apply a class to as many elements as you want.

You should use class and ID names that are descriptive. The browser doesn't care if they are semantic, as with HTML, but it is easier for the developer when it's apparent what the classes and IDs correspond to. For example:

```
<p class="intro">...</p>
<nav id="main">...</nav>
```

You can also target items more specifically with *descendant* selectors, which just means something that's inside something else:

```
.classname p { color: purple; }
```

In this case, we're telling the browser to first find any elements with the classname class, and then that the <p>s *inside* those elements should be purple (but not the <p>s that are not inside a classname element).

If you want the same style to apply to more than one selector, you can group them using commas, instead of creating two separate rules:

```
h1, h2 { color: green; }
```

This example tells the browser that both <h1> and <h2> elements should be green.

When you're writing CSS, the spaces and line breaks are optional, except for the spaces in the descendant selectors, such as .classname p in the earlier example.

So, some stylesheets might look like this, which is perfectly all right (although hard to read):

```
p{color:green}div{width:50%;background-
color:blue}.classname{color:yellow}
```

By removing the spaces, or *optimizing* the stylesheet, you're reducing the file size of the CSS document (every byte counts). This can help make your page load faster (we'll talk about how to use software to remove the spaces automatically in Chapter 11).

[NOTE]

It's hard to read a stylesheet that's been optimized, because everything runs together. There are several online tools that can add spaces and line breaks back in at the appropriate places, so it's easier to read. Try Clean CSS (*http://www.cleancss.com/*), or just search online for CSS optimizers.

Versions of CSS

Just as with HTML, there are different versions of CSS. The first version of CSS came out in 1996, just a couple years after HTML was first used to create web pages. The most recent version is CSS3.

Each version of CSS is made up of all the properties that can be styled using CSS. Properties are the qualities of your HTML elements that are affected by the styles. Some of these qualities include color, typeface, size of elements, and location of elements on the page.

Several new properties were added in CSS3. One of the most significant changes in CSS3 was to media queries, which made responsive design possible. You'll learn more about how media queries work in Chapter 5.

Just as with HTML, you need to keep in mind that not all browsers have the ability to *render*, or display on the page, all of the properties in the latest version of CSS. I've noted in the book which properties you'll need to pay attention to.

And like with HTML, not all browsers will render everything in CSS exactly the same way. You should be aware of the differences, and remember to test your website in various browsers and devices to make sure it looks the way you want it to look.

In Figure 4-1 you'll see the Mozilla website displayed as intended, but in Figure 4-2, you'll see the same website displayed with all the CSS removed.

Figure 4-1. The Mozilla website displayed as intended.

Figure 4-2. The Mozilla website displayed without any CSS applied to the page.

BROWSER PREFIXES

Parts of CSS3 are still being worked out by the W3C and tested by the browser vendors. So, the final specification for any new style may be slightly different from how the browsers are currently rendering it.

Rather than leaving developers in limbo, not knowing how their code will look in any given browser, the browsers support *browser prefixes* (often called *vendor prefixes*) that allow developers more control when using the new parts of CSS.

We don't actually have to worry about *all* of the different browsers, because most of them rely on one of four *browser rendering engines*, which determine how web pages are displayed. To render a page, the browser will take all the content (HTML and images) and styles (CSS) as well as any JavaScript and put it all together to determine how to display the page on the screen. All of the browsers that use the same rendering engine will display a particular set of code in the same way.

The four rendering engines, which will be referenced in the code snippet a few paragraphs ahead, are as follows:

- *WebKit*, which is used by Apple's Safari and Google's Chrome browser
- Mozilla's rendering engine, called *Gecko*, which is used in Firefox
- Microsoft's rendering engine, called *Trident*, used in IE
- Opera's rendering engine, called *Presto*, which is used in the Opera web browser

Because each of the browser rendering engines may render a still-in-progress style differently, each rendering engine has its own prefixed CSS property to correspond with these styles, which are variations on the actual property.

For example, the hyphens property is not yet finalized, so it has variations for the four browser rendering engines, and you need to list each one in your code:

```
p {
    -webkit-hyphens: auto;
    -moz-hyphens: auto;
    -ms-hyphens: auto;
    -o-hyphens: auto;
    hyphens: auto;
}
```

The five declarations all have a different property, the last being the non-prefixed hyphens, the property that will eventually be finalized by the W3C.

The four before it correspond to each browser rendering engine listed—you can tell which is which by the first part of the property name, webkit, moz, ms, or o. Note that the prefixed properties also *start* with a dash.

In this example, if WebKit is still testing the hyphens property, WebKit browsers will see -webkit-hyphens and render that declaration. They won't recognize the other prefixed properties, or the non-prefixed property, and thus will ignore them.

But then what happens when the specification is approved? Once WebKit implements the actual hyphens property, the -webkit-hyphens property will still be recognized by WebKit browsers, at least for a little while. However, because the non-prefixed hyphens is further down the stylesheet, and it is now valid, it will be recognized by WebKit browsers too and will override -webkit-hyphens.

Most of the time, when using a property that has not yet been finalized, you will need to include all four of the prefixed properties, similar to what is displayed in the example just shown.

The order of the four browser prefixed properties does not matter. Many people prefer the order used in the previous example (i.e., longest to shortest), just because it looks neater in your stylesheet. But the non-prefixed property always has to come last.

You'll notice in this code that I placed each declaration on a separate line, which I don't otherwise do in CSS. I make the exception in this case because separate lines make it much easier to make sure all the prefixes are included, and to see that each one includes the same value (although in some cases, you may need to use different values for some of them).

Eventually, you'll be able to stop using the prefixed versions of each property and only use the non-prefixed property (although there will always be more new properties being introduced that will require prefixes).

Several new properties in CSS3 are already supported by some or all of the major browsers. It doesn't hurt the rendering of the page to keep the prefixed properties in your CSS when they're no longer needed— that's why the non-prefixed property comes last, to override the rest. However, they'll add a little unnecessary weight to your CSS.

If a CSS3 property requires prefixes at the time that this book goes to press, it will be noted, but by the time you read this, that status may have changed.

Check Can I Use... (*http://caniuse.com/*) to find out which CSS properties are supported by which browser versions, and whether you need to use prefixes.

Where CSS Goes

Styles can be applied to your web page in a few different ways, either through a separate file called a stylesheet or included in the code of the web page. Where you choose to include your CSS has an effect on how it is applied to the page.

EMBEDDED STYLES

If you want styles to apply to only one page on the site, you can add them directly in the `<head>` of the HTML file, using the `<style>` element. You just place one or more CSS rules inside the element, as follows:

```
<head>

<style>
p { color: blue; }
</style>

</head>
```

Normally, though, you don't want styles to apply to only one page; you want them to apply to the whole website. Even if a particular style will only apply to a particular page, it's still best to include it in a separate stylesheet so that everything is in one place and easy to find, especially if more than one person will be working on the code for the site.

However, embedded styles should be used when you're coding an HTML email, because email clients usually can't import external stylesheets.

STYLESHEETS

Generally, your CSS declarations will be collected in one or more separate files called stylesheets, which are linked to from your HTML files. You want styles such as typeface, colors, and layout to be consistent throughout the website, and using stylesheets means that you can declare a style once and have it apply to every page of your site.

The <link> element allows you to link documents (files) to your HTML page, including CSS and JavaScript files. The <link> element is included in the <head> of the HTML file:

```
<head>
<link rel="stylesheet" href="styles/mystyle.css">
</head>
```

Any particular web page can link to more than one stylesheet.

You can also use @import to link styles to a page. Inside the <head> of the document, you would add an @import rule inside a <style> element:

```
<head>

<style>
@import url(styles/mystyle.css)
</style>

</head>
```

Linking to and importing a stylesheet effectively do the same thing, as far as getting the styles to the browser. However, choosing one or the other can have an effect on the site's performance, which we'll look at in Chapter 11. Generally, you should use <link> and minimize the number of stylesheets that you're using.

INLINE STYLES

Occasionally you will want to be even more specific and apply a style to only one occurrence of an element, directly inside the HTML.

To do this, you simply add a style attribute (style="...") to the element, and any styles you wish to apply go inside the quotation marks:

```
<p style="color: green; font-size: 2em;">This is a
paragraph.</p>
```

You should avoid using inline styles on websites, because it's easy to lose track of where all your CSS is and what it's doing, making the website harder to maintain. However, it can be useful when testing out changes to a page.

The Cascade

If you're already comfortable using CSS, this section will contain familiar material, but it's worth a review.

So far, we have styles in external stylesheets, styles in the page <head>, and inline styles. We also learned that styles can be attached to elements, classes, and IDs. If more than one conflicting style is assigned to the same element, how does the browser know which to pick?

CSS has very detailed rules about what order to apply styles in, which is the *cascade* in Cascading Style Sheets. The cascade determines which rules take precedence over other rules.

The cascade can be pretty difficult to comprehend, but most of the time your CSS will be straightforward and it will be clear what's going on. I'm going to present a somewhat simplified version of how the cascade works, but if you're going to be working with code a lot this is something you should learn more about.

HOW IT WORKS

Every HTML element has several properties that apply to it. For example, the properties of a <p> include text color, background color, font size, typeface, whether it's bold, whether it's italic, if there's a border and if so what the border looks like, where the paragraph is positioned on the page, and so on (there are dozens more).

As the browser is rendering the web page, it looks at each individual element one at a time and decides how to render that element, by determining the values for each of those properties.

The browser goes through a very specific routine—a hierarchy—to decide which style to apply to the particular element. These steps are in order of priority, starting with the highest priority:

1. Rules that are marked as important

2. Inline style rules

3. Rules containing IDs

4. Rules containing classes, attributes, and pseudo-classes

5. Rules containing elements and pseudo-elements

6. Inherited rules

7. Default values

The order of the steps is often called the *CSS specificity*, as it goes from the most specific rules (applying to only one or a few instances of an element) to the least specific rules (applying to all instances of an element).

For each element on the page, the browser will go through the hierarchy in order until it finds a style for each particular property. For example, let's say it needs to know the color of the text (`color`) for a paragraph. It will start by looking for rules marked as important, and go on to inline styles, IDs, and so on. Once it has found all the `color` values for the paragraph, it will choose which one takes priority according to the cascade.

IMPORTANT

If you want a particular rule to apply no matter what, you can mark it with `!important`. This can be used either in your regular styles or in inline styles. The browser will look for `!important` everywhere before moving on to the next rule.

In the following example, the `color` has been marked as `!important`, but the `font-weight` has not. `!important` comes directly before the semicolon and applies to only one declaration, not the whole declaration group:

```
p { font-weight: bold; color: blue !important; }
```

This paragraph will have blue text, no matter whether other colors are applied to that same element in other declarations.

Although `!important` seems like a useful tool, you should use it only very, very rarely, if you absolutely can't accomplish what you want using classes, IDs, or other selectors. Once you apply `!important`, you're at the top level, so there's really no way to go over its head, so to speak.

INLINE STYLES

If the browser doesn't find any !important rules to apply to our color, next it will look for inline styles. These are styles that are attached directly to elements within your HTML document. All inline styles take precedence over any styles found in external stylesheets or embedded in the <head> of the document:

```
<p style="color: blue;">Paragraph text.</p>
```

IDS

If there are no inline styles for the color, next the browser will look for any IDs that apply to the element, either directly or through a descendent selector:

```
<p id="example">Paragraph text.</p>

#example { color: blue; }
```

CLASSES, ATTRIBUTES, AND PSEUDO-CLASSES

If there are no ID styles for the color, the browser will next look for any classes, attributes, and pseudo-classes that apply to the element. Again, it can be included in a descendent selector:

```
.example { color: blue; }
.example p { color: green; }
```

ELEMENTS AND PSEUDO-ELEMENTS

If there are no styles for the color that contain classes, attributes, or pseudo-classes, the browser will next look for any styles that only contain elements or pseudo-elements in the selector:

```
<p>Paragraph text.</p>

p { color: blue; }
```

INHERITED RULES

At this point, if the browser has found no styles that directly apply to the color of our <p>, it will look for any inherited styles that might apply.

Inheritance is pretty simple. This just means that if an element does not have a style applied to it, it will inherit the style of its parent element:

```
<p>This is a paragraph with <strong>bold text</strong>.
</p>

p { color: blue; }
```

Because the `<strong>` doesn't have a `color` value assigned to it, it will inherit the value from its parent element, which is the `<p>`. The `color` of the `<p>` is set to blue, so that will be the color of the `<strong>`.

Not every property is inherited, but it will be pretty obvious which ones are. For example, font size is inherited, because once you set the size for your `<p>`, you want everything inside the `<p>` to be the same size—even text that's also inside a `<strong>` or `<em>`.

On the other hand, borders *aren't* inherited. If you gave your `<div>` a border, you wouldn't want or expect each individual paragraph in the `<div>` to have its own border as well.

DEFAULT VALUES

If we've gotten this far without finding a `color` for our `<p>`, all is not lost: every element has a default value.

For most properties, the default value is part of the CSS specification. For example, the default color for any text element is black. If you don't specify a color, the browser will use the default color.

So, if there are no styles at all that would apply a `color` to our `<p>`, it will be black text.

WHAT IF ANYTHING CONFLICTS?

There's still a bit more to it than what I've already explained.

Beyond the hierarchy, specificity looks at how many items are in a selector. More items equals higher priority (i.e., a rule with two IDs has priority over a rule with only one ID).

If two style rules are still equal, and it doesn't know which one to pick, it uses the one that comes *last*, after putting all your styles in order (from the top of your first stylesheet to the end of your last stylesheet).

What you've read here is a summary that will cover pretty much everything you need to know. But if you want to learn more about specificity, or use it to do more powerful things with your CSS, refer to Vitaly Friedman's *Smashing Magazine* article, "CSS Specificity: Things You Should Know" (*http://coding.smashingmagazine.com/2007/07/27/css-specificity-things-you-should-know/*).

Using the Cascade

All of that probably seemed really confusing, but in reality it's simple, because *you* are deciding what to apply styles to.

As you're styling a page, you'll actually go in the opposite order of what we just discussed. You want to apply styles as broadly as possible, so you'll rarely get into the specifics.

For example, you aren't likely to have dozens of text colors for paragraphs on your page, with numerous competing style rules to sort through. You might have one or two, but you'll know exactly how you applied them. This is the order you will follow:

1. Default values

2. Inherited rules

3. Rules containing elements and pseudo-elements

4. Rules containing classes, attributes, and pseudo-classes

5. Rules containing IDs

6. Inline style rules

7. Rules that are marked as important

DEFAULT VALUES AND RESET

First, start with the default values. For most things, this is pretty obvious. Without any styles, as we saw in the HTML page we were working on in Chapter 3, the text is black, heading text is larger than paragraph text, and nothing has a border. Those are default values.

However, browsers don't always use the default values they're supposed to, so to make sure we're starting at the same place no matter what browser is being used, we're going to reset some values to zero. Otherwise we might have little leftover remnants of incorrect defaults that may affect our design and make it display differently in different browsers.

Reset

To reset the CSS, we'll set all the margins and padding to zero, and set some of the font properties to a standard base size. After everything is reset, we'll add all of our styles to set everything to the properties we want. The section of CSS that resets everything is often called a *reset CSS* or *reset stylesheet*.

For example, if we use a reset CSS on our Pandas Forever site, we get what you see in Figure 4-3.

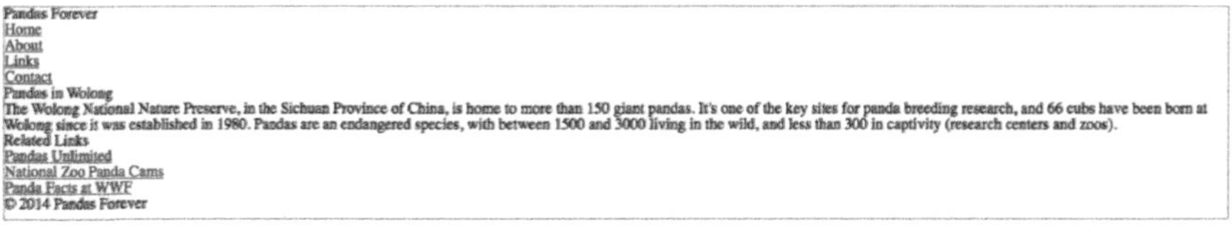

Pandas Forever
Home
About
Links
Contact
Pandas in Wolong
The Wolong National Nature Preserve, in the Sichuan Province of China, is home to more than 150 giant pandas. It's one of the key sites for panda breeding research, and 66 cubs have been born at Wolong since it was established in 1980. Pandas are an endangered species, with between 1500 and 3000 living in the wild, and less than 300 in captivity (research centers and zoos).
Related Links
Pandas Unlimited
National Zoo Panda Cams
Panda Facts at WWF
© 2014 Pandas Forever

Figure 4-3. Our example page, with all the styles reset.

It looked better before, right? Don't worry, we'll fix it in a bit.

It would be a lot of work to figure out all the different elements you're using in your CSS, and then write the style declarations to reset all of them. Luckily, a few people have already done this for us, creating blocks of CSS containing all the reset styles you need, that you can simply copy and paste into your own stylesheet.

One of the most popular is Eric Meyer's Reset CSS (*http://meyerweb. com/eric/tools/css/reset/*). It's in the public domain, so it's free for you to use and modify in any way you wish.

An alternative is Normalize.css (*http://necolas.github.com/normalize. css/*) from Nicolas Gallagher.

You can also create your own reset—see "Quick Tip: Create Your Own Simple Reset.css File" (*http://net.tutsplus.com/tutorials/html-css-tech-niques/weekend-quick-tip-create-your-own-resetcss-file/*) by Jeffrey Way on Nettuts+ for details.

The reset needs to be the very first CSS rendered by the browser, to make sure that it doesn't override any of your other styles. So, it should either be the first CSS file linked to in your <head> or, if you don't have it in a separate file, the first lines of code in your first CSS file.

INHERITED RULES

The next step we'll look at is inherited rules. Most styles on your site will be inherited.

So, if you set the text color of your <body> to be pink (although I don't think you'd want to), all text on the site will be pink. You don't need to worry about setting the color for paragraphs, lists, <div>s, and so on, unless you want them to be something other than pink:

```
body { color: pink; }
```

There's one exception to this: links (<a>) don't inherit color; they are blue by default (and purple for visited links) so that they will be visually differentiated on the page. You can leave them blue/purple, or give them a different color by assigning a color to the <a> element.

Also, make sure not to add style declarations that are redundant. If the <body> is set to pink, don't also add a rule to make all the <p>s pink. They're already pink, so you're just adding code you don't need.

ELEMENTS

Apply styles first in the broadest stroke. For example, if you want all your text to be in Helvetica, apply that style rule to the <body> element, and everything else on the page will inherit.

If you want all your top-level headings to be Georgia instead, apply that style to the <h1> element, and all your headings will be Georgia while everything else remains Helvetica.

Whatever style you are applying, try to find the highest-level element that it can apply to.

In our case, we want to change the size of the headings on our site to be larger than the other text on the page, and bold:

```
h1 { font-size: 2em; }
h2 { font-size: 1.3em; }
h1, h2 { font-weight: bold; }
p, ul { font-size: 1em; }
```

The em unit is a relative unit, and 2em means that the <h1> text will be two times as large as the base font size (the size of all other text on the site). We'll talk about ems in more detail in the "Measurements" section later in this chapter.

Even though the paragraphs and lists will be the default font size, we'll include that in our CSS just so there's no confusion, so we'll give them a value of 1em.

EVERYTHING ELSE

If a style needs to be more specific than all instances of an element, you can differentiate those in a few ways. For example, if you want the links in the <nav> to be larger:

```
nav li { font-size: 1.5em; }
```

All the other `<li>`s on the site will continue to inherit their size, so you'll see in Figure 4-4 that the links in the "Related Links" section didn't change size.

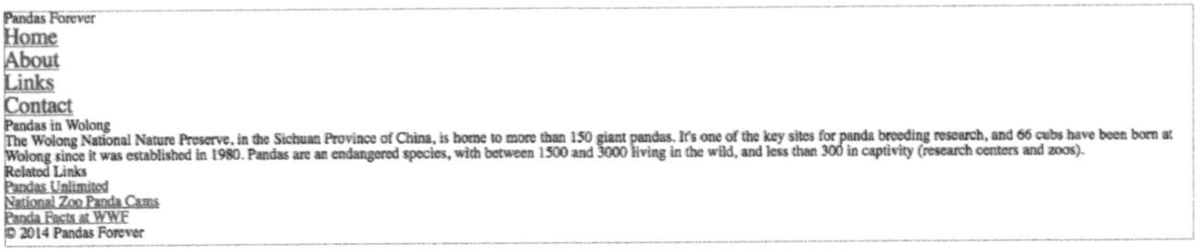

Pandas Forever
Home
About
Links
Contact
Pandas in Wolong
The Wolong National Nature Preserve, in the Sichuan Province of China, is home to more than 150 giant pandas. It's one of the key sites for panda breeding research, and 66 cubs have been born at Wolong since it was established in 1980. Pandas are an endangered species, with between 1500 and 3000 living in the wild, and less than 300 in captivity (research centers and zoos).
Related Links
Pandas Unlimited
National Zoo Panda Cams
Panda Facts at WWF
© 2014 Pandas Forever

Figure 4-4. The size of the list items in the navigation got bigger, but other list items stayed the same size.

Start by using descendant selectors as in the previous example, before moving on and adding classes to elements to differentiate them from others.

But don't use descendants and classes unless you actually need them. In the previous example, because the links were actually the only text inside the `<nav>`, we could have applied the style directly to the `<nav>` instead of using a descendant selector. This would have the exact same effect:

```
nav { font-size: 1.5em; }
```

The most specific selectors are IDs, inline styles, and `!important`, but you should avoid using those unless you really know what you're doing.

KEEPING IT SIMPLE

You might be wondering why it's necessary to keep CSS as simple as possible. Why not just add in some classes and `!important`s if they'll do what you want them to do?

The reason is that for any website, you're almost certainly going to be making changes to the CSS later on, whether it's tiny tweaks or a major site overhaul. The simpler the CSS is to start, the easier it is to make changes, especially if someone other than the original developer is the one making the changes.

And as I mentioned, this book only tells you the very basics of how CSS works.

If something doesn't look as expected on your page, it may be that the cascade is rendering a different style than you intended. Test and make changes until you figure out what's going on. The easiest way to learn how everything works is to try out different things and see what happens.

And always make sure to test your site in multiple browsers and devices, to make sure that the CSS is applied the same in all of them. We'll talk about testing more in Chapter 8.

Comments

As with HTML, you can add comments to your CSS files, although you use different symbols to mark your comments as such.

The browser will simply ignore everything inside the comment.

Common ways to use comments in a stylesheet are to provide a description or explanation of what something is used for or to make notes of when changes are made:

```
/* this is a CSS comment */

/* they can be on one or multiple lines
or on the same line as your style code */ h1 { color:
#7b0000; }
```

Organizing Your Stylesheet

Other than when styles need to go in a specific order to be applied correctly, your stylesheet can be in pretty much any order. But it's best to go about it in a systematic way to make it easier to find everything later. Once you start adding media queries to the mix, you'll need to know where everything is.

You're always going to start with the reset CSS. That may be a separate file, or it may be the first lines of CSS in your primary stylesheet.

Some people like to arrange their stylesheets by page or site section, with comments labeling each section of the stylesheet. You can add dashes or other symbols inside a comment to draw "lines" between the sections of your stylesheet, making it easier to find particular code:

```
/* Main Content ---------------------------- */

styles for typography, layout, etc. in main content

/* Header ------------------------- */

styles for typography, layout, etc. in header

/* Footer ------------------------ */

styles for typography, layout, etc. in footer
```

Other people prefer to put like items together, regardless of what section of the page they are styling, for a better idea of what's happening:

```
/* Typography ---------------------------- */

p { ... }
header p { ... }
footer p { ... }
.classname p { ... }

li { ... }
footer li { ... }
.classname li { ... }

/* Layout ---------------------------- */

header { ... }
footer { .... }
```

In your web browser, you can view the HTML and CSS files from any website. Look at the CSS from various websites to see how the styles are arranged. There isn't a right way to do it, but be consistent.

The Box Model

The most important concept in CSS layout is the "box model." This just means that every single HTML element on the page is a rectangular box. Each box may or may not have borders, padding (empty space inside the edges of the box), and margins (empty space outside the edges of the box).

As you see in Figure 4-5, the content of the box is in the center. The content of an element can be text, images, or child elements (like a paragraph inside a <div>). The element is surrounded by padding, then a border, then margins, any of which can be set to a width and height of zero (a border with zero width and height would be invisible).

MEASUREMENTS

The height, width, padding, margin, and borders of elements can be set using any one of a variety of units of measurement.

Traditionally, absolute units of measurement have been used, to ensure an element's exact placement on the screen. In responsive design, you'll generally use relative units of measurement, so that each element can respond to the size of the viewport.

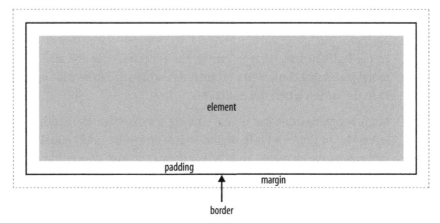

Figure 4-5. This element is surrounded by padding, a border, and margins

These are the most common relative units of measurement:

%
> Percent is measured against the containing element.

em
> Ems are relative to the **font-size** of the element.

rem
> Rems are relative to the **font-size** of the document (i.e., the html element).

And these are the most common absolute units of measurement:

px
> Pixels are an absolute measurement, but they aren't necessarily consistent across devices.

in, cm, *and* mm
> Physical measurements map to pixels, but also aren't consistent across devices. One inch is 96 pixels, one centimeter is 37.8 pixels, and a millimeter is 3.78 pixels.

pt
> Points are equal to 1/72 of an inch, and are much more common in print design. On the Web, they can be useful for making a print stylesheet.

EMS

You'll use ems for measurements a lot in responsive design.

In old-fashioned metal typesetting, the *em* referred to the size of the metal plates that contained a raised letter, which had to be wide enough to fit the widest letter, the capital M.

Many people assume that digital ems are also based on the width of the letter M, but they aren't. In digital terms, an em is simply equal to the font size of the element. And the em doesn't change depending on the font chosen, as you can see in Figure 4-6.

Figure 4-6. These boxes are exactly one em in height and width.

HEIGHT AND WIDTH

In the box model, every element has a height and width, which can sometimes be changed by CSS.

Inline elements have an inherent height and width, which cannot be overridden. An inline element will, by default, only be as wide and high as it needs to be to display its content, as shown in Figure 4-7.

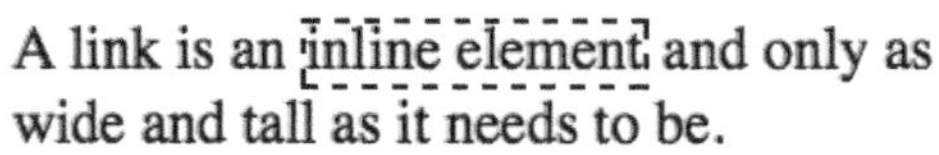

A link is an inline element and only as wide and tall as it needs to be.

Figure 4-7. Inline elements are only as wide and tall as they need to be to display their content.

Block elements are, by default, 100% the width of the containing element, even if the content doesn't fill the space.

The height is, by default, as high as it needs to be to contain the content. For example, a paragraph will be the height necessary to contain all the text as it wraps onto multiple lines, as you can see in Figure 4-8.

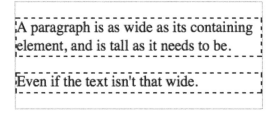

Figure 4-8. Block elements are by default as wide as their containing element, and as tall as they need to be to contain their content.

You can change the width or height of a block element with CSS:

```
div { width: 75%; height: 200px; }
```

Keep in mind that a percentage width is based on the width of the containing element. So, in the preceding code, the <div> will be 75% of the width of whatever element it is in.

MARGINS AND PADDING

Every element has margins to provide space around the *outside* of the element in the layout of the page. Each element also has padding, which provides space on the *inside* of the element, around the content. The effect is often similar, unless the element has a border, which is outside the padding and inside the margin.

Browsers have a default margin and padding for each of the elements, but it's not always consistent from browser to browser. That's why we used the reset CSS earlier to set the margins and padding to zero for every element. That way, you won't accidentally have margins and padding that are different sizes on different browsers, making things not line up the way you expect.

Generally, in responsive design you'll use percent to set the horizontal (left/right) margins and padding of elements, so that the layout can respond to the size of the viewport. On a wide screen, you have space for ample margins around content. On a small screen, you don't want to waste valuable screen space with huge margins.

Vertical margins and padding (top/bottom) can be set in pixels, because they don't need to respond to the size of the viewport.

Each of the four sides of the element can have different values for the width of the padding or margin.

This example sets each of the four sides separately. The order goes clockwise—top, right, bottom, left (as an easy way to remember the order, think of it with the mnemonic TRBL, or "trouble"):

```
div {
    padding: 1px 2px 3px 4px;
    margin: 1px 2px 3px 4px;
}
```

In this example, the top margin/padding is set to 1 pixel, the right to 2 pixels, the bottom to 3 pixels, and the left to 4 pixels.

If the measurements are the same on opposing sides, or on all four sides, the values can be consolidated.

You still use the same mnemonic TRBL, and the missing numbers will mirror the opposite side of the box. So in the following example, top is 1 pixel and right is 2 pixels, and bottom will be the same as top (1 pixel) and left the same as right (2 pixels):

```
div {
    padding: 1px 2px;
    margin: 1px 2px;
}
```

If there are three numbers, the same thing goes. If you give numbers for top, right, and bottom, the missing number for left will mirror the right (2 pixels):

```
div {
    padding: 1px 2px 3px;
    margin: 1px 2px 3px;
}
```

If there is only one number, it will be used for all four sides of the box:

```
div {
    padding: 1px;
    margin: 1px;
}
```

You can also set one side individually—for example, if you had set margins for all paragraphs, but wanted to override that for one margin on a particular paragraph:

```
p { margin: 5px 10%; }
.other p { margin-top: 10px; }
```

You can set any side individually, with padding-top, padding-right, padding-bottom, padding-left, margin-top, margin-right, margin-bottom, and margin-left. Of course, if any of these are being applied to the same element, you would want to combine them into one declaration as noted previously.

If you want to center a block element in its containing element, you can do so by setting the left and right margins of the element to the value of auto. This sticks the element in the middle of the container, and the remaining space is split evenly between the left and right margins, effectively centering the element, as you see in Figure 4-9.

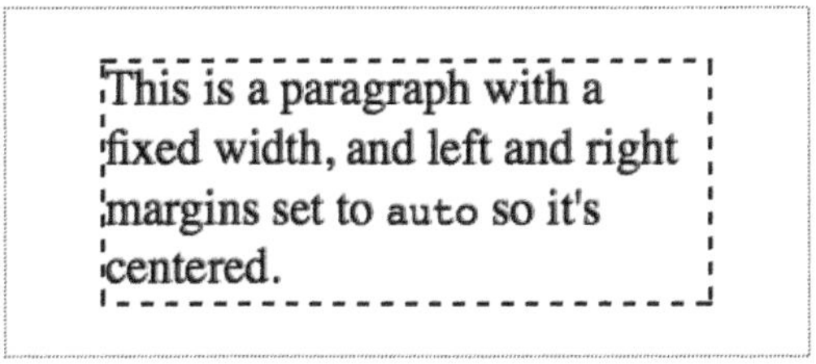

Figure 4-9. Setting the left and right margins of a block element to auto will center it in the containing element.

This only has a visual effect if the element you're centering has a width of less than 100%; otherwise, it will just fill the whole space.

BORDERS

Borders are placed between the padding and margin and provide an outline for an element.

When declaring a border, you need to specify the width of the line, the style of border, and the color.

Border width is commonly declared in pixels.

border-style values include solid, dotted, and dashed. double provides a double line, and groove, ridge, inset, and outset all provide 3D borders in different directions. You can see examples of these in Figure 4-10.

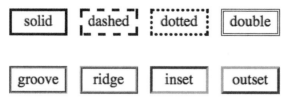

Figure 4-10. The options for border styles.

To declare borders all in one declaration, you can include the values in any order. The following code sets the <div> border to 1 pixel, with a style of solid and a color of red:

```
div { border: 1px solid red; }
```

You can also set each of the three properties separately, if you only need to do one at once:

```
div { border-width: 2px; }
div { border-style: dotted; }
div { border-color: green; }
```

You can set each side of an element separately, as well:

```
div { border-left-width: 2em; }
div { border-right-style: inset; }
div { border-top-color: blue; }
```

And so on: each of the three properties can be set for top, bottom, left, and right.

BOX-SIZING

Now that you've learned how to measure all the pieces of the box, you need to know that unfortunately it's kind of tricky to figure out the size of the box on the web page. Do the padding, borders, and margins count as part of the width and height of an element? It depends.

There are actually two separate ways to tell the browser how to measure everything. The box-sizing property, which is new in CSS3, allows you to choose between the two methods, which are border-box and content-box.

With border-box, once you set the width of your block element, any padding and borders you add will be inside that width. In contrast, with the default content-box, any padding and borders will be outside the width.

border-box is generally easier to use. However, this is not the default, so to use it, you have to set your element to box-sizing: border-box.

This property isn't fully supported by all browsers, so you have to use the vendor prefixes. IE8+ and Opera already support this property, so you only need prefixes for WebKit and Mozilla:

```
div {
    -webkit-box-sizing: border-box;
    -moz-box-sizing: border-box;
    box-sizing: border-box;
}
```

You may want to apply **border-box** to your whole website. The code to do so is:

```
*, *:before, *:after {
    -moz-box-sizing: border-box;
    -webkit-box-sizing: border-box;
    box-sizing: border-box;
}
```

Those asterisks just mean that the CSS should be applied to every element.

[NOTE]

box-sizing doesn't work in IE 7 and older, so even if you set something to border-box, it will render as the default content-box. When you're testing your site, you may decide you need to add additional CSS to fix any layout issues. You can also find a polyfill to make box-sizing work in IE 6 and 7 at HTML5 Please (*http://html5please.com/#box-sizing*), from the people behind HTML5 Boilerplate, Modernizr, and CSS3 Please.

In Figure 4-11, both paragraphs have a width of 300 pixels, padding of 20 pixels on each side, and a border width of 5 pixels. In the first paragraph, the padding and border are inside the 300-pixel width. In the second paragraph, the padding and border are added on outside the 300-pixel width.

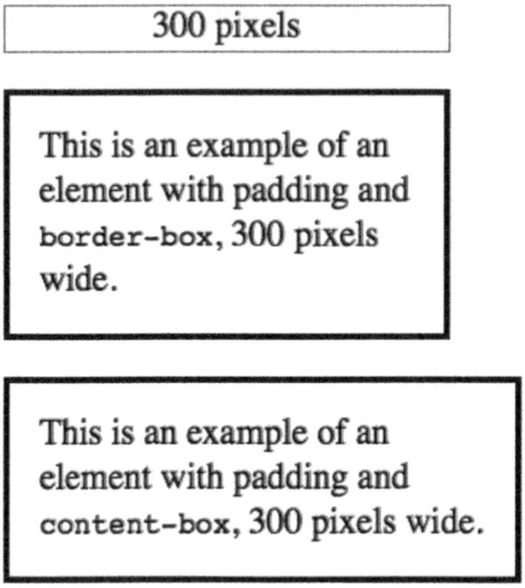

```
300 pixels
```

```
This is an example of an
element with padding and
border-box, 300 pixels
wide.
```

```
This is an example of an
element with padding and
content-box, 300 pixels wide.
```

Figure 4-11. The difference between how a block element is rendered with the only difference in style being setting box-sizing to a value of border-box or content-box.

display

One of the key properties of HTML elements is display, which affects how an element takes up space on the screen. Most elements have a value of either block or inline. The difference is just like it sounds—block elements are rendered as stacked blocks, and inline elements are rendered inline with the flow of text, as you see in Figure 4-12.

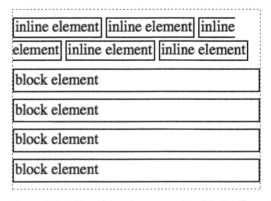

Figure 4-12. Inline elements are rendered in the flow of text, while block elements are stacked blocks.

display is a CSS property, so you can change the value for any element, but you should know the default values for the elements you're working with.

An example of a block element is a paragraph. Look at Figure 4-12, and imagine each block element as a paragraph. Each one automatically starts on a new line, and whatever is after it also starts on a new line. Some other block elements include structural elements like <nav> and <article>, headings, and <div>.

Block elements always fill their containing element horizontally, unless you manually set the width to be different. So, a block element that is only inside the <body> will be as wide as the browser window. Each block element starts on a new line, and the following element starts on a new line, whether or not it's a block element.

Inline elements, on the other hand, are *inline*, in the middle of other text. For example, an inline element might be <strong>, which contains just a few words in the middle of a paragraph that you have set to appear in bold. Other inline elements include <em>, <span>, and links.

Inline elements are only as big as they need to be. The words inside an inline element stay where they're supposed to be inside the paragraph or other block element, without starting on a new line and without making the following text start on a new line.

Besides the block and inline elements, there are also list-item elements, which are the items in a bulleted list, <li>. They behave similarly to block elements in most respects. Tables, table rows, and table cells have their own display properties.

There are a few other values for the display property, which you will likely not use much (if at all). You can see a full list in the Mozilla Developer Network's "display" article (*https://developer.mozilla.org/en-US/docs/CSS/display*).

Although you'll keep the default display value for most elements, you can use CSS to change it. For example, it's common to change list items from list-item to inline so that they will display in a horizontal row instead of a vertical row:

```
li { display: inline; }
```

Positioning

The key to putting things where you want them on a page is position-ing. This is a little tricky, so if you're not a coder, don't worry if you don't understand exactly how it works—you just need to understand the gist of the differences.

By default, the flow of the page goes from left to right for inline ele-ments, wrapping onto a new "line" when necessary, and from top to bottom for block elements, as you saw in Figure 4-12. The various position values can change that.

STATIC

The default position setting is static. Things just go where you think they're supposed to go, as in Figure 4-13.

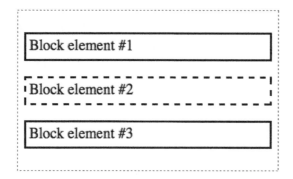

Figure 4-13. Block elements with default position appear stacked, as usual.

RELATIVE

An element can be given a relative position, which moves it to a dif-ferent location but ignores the flow of other content on the page. For example, in Figure 4-14, the second paragraph has relative positioning, moving it 40 pixels from the top and 40 from the left:

```
p.2nd { position: relative; left: 40px; top: 40px; }
```

The browser leaves a space where the element *should* be, but then just moves the element, relatively, in the direction(s) specified.

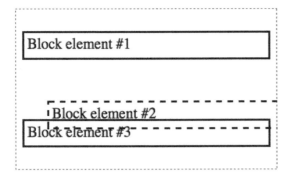

Figure 4-14. The second block is positioned relatively.

As you can see, it simply overlaps other elements on the page, rather than pushing them out of the way to make space. On the right side of the screen, there is no room for the edge of the box to go 40 pixels to the right, so part of the box moves off-screen and is no longer visible to the user.

Note that the positioned element is *on top* of the other elements on the page.

To make this work you need to set the **position** to **relative**, and then also define the change in position, either horizontally, vertically, or both.

ABSOLUTE

Absolute positioning is different. The browser moves the element as you request, but it doesn't leave a space where the element should have been.

And instead of the directions being in relation to where the element should be in the document flow, they position it in the first containing element that doesn't have a **position** of **static**.

In the following example, the three blocks are in a containing **<div>**:

```
p.2nd { position: absolute; left: 40px; top: 40px; }
```

Box #2 is absolutely positioned, so it's ignored in the flow of the other elements. Instead, it's placed 40 pixels down from the top-left corner of the containing element, and 40 pixels to the right of the top-left corner of the containing **<div>**.

Because there is no empty space left for it, it simply overlaps the other elements, as you can see in Figure 4-15.

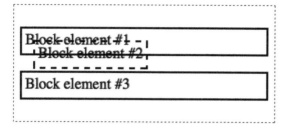

Figure 4-15. The second block is positioned absolutely.

An odd thing you'll notice about the absolutely positioned element shown in Figure 4-15 is that its width is only as wide as the content, and not the full width of the containing element, as would be normal for a block element. Absolutely positioned elements don't have the default width of 100% that other block elements do.

If there was more text in the element, it would expand until it hit the right edge of the containing elements, and then the text would wrap.

[NOTE]

You'll have noticed that in some of these cases, elements overlap. To change which element is in front, you can give elements a z-index value: The element with the highest value will be in front. Negative numbers are allowed:

```
p.1st { z-index: 50; }
p.2nd { position: relative; left: 40px; top: 40px;
z-index: 25; }
```

FIXED

Fixed positioning is very similar, but the element will be positioned relative to the entire page, not just the containing element. So, in the previous example, if we used fixed positioning, box #2 would be positioned in the top-left corner of the web page, 40 pixels down and 40 pixels to the right of the lefthand edge.

Any element with a fixed position will stay in place even if the user scrolls the page, so if you want a navigation section or another element to always be at the top of the page, this is the way to do it. Keep in mind that the other elements will ignore the fixed element, so it will overlap.

Fixed positioning is a little quirky in mobile browsers. Brad Frost's article "Fixed Positioning in Mobile Browsers" (*http://bradfrostweb.com/blog/mobile/fixed-position/*) explains why in more detail.

MEASUREMENTS FOR POSITIONED ELEMENTS

When an element is given a `relative`, `absolute`, or `fixed` position, the offset numbers will be given from the left, right, top, or bottom.

You can use either `left` or `right` (but not both) to move it horizontally, and/or either `top` or `bottom` (but not both) to move it vertically. If you accidentally give it conflicting directions (i.e., both `left` and `right`), the browser will ignore the first declaration.

You don't have to move an element *both* horizontally and vertically; you can declare only one of the direction properties.

Note that when using the directions, the element is being moved *from* that direction, not *toward* that direction. So, `left: 40px;` will move the box 40 pixels *away* from the lefthand side of its original location, so it's actually moving to the right.

You can also use negative numbers. If you're doing relative positioning, moving an element 40 pixels to the left has the same effect as moving it −40 pixels to the right. The same is true with top and bottom, because you're only moving it in relation to itself.

However, the same isn't true of absolute and fixed positioning. Positioning the element 40 pixels from the top and 40 pixels from the left, as shown in the following code, will place it 40 pixels from the left edge of the containing element (see Figure 4-16):

```
p.2nd { position: absolute; left: 40px; top: 40px; }
```

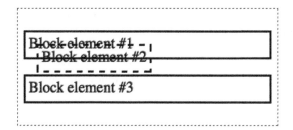

Figure 4-16. The second block is positioned absolutely, and 40 pixels from the left and top.

Positioning it −40 pixels to the right, on the other hand, will start it flush against the right edge of the containing element and then move it 40 more pixels to the right (see Figure 4-17):

```
p.2nd { position: absolute; right: -40px; top: 40px; }
```

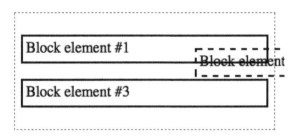

Figure 4-17. The second block is positioned −40 pixels from the right.

Positioning can be kind of tricky. The best way to learn it is to put together a test page and try out all these properties to get a better feel for how they work.

float and clear

The **float** and **clear** properties also allow you to change where an element is positioned on the page, although they are separate from the **position** property.

float is what you use to make content flow around a particular element. For example, let's say you have an image in between two paragraphs, as in the following code (see Figure 4-18):

```
<p>...</p>
<img src="image.jpg">
<p>...</p>
```

You don't want all that empty space in there, so you will want to fill it up with text, as in Figure 4-19.

Using the **float** property tells the browser to float the element on the left or right side of its containing element, and the following elements, whether block or inline, will wrap around that floated element.

Of course, you don't want to float all the images on your website, so you will need to differentiate that image somehow, such as with a class. You might make a class such as **floatleft** that you could apply to any element that you want to float to the right:

```
.floatleft { float: left; }
```

The Wolong National Nature Preserve, in the Sichuan Province of China, is home to more than 150 giant pandas. It's one of the key sites for panda breeding research, and 66 cubs have been born at Wolong since it was established in 1980.

The Wolong Nature Reserve covers around 200,000 hectares (772 square miles) in the Ming Shan mountain range, in the ABA Tibetan Autonomous Region, near the Tibetan Plateau. Elevations in the reserve range from 1555 to 4600 meters (4,000 to 11,000 ft).

Figure 4-18. The image is between two paragraphs with no float.

The Wolong National Nature Preserve, in the Sichuan Province of China, is home to more than 150 giant pandas. It's one of the key sites for panda breeding research, and 66 cubs have been born at Wolong since it was established in 1980.

The Wolong Nature Reserve covers around 200,000 hectares (772 square miles) in the Ming Shan mountain range, in the ABA Tibetan Autonomous Region, near the Tibetan Plateau. Elevations in the reserve range from 1555 to 4600 meters (4,000 to 11,000 ft).

Figure 4-19. The image is floated to the left.

Keep in mind that all following elements will wrap around the floated element until there is no more space. You might end up with things wrapping that you don't want, such as the heading in Figure 4-20.

If you don't want everything to float, just apply the clear property to the first element that you want to clear onto a new line:

```
ul { clear: left; }
```

When you clear, the left or right needs to match the previous float.

The Wolong National Nature Preserve, in the Sichuan Province of China, is home to more than 150 giant pandas. It's one of the key sites for panda breeding research, and 66 cubs have been born at Wolong since it was established in 1980.

 The Wolong Nature Reserve covers around 200,000 hectares (772 square miles) in the Ming Shan mountain range, in the ABA Tibetan Autonomous Region, near the Tibetan Plateau. Elevations in the reserve range from 1555 to 4600 meters (4,000 to 11,000 ft).

Additional Panda Facts

Pandas are an endangered species, with between 1500 and 3000 living in the wild, and less than 300 in captivity (research centers and zoos).

The Wolong National Nature Preserve, in the Sichuan Province of China, is home to more than 150 giant pandas. It's one of the key sites for panda breeding research, and 66 cubs have been born at Wolong since it was established in 1980.

 The Wolong Nature Reserve covers around 200,000 hectares (772 square miles) in the Ming Shan mountain range, in the ABA Tibetan Autonomous Region, near the Tibetan Plateau. Elevations in the reserve range from 1555 to 4600 meters (4,000 to 11,000 ft).

Additional Panda Facts

Pandas are an endangered species, with between 1500 and 3000 living in the wild, and less than 300 in captivity (research centers and zoos).

Figure 4-20. In the example on the right, the heading is cleared after the floated image.

Basic Styles

Going back to our Pandas Forever site, let's add in some basic styles to make it look a little nicer.

First, to do it the easy way instead of the hard way, we're going to use box-sizing as discussed earlier in the chapter. We'll apply it to all elements:

```
*, *:before, *:after {
    -moz-box-sizing: border-box;
    -webkit-box-sizing: border-box;
    box-sizing: border-box;
}
```

We already set a font size for the headings, paragraphs, and lists, and we made the headings bold. Next, we'll add some margins and padding to separate things a bit, and add bullets on the list items, which you'll see in Figure 4-21:

```
h1 { font-size: 2em; }
h2 { font-size: 1.5em; }
h1, h2 { font-weight: bold; margin: 5px 0; }
p { font-size: 1em; margin: 5px 0; }
ul { padding-left: 10px; margin: 10px 0; list-style-
type: disc; }
li { margin-left: 10px; padding-left: 10px; }
```

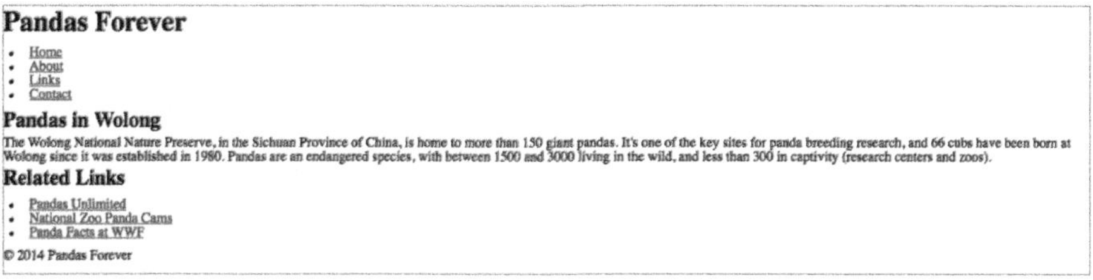

Figure 4-21. The example site with margins, padding, and bullets added.

Next, we're going to add a border to the structural elements of the page, just to make it easier to see where everything is. Even if you don't have borders on the final design, it's often helpful to add borders to elements while you are working on creating a design, just so you can easily see what's going on with the margins and padding. Here's the code (you'll see the results in Figure 4-22):

```
header, article, aside, footer { border: 1px solid #111;
}
```

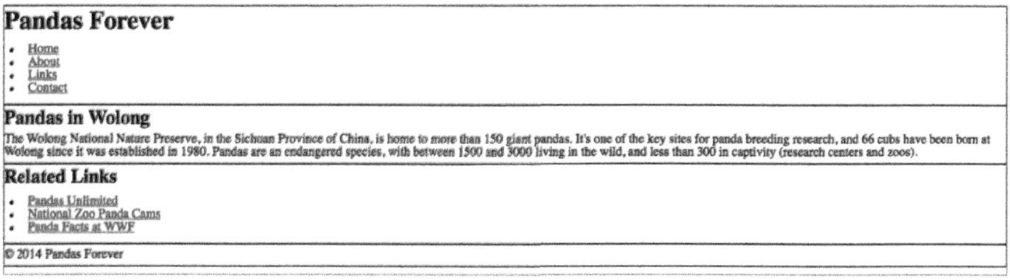

Figure 4-22. The example site with borders around the structural elements of the page.

To make things look a little neater, we'll add some padding and margins to the structural elements, resulting in Figure 4-23:

```
header, article, aside, footer { border: 1px solid #111;
padding: 10px 1em; margin: 0 5% 10px; }
header { margin-top: 10px; }
```

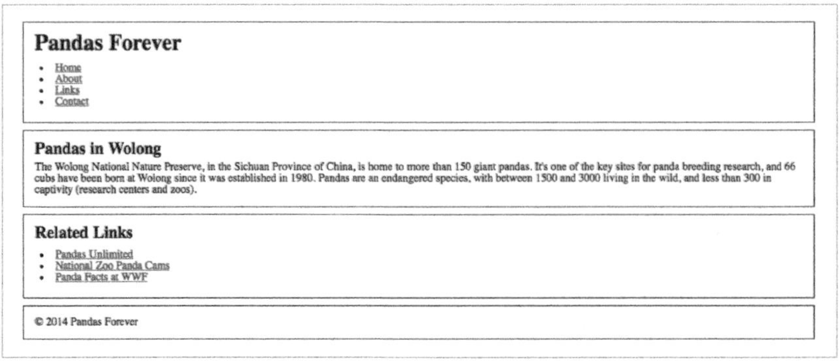

Pandas Forever

- Home
- About
- Links
- Contact

Pandas in Wolong

The Wolong National Nature Preserve, in the Sichuan Province of China, is home to more than 150 giant pandas. It's one of the key sites for panda breeding research, and 66 cubs have been born at Wolong since it was established in 1980. Pandas are an endangered species, with between 1500 and 3000 living in the wild, and less than 300 in captivity (research centers and zoos).

Related Links

- Pandas Unlimited
- National Zoo Panda Cams
- Panda Facts at WWF

© 2014 Pandas Forever

Figure 4-23. The example site with padding and margins to separate the elements.

You'll notice that I haven't been talking about responsive design as we've added styles to our site. If you'll remember, we started out with just HTML and no styles, which is a responsive site by default. So far we haven't done anything to make it *not* responsive. The site works in various screen sizes, such as in Figure 4-24 and Figure 4-25, although in wider screen sizes the text is wide and difficult to read.

When we move on to talking about media queries in Chapter 5, you'll learn how to have the site change its layout in regard to the screen width.

Summary

In this chapter, we learned that CSS has been released in versions, similar to HTML versions. The latest version, CSS3, gives us several new properties to use, including media queries, which are the backbone of responsive design.

Although some of the CSS3 properties are still in the testing phase, we can include them in our designs by using browser prefixes to allow browsers to render their testing versions of a property.

CSS can be applied to your web page either through separate files called stylesheets, or by including it in the code of the web page as embedded or inline styles. Generally, using stylesheets is the best option, as it allows you to apply styles globally across a whole site or sections of a site.

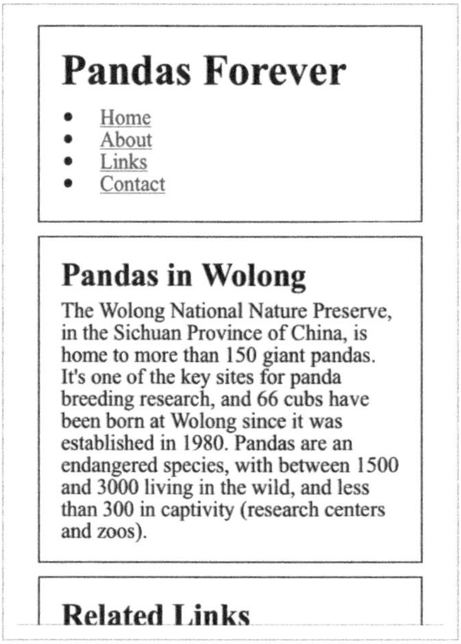

Figure 4-24. The example site viewed on a narrow screen, about the size of a mobile phone.

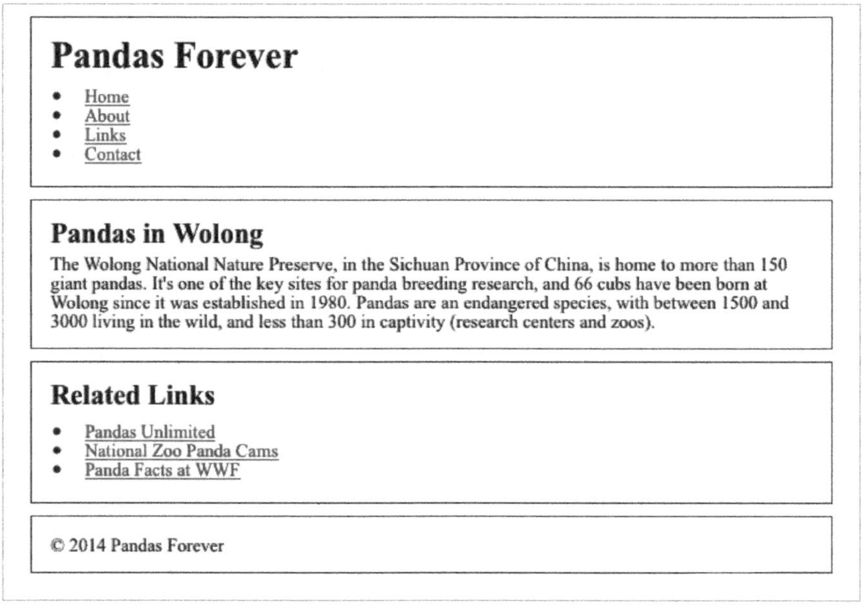

Figure 4-25. The example site viewed on a medium-width screen, about the size of a tablet.

The cascade is a set of very detailed rules about how browsers apply styles to a web page—what order the styles are applied in, and which rules take precedence over one another. Rules that are marked as important take top priority, followed by inline style rules, then rules containing IDs, classes, and elements, inherited rules, and default values. As tiebreakers, the browser will look at specificity and the order of the styles.

Although the cascade can be very complex, if you plan ahead when adding styles to your website, adding them broadly and consistently wherever possible, you can make a style implementation that's simple and straightforward, requiring less maintenance and giving you fewer headaches.

Starting out your CSS by resetting the default values will ensure that all browsers will render the styles as you expect. You can find various reset stylesheets online, if you don't want to create your own.

There isn't one particular correct way to organize the code in your stylesheets, but it's best to use a consistent system so it's easier to find things later. You may want to group styles by page or site section, or group like items together, such as typography styles.

The most important concept in CSS layout is the box model, which determines how elements are displayed on the web page, with each element represented as a rectangular box. Each box has a width and height, and may or may not have borders, padding, and margins.

Elements will start out with default values for all those properties, but the values can be changed using various units of measurement. For responsive design, most measurements should be in relative units such as percent, ems, and rems. Vertical measurements can sometimes be in absolute units like pixels. You can also use **auto**, which calculates the value based on adjacent or containing elements.

The **box-sizing** property allows you to change how the browser renders padding and borders—that is, whether their measurements are included inside the width of an element or outside the width. Positioning allows you to determine where elements appear on the page.

Now that you have seen the basics of how CSS works, in Chapter 5 we're going to learn how to use CSS media queries to make a website responsive.

[5]

Media Queries

Media queries are what make responsive websites responsive to the devices the sites are being viewed on. Up until now, all of our CSS declarations have applied to the web page without regard for screen size.

CSS media queries allow you to apply different style declarations based on qualities of the device the website is being viewed on, most commonly the width of the viewport: *arrange the site in two columns, but if the screen is wider than 40 ems, arrange it in three columns instead.*

This is the part of responsive design that means you can see a different layout on a mobile phone than you see on a tablet or on a desktop monitor. Media queries are sometimes referred to as the *special sauce* or the *magic pixie dust* of responsive design, because they go on top of all the other pieces of your design and make magic happen.

In this chapter, you'll learn how to structure a media query, and where to add it to your styles. You'll learn what media queries can be used for—not just the obvious viewport width—and how media queries are supported by browsers.

You'll learn how to starting thinking about the design of your site, starting with the smallest screen widths and working upward with progressive enhancement. You'll learn what a breakpoint and a design range are, and how to use them in your designs.

Finally, we'll go back to our example site and add some media queries to create a two-column version of the design for wider screens, and make other layout changes that depend on the width of the viewport.

What's a Media Query?

Although media queries can do pretty awesome things on the screen, the syntax is actually fairly simple.

Basically, you're going to start with a question, such as "Is the screen wider than 40 ems?" You'll follow that with some CSS. If the answer to the question is "true," then the browser will apply that CSS to the web page. If the answer is "false," the browser will ignore that CSS.

If you're a programmer, you can just think of it as an **if/then** statement.

Although CSS2 supported media queries for media *types* (such as screen or print), it wasn't until CSS3 that we were able to do media queries based on *qualities* of the device, such as viewport width. That's why responsive design didn't exist until 2010—it wasn't possible before then.

Here's an example of a simple media query:

```
body { background-color: green; }

@media only screen and (min-width: 40em) {
    body { background-color: blue; }
}
```

The first line of CSS gives the website's **<body>** a background color of green. The second line of CSS says that if the viewport is a minimum width of 40 ems, then the **<body>** should have a background color of blue.

The narrow-width screens get a green background, and the wider screens get a blue background. (Note: not quite all browsers support media queries, and we'll address that issue in a bit.)

Keep in mind that each CSS declaration in your stylesheet will override any declarations that come before it (or in previous stylesheets), so your media query needs to come *after* any non-query declarations for the same selector/property.

Some examples of what media queries are commonly used for:

Columns
Start with one column on a narrow screen, and change to two, three, or more columns when there's enough space.

Navigation
Display a hidden navigation (e.g., a drop-down menu) on a narrow screen, and a full navigation (where you can see all the menu items at once) on wide screens.

Typography

Change the type size depending on the width of the viewport, or adjust column widths so that you display the optimum number of characters per line for ease in reading.

Images

Display different sizes or crops of the same image (a small close-up image versus a large zoomed-out image) depending on the amount of space available on the page.

[NOTE]

Using background colors is a good way to test out the expressions in your media queries, because when you resize your browser to make sure your media query works, you can easily see the change.

Media Query Structure

The most common way to use media queries is to include them directly inside your regular stylesheet along with all your other CSS:

```
@media only screen and (min-width: 40em) {
    body { background-color: blue; }
}
```

Looking at this example, it seems like a lot of code, but it's easy to dissect into parts that make sense. Let's start going through it one piece at a time.

```
@media
```

First, media queries inside a stylesheet always start with **@media**. That's what defines them as media queries.

Following the **@media** are one or more *expressions*, which are the questions that are evaluated as being true or false. When you create a media query, it *always* needs to start with the media type as the first expression (in this case, **screen**):

```
@media only screen
```

Despite just being one word, that's a whole expression, meaning "Is the media type equal to **screen**?" That's opposed to other options of **print** or **braille** or **all** or something else. For the purposes of responsive web design, we'll pretty much always use **screen**.

You'll notice there's an extra word before the media type—only. This is a bit of a hack, actually. Some older browsers only support the CSS2 media type queries, and not newer CSS3 queries. So, they would read our initial example and understand screen but not and (min-width: 40em). Browsers are supposed to just skip any CSS declarations they don't understand, but when it comes to media queries, they're a bit quirky: they won't skip the whole declaration, only the and (min-width: 40em) part of the query. The result is that an older browser would see screen, say "yes, that's true," and apply the CSS—on any size screen, regardless of the viewport width.

Because we don't want that to happen, we add in the word only, which doesn't actually change the overall meaning of the media query but does cause those older browsers to ignore the whole query, which is what we want to happen (we'll talk later about how to give the proper styles to those older browsers).

[NOTE]

The media type screen covers computers and mobile devices—anything with a screen—and print is for printers.

You can use all if you want to target any media type, but simply omitting the media type will cause it to default to all.

There are a few other media types, such as braille, projection, speech, and tv, but they aren't commonly used and don't always work like you'd think they would. For more information, see "Media types" (*http://www. w3.org/TR/CSS2/media.html*) on the W3C site.

Next is the and:

```
@media only screen and
```

You need that word because you have multiple expressions—the screen was your first expression, and now you're going to add another expression to evaluate a quality of the device. Because it's an and, both expressions in the media query need to be true in order for the whole query to be true and the CSS to be applied.

Media queries can also use or or not, or have multiple, nested expressions, but you normally wouldn't have any reason to do such complicated queries, so we won't delve that deep in this book.

Next we get to the meat of the media query, where we're evaluating expressions that look at *media features* (e.g., the width of the viewport or screen, the orientation of the device, or the color capabilities):

```
@media only screen and (min-width: 40em)
```

Here, your second expression, after the `and`, is `(min-width: 40em)`. Note that the expression is inside parentheses. Each expression goes inside parentheses except when it's a one-word media type expression, such as `screen` or `print`.

The `min-` prefix, which means "a minimum of," is the same as saying "greater than or equal to." So here you're saying *if the viewport is a minimum of 40 ems wide* or *if the viewport is greater than or equal to 40 ems wide.*

If the viewport is any width *less* than 40 ems, then the query is not true. If it is exactly 40 ems wide, or any width *greater* than 40 ems, then the query *is* true.

The opposite, the `max-` prefix, means "a maximum of" and is the same as saying "less than or equal to."

Finally, you include a set of curly braces surrounding all the CSS that will be applied if the entire media query is true:

```
@media only screen and (min-width: 40em) {
    ...
}
```

One thing to take a special look at: it can get a bit confusing because you use curly braces both to contain all the declarations in the media query, and to contain each style declaration. Make sure that you have the right number of braces—if you leave one out, the browser will get confused trying to apply your styles.

You can have as many declarations as you want inside the media query:

```
@media only screen and (min-width: 40em) {
    body { background-color: blue; }
    p { padding: 5px 5%; }
    .example { color: red; }
}
```

Keep in mind that once you start using media queries, you won't be putting *all* of your styles in media queries to account for every possibility. You'll start with non-media-queried style declarations that apply to all viewport widths, then only override them for certain widths with media queries.

So, in the example from the start of the chapter, we start with green for the background color at all viewport widths. The media query overrides that with blue for widths of 40 ems or wider, but leaves everything else—viewports narrower than 40 ems—with the original green:

```
body { background-color: green; }

@media only screen and (min-width: 40em) {
    body { background-color: blue; }
}
```

Using Media Queries in Stylesheet Links

You'll remember from Chapter 4 that in the <head> of our HTML page, we can link to one or more CSS files:

```
<link rel="stylesheet" href="styles/mainstyles.css">
<link rel="stylesheet" href="styles/otherstyles.css">
```

The browser simply reads and applies all of the style declarations from all of the stylesheets, starting with the first stylesheet that is linked to.

Rather than writing media queries inside our stylesheets, we can tell the browser that entire stylesheets should only be applied if a media query is true—and ignored if the media query is not true.

If you've been working on websites for a while, you may have seen the CSS2 version of this used for print stylesheets:

```
<link rel="stylesheet" href="styles/mainstyles.css">
<link rel="stylesheet" href="styles/printstyles.css"
media="print">
```

In this example, we're telling the browser that if the user is printing the page instead of viewing it on the screen, then additional styles should be added. For example, we might hide a repeating background image for print, to avoid wasting the user's printer ink or toner.

To designate a stylesheet only for print, we simply add media="print" as part of the link element, which tells the browser that when the query "is the media type print?" is true, it should apply the *printstyles. css* stylesheet; if false, it should ignore that entire stylesheet.

The other stylesheet links have no media type designation, so they are applied whether the media type is screen, print, or anything else.

As we generally would add print styles to override regular styles, that stylesheet link is listed last.

Telling the browser that a stylesheet is for print is pretty easy—it only takes one word, `print`. But we can also do this with CSS3 media queries, using syntax that's similar to how we embed media queries in stylesheets.

You simply put your query, starting with `only screen`, inside the quotation marks of a `media` attribute on the `link` element:

```
<link rel="stylesheet" href="styles/mainstyles.css">
<link rel="stylesheet" href="styles/widerscreen.css"
media="only screen and (min-width: 40em)">
```

Here, the first stylesheet is applied for all devices, while the second stylesheet is applied only if the query is true—if it's on a screen and the viewport is a minimum width of 40 ems.

Other Ways to Use Media Queries

You just learned the two primary ways to use media queries: by including the media queries in your stylesheets, or by using media queries to link to separate stylesheets.

These two methods have the same end result, so deciding between them is more of a personal preference in how you like to organize your CSS.

Additionally, there are a couple of other methods for adding media queries to your website—the same alternate ways to add CSS that we learned about in Chapter 4.

First, you can include a media query as an attribute to the `<style>` element in the `<head>` of a page:

```
<style media="only screen and (min-width: 40em)">
    ...
</style>
```

Doing that would mean that all the styles inside that `<style>` element are only applied if the query is true.

We already learned in Chapter 4 that applying style to a single page of your site isn't generally a good idea, so you probably won't use that method often, if at all.

You can also import a stylesheet, which works similarly to linking to a stylesheet:

```
@import url(styles.css) only screen and (min-width:
40em)
```

Generally, using `<link>` is preferable to importing a stylesheet.

What We Can Query

There are many possible media features that can be queried with a media query, such as viewport width and height, screen width and height, orientation, aspect ratio, and resolution (the number of pixels in each dimension of the screen).

Most of these can be prepended with `min-` or `max-`.

However, not all of these are currently supported by the major browsers. We'll look at that in more detail in this section. In addition, IE 8 and earlier versions don't support any media queries. Later in this chapter, you'll learn what to do about that.

VIEWPORT WIDTH AND HEIGHT

`width`
>Width of viewport

`height`
>Height of viewport

These are the device qualities that you will most often use in your responsive design media queries (`width` more often than `height`).

In the following example, the first media query asks whether the viewport is *at least* 40 ems in width. The second asks whether the viewport is *exactly* 60 ems in height (it's unlikely you'd ever need to use an exact measurement, rather than `min-` or `max-`):

```
@media only screen and (min-width: 40em) { ... }
@media only screen and (height: 60em) { ... }
```

Although we tend to talk about screen size when we're doing responsive design, as I explained earlier in the book, we're actually doing queries based on *viewport* size, not *screen* size. That's why you can change the width of your browser window to see a responsive design change.

The viewport is the part of the browser window that actually contains the web page. So when you look at your browser window, you subtract the *chrome*, which is the scrollbar at the side of the page, and any toolbars or menus at the top or bottom.

What's left is the viewport.

Even on the same monitor screen, the viewport can vary based on the browser, or user preferences like which browser toolbars are being used. The width of the sidebar might be a few pixels different, or the user may not have the window maximized.

SCREEN WIDTH AND HEIGHT

device-width
> Width of device screen

device-height
> Height of device screen

These work similarly to **width** and **height**, except they measure the dimensions of the actual screen on the device rather than the viewport. So, resizing your browser window will have no effect, and if the user doesn't have his window maximized, he may not get the layout you intended.

Example:

```
@media only screen and (max-device-width: 40em) { ... }
```

ORIENTATION

orientation
> Landscape or portrait

This quality looks at whether the screen is in landscape orientation (width is greater than height) or portrait orientation (height is greater than width). Although this is potentially very useful, it's not supported by all browsers yet.

Example:

```
@media only screen and (orientation: landscape) { ... }
```

ASPECT RATIO

aspect-ratio
> Ratio of the viewport

device-aspect-ratio
> Ratio of the device screen

The viewport aspect ratio or device aspect ratio is the ratio of the width to the height. So, if a screen were 1,000 pixels wide and 500 pixels high, the **device-aspect-ratio** would be 2:1, because 1,000 is twice 500.

The ratios of screens vary widely, even though at first glance they pretty much all just look like a similar rectangle.

Common monitor aspect ratios are 16:9 (such as 1920 × 1080 or 1366 × 768 pixels) or 16:10 (1280 × 800). The iPhone 3 and 4S are 3:2 (480 × 320 and 960 × 640) and the iPhone 5 is 16:9 (1136 × 640). Android phones are commonly 4:3, 3:2, 16:10, or 16:9.

Examples:

```
@media only screen and (device-aspect-ratio: 16/9)
{ ... }
@media only screen and (min-device-aspect-ratio:
1920/1080) { ... }
```

RESOLUTION

resolution
> Resolution of the device screen

resolution replaces, and does something similar to, an older media query type, **device-pixel-ratio**. Although this might be useful for displaying the appropriate-resolution images for a screen, it is not yet supported in Safari or Chrome.

Example:

```
@media only screen and (min-resolution: 300dpi) { ... }
```

OTHER MEDIA FEATURES

A few more that you are not likely to use in the near future but that may come in handy someday include:

color

> The number of bits per color component of the output device. Use `min-` to query against a number. The word `color` by itself simply asks if the device has a color screen or not. Not supported by Opera.

color-index

> The number of entries in the color lookup table of the device, such as 256. Only supported by Opera.

monochrome

> Whether the device screen is monochrome (remember the old monitors with green text on a black screen?). Not yet supported by any browser.

scan

> Whether the device uses progressive scan—which only applies to TVs, not to other devices. Not yet supported by any browser.

grid

> Whether the output is grid-based (such as teletype or TTY, which have a fixed font) or bitmap (a "normal" screen with pixels). Not yet supported by any browser.

Browser Support

So all this media query stuff sounds wonderful, but we have a problem: some browsers don't support media queries at all.

This is why you need to make sure that your basic layout and design, without media queries added in, will work on any device or screen size. It may not look great, but it will be usable.

Feature phones won't support media queries. This is one of the benefits of starting with a design for small screens first: your default layout, without media queries, will work on small-screen devices that don't support media queries. If you started with a wide-screen design first, you'd get the wide layout on those devices, and it might not be usable.

Most modern browsers do support media queries—at least, the basic `min-width` and `max-width` that we use in responsive design (see "Can I Use CSS Media Queries?" [*http://caniuse.com/css-mediaqueries*] for details). Pretty much the only browsers we really need to worry about are IE 8 and earlier.

Luckily, there's a solution. Whether or not you use it will depend on whether very many of your site's users are using IE 8 or earlier. If there are not many, it may be enough to give them the default design. Even though it's a layout for small screens (probably one column), it will still work on larger screens.

CONDITIONAL COMMENTS FOR INTERNET EXPLORER

If you decide your site needs to support media queries in IE 8 and earlier, you can use something called *conditional comments* to target code only to Internet Explorer.

The downside is that this can add a lot of extra code to your site, depending on how you implement it.

A conditional comment is a type of query, but it goes in your HTML instead of your CSS. You can use it to send a specific stylesheet to IE 8 and earlier.

It will look like this, with HTML in the middle:

```
<!--[if (lt IE 9)&(!IEMobile)]>
    ...
<![endif]-->
```

The code you use for conditional comments is kind of difficult to remember, with all those parentheses and punctuation marks, so it's best to just copy it when you need it, rather than trying to remember how to type out all this code.

The first line is essentially saying this: if the browser is an IE version less than ("lt") version 9, *and* the browser is not IE Mobile (the exclamation point means "not"), then the browser should render the HTML inside the conditional comment. Otherwise, it shouldn't.

The whole thing starts and ends with the symbols for an HTML comment (<!-- ... -->), so any non-IE browsers will see it as a comment and ignore the whole thing. However, IE is built to recognize this as a query that needs to be evaluated.

Although you can use conditional comments to target code to IE 8 and earlier, this doesn't actually add support for media queries, so how do you know which code to send to these browsers?

You can actually make a pretty good guess. Your conditional comment excluded IE Mobile, so you know the device in use is almost certainly a desktop/laptop computer.

Thinking of common monitor sizes, the screen is almost certainly a minimum of 1,024 pixels wide, and probably at least 1,280. It can be much wider, but at least you have a starting point. Instead of giving it a whole separate layout, you can give it the stylesheet or CSS you would give to a viewport width of about 1,280 pixels (80 ems), and you'll likely be in the ballpark for nearly every user.

So, if you want to tell IE 8 and earlier desktop browsers to use the *mid-size.css* stylesheet, you would just include this code in the <head> of the web page:

```
<!--[if (lt IE 9)&(!IEMobile)]>
    <link rel="stylesheet" href="midsize.css">
<![endif]-->
```

But if your styles aren't broken out into stylesheets for particular screen widths (e.g., if your media queries are mixed in with your other CSS), this won't work.

Another way to deal with IE 8 and earlier browsers is to start with your default single-column view (which is what they'll get if all the media queries are ignored) and then use conditional comments to add supplemental styles for an IE-specific layout:

```
<!--[if (lt IE 9)&(!IEMobile)]>
    <link rel="stylesheet" href="ie-styles.css">
<![endif]-->
```

[NOTE]

Another option is a polyfill that adds support for media queries in older versions of Internet Explorer. Check out Respond.js (*https://github.com/scottjehl/Respond*), a fast and lightweight JavaScript polyfill that adds support for min-width and max-width media queries in IE 6–8. The downside is that this adds more code to your site, and won't work in browsers without JavaScript; also it can only be used for min-width and max-width queries.

TESTING MEDIA QUERY ANSWERS

To find out what values your browser is using to answer media queries, visit MQtest.io (*http://mqtest.io/*) from Viljami Salminen. As seen in Figure 5-1, it will tell you the exact numbers your browser is sending for height, width, device height/width, aspect ratios, orientation, and resolution. You can watch the width and height values change as you resize your browser window. This is handy if your media queries aren't acting as expected on a certain device: you might determine that your browser is sending different information than what you assumed.

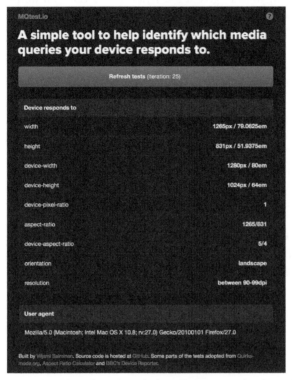

Figure 5-1. The MQtest.io website will show you the dimensions of your browser window.

Breakpoints

An important concept in responsive design is *breakpoints*. A breakpoint is the point at which you use a media query to change the design. It breaks your design into two (or more) variations.

Sometimes it's a very visible change, like the number of columns (e.g., changing from one column to two columns at 40 ems). But other times it's a very subtle change, like changing the text size slightly to fit better.

A good way to think of it is to imagine a row of all the possible screen sizes, with the smallest screens on one end and the widest screens on the other end.

In Figure 5-2, there's a line at each breakpoint, where the design changes based on viewport width.

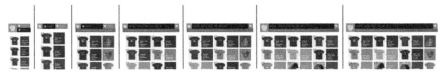

Figure 5-2. Each line represents a breakpoint.

[NOTE]

You learned earlier in the chapter that media queries can be used for all sorts of things—viewport width, height, orientation, aspect ratio, and even whether or not the display is in color.

But because `width` is the only media feature that's currently supported by most browsers, it's essentially the only media feature that's being used in responsive design right now. Thus, this book will focus on using only media queries for the `width` property.

Design Ranges

As we create responsive websites, we tend to focus on the breakpoints, because those are the numbers we're adding to our CSS, and those are the points where something is *happening*.

But as important as those points are, they're only a small part of the picture. The design needs to look good at any width, not just at certain points.

A *design range*, then, is the range of screen sizes on each side of the line. Each design range gets a different variation of the design.

In the next section, we'll add a media query to our web page that will change the design from one column to two columns at 36 ems, giving us two design ranges: 0–35 ems, as Figure 5-3, and 36-infinity ems, as in Figure 5-4. In practice, we only design for screens as small as about 240 pixels (usually about 15 ems) wide and perhaps as large as 3,200 pixels (about 200 ems) wide, so our two design ranges would be 15–35 ems and 36–200 ems.

Figure 5-3. Examples in the design range of 15–35 ems.

Figure 5-4. Examples in the design range of 36–200 ems.

Of course, the screenshots in Figure 5-3 and Figure 5-4 only represent a few points in each design range, as it isn't feasible to include screenshots of every possible viewport width in this book.

This is why responsive prototypes, which you will learn about in Chapter 7, are so helpful during the design process—you can open up the prototype in your browser and resize the browser window slowly to see how the design looks at every screen width.

As we add additional media queries to our example, it will break our design into additional ranges.

Designing Responsively

Before we start adding media queries to our example site, we need to talk a little bit about the best way to put together a responsive website.

PROGRESSIVE ENHANCEMENT

Progressive enhancement is the idea that you start with the basics, and add on from there for browsers and devices that can handle more.

Your default design (before media queries) is for the narrowest screens, but it also needs to be adequate for the most basic devices—those that may not be able to recognize media queries, CSS3, or JavaScript.

When you're making a website, you start out with the content and use HTML to give it semantic structure. This is the first layer. Any browser will be able to read your HTML.

The next layer is for presentation. In the presentation layer, you use CSS to determine how everything will appear on the page: layout, colors, typography. Some browsers won't support all of your CSS, but the site is still usable without it. But for nearly all browsers, the CSS makes the site look much better, and makes it easier to navigate the content.

The third layer is behavior, which is done with JavaScript. Not all browsers support JavaScript, or a user might have turned it off for security reasons. Although you can use JavaScript to make a site do neat things, such as menus that move around, you need to try to make sure that the essential site functionality will work without JavaScript (which may not be possible on extremely interactive sites).

Don't put in place technical restrictions that aren't necessary; this just leaves people out.

This doesn't mean you need to make your website simple and boring, without any bells and whistles. It just means you need to start with the simplest site possible, make sure it works, and then add on the bells and whistles on top of that. You're not "designing for the lowest common denominator," which is a frequent criticism of progressive enhancement; you're just *starting* there, and then designing for *everybody*.

DESIGNING WITH GRIDS

We're going to step back from the technical bits for a second and talk about how you decide where everything goes on the page.

There's a lot more to the *process* of creating a design, which we'll talk about in Chapter 7, but right now we're just going to look at the basics of how grids and columns are used to create what you see on a web page.

As you're putting your design together, you need to think about how the pieces will fit together on the screen.

Responsive design is often described as involving "flexible grids." Although the flexibility is inherent to responsive design, grids are not actually required.

However, grids are a key part of creating a *well-designed website.*

In his book *Ordering Disorder: Grid Principles for Web Design* (New Riders), Khoi Vinh explains that the purpose of successful designs is to "create order out of disorder." Using grids, rather than haphazardly creating columns, gives your web page "order, continuity, and harmony," which makes it more visually appealing as well as creating a more pleasant experience for the user.

The idea of designing with grids comes from graphic design. A grid simply means that the design is made up of multiple columns of equal widths, with equal gutters (margins) between them, and everything on the page is based around those columns. For example, Figure 5-5 is a typographic grid based on five columns.

Figure 5-5. An empty five-column grid, and an example of a layout in that grid.

You can see that just because the grid has five columns of text, that doesn't mean that the whole design is divided into five columns. The grid columns can be combined to create the actual "columns" in the layout.

USING COLUMNS

It's fairly common to use 12-column grids for websites, because it gives you a lot of flexibility: 12 is divisible by 2, 3, 4, and 6, so your layout can include sections that use any of those numbers of columns—even all on the same page.

For example, the Monocle website shown in Figure 5-6 (left) is built on a 12-column grid. You can see that different sections of the page have different numbers of columns, but the fractions always add up to 12. For example, four equal columns is 3/12 + 3/12 + 3/12 + 3/12, and three equal columns is 4/12 + 4/12 + 4/12.

Even though there are different columns as you scroll down the page, it looks orderly and cohesive.

Of course, on a responsive site the boxes can simply be rearranged at different viewport widths, so that they fit into either the same or a different grid.

Compare the visual cohesion of the Monocle site to a site like Yahoo!, seen in Figure 5-6 (right), which has content components that look like they were randomly put together. I added lines on the page to show the columns in the various sections of the page.

As we work on our example site later in this chapter, we'll use a grid to determine where our columns should go on the page.

[NOTE]

To learn more about how grids work on responsive sites, see Chris Coyier's "Don't Overthink It Grids" (*http://css-tricks.com/dont-overthink-it-grids/*) on CSS-Tricks.

If you want to dive deeper into the theory and methodology of grid-based design, read Khoi Vinh's *Ordering Disorder: Grid Principles for Web Design* (*http://grids.subtraction.com/*).

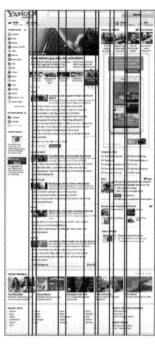

Figure 5-6. The Monocle website is built on a 12-column grid (left); The Yahoo! website has columns all over the place (right).

DESIGN FOR SMALL SCREENS FIRST

When you're working with media queries to change your site's design at different page widths, you're generally going to be working from one direction or the other, either making your default design for the narrowest width and then adding media queries for wider viewports, or starting with the widest width and adding media queries for smaller viewport widths.

Generally, it works better to design for small screens first. Even though you're probably more comfortable working with desktop-sized website designs, it's far easier to start your design with the narrowest screen width, which forces you to focus on the content and only include what you actually need.

It's much easier to create a layout and then make it bigger than it is to make a layout smaller. Once you've created a pleasing layout for a narrow viewport, you'll have plenty of space at wider widths to move things around and give them more room. But if you try to take a desktop-sized site and squish everything into a tiny screen—well, the key word there is "squish."

If you look at where we left off with our example site in Chapter 4, you'll see that we have a layout that works on all sizes of screen but looks best on narrow screens like those on a mobile phone (Figure 5-7).

We're going to take this design and add media queries to make it look good on all screen sizes.

Using Media Queries

Breakpoints are arbitrary. Your website can have any number you want, including zero. So where do you start? Your initial design planning will give you an idea of how many breakpoints you need, but you'll need to turn to the browser to find the best place to add a media query, which will break your design into two design ranges.

We're going to start by looking at our example website in the browser at the narrowest width, and then slowly make the browser window wider and see what happens.

Figure 5-7. The example site viewed on a narrow screen, about the size of a mobile phone's.

Two-Column Layout

We're going to first concentrate only on the article section, and the number of characters per line (in Chapter 10 we'll make changes to the navigation and other parts of the page). As you'll learn in Chapter 9, text is easiest to read with 45 to 75 characters on each line. That's not a hard-and-fast rule, but if your text isn't in that ballpark, it's generally going to decrease the ease of reading.

At the narrowest screen width, there are 45 characters per line, which is slightly less than our optimal range but still good.

When the site is viewed at wider screen widths, we want it to have no more than 75 characters per line. To find this point, we'll slowly make the browser window wider and stop when the text exceeds 75 characters per line, as you see in Figure 5-8. We need to add a breakpoint there.

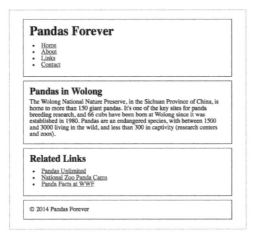

Figure 5-8. Once there are more than 75 characters per line, add a breakpoint.

If we measure the viewport width at that point, we'll find that it's about 36 ems wide. The easiest way to do this is to have a tool like MQtest.io (*http://mqtest.io/*) open in a separate tab in the same browser window. You can just switch to that tab, and it will tell you how wide the window currently is.

You can round to the nearest whole number—you're only going for an average of 75 characters per line, so it doesn't need to be exact.

USING FLOATS

Now, we want to change the layout so that the content displays in two columns. We'll first go over the CSS necessary for that layout, and then add a media query to tell the browser to only use that CSS when the viewport is 36 ems or wider.

The `<article>` will be in a wider column with a `float` to place it on the left side of the page, and the Related Links section `<aside>` will go in a narrower column to the right. We'll then add a `clear` to the footer so it starts out on a new line.

We want it to look like what you see in Figure 5-9.

Here's the CSS we'll use:

```
article { float: left; }
aside { float: right; }
footer { clear: both; }
```

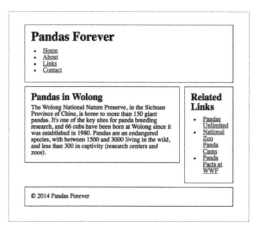

Figure 5-9. We are going to make the layout change to two columns at this breakpoint.

When we add that to the CSS, though, we find it's not quite right, because we get what you see in Figure 5-10.

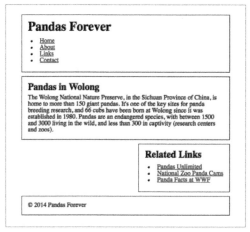

Figure 5-10. Without any specified widths, the article fills the page width, and the Related Links section ends up below it.

The problem is that when you're floating a block element, the default width of **auto** means the element will be as wide as the content requires. For the article, there's enough text to fill the whole width of the screen, so it's still as wide as it was before. The Related Links, however, has narrow content, so its **auto** width is very narrow.

USING A GRID

To fix this, we need to manually give those two elements a width. We're going to use the grid system to figure out how wide they should each be.

All the widths are based on percentages. I'm going to use a four-column grid, with each of the four columns being 21% wide, the gutters between them 2%, and 5% margins on the left and right. All those numbers add up to 100%, the full width of the page. You can see how the percentages all work out in Figure 5-11.

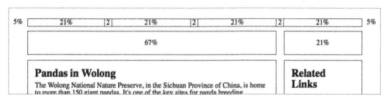

Figure 5-11. The page is divided into four equal columns, with equal gutters between them.

The left column, the `<article>`, will be three columns wide. Together, the widths of the columns and gutters it contains add up to 67%. The right column is 21% of the total page width, and there's a 2% gutter between them. Let's go ahead and add the column widths to the CSS:

```
article { float: left; width: 67%; }
aside { float: right; width: 21%; }
footer { clear: both; }
```

We're getting closer, but we still have a problem, as you see in Figure 5-12: the columns should be right next to each other, but there's an issue with the margins.

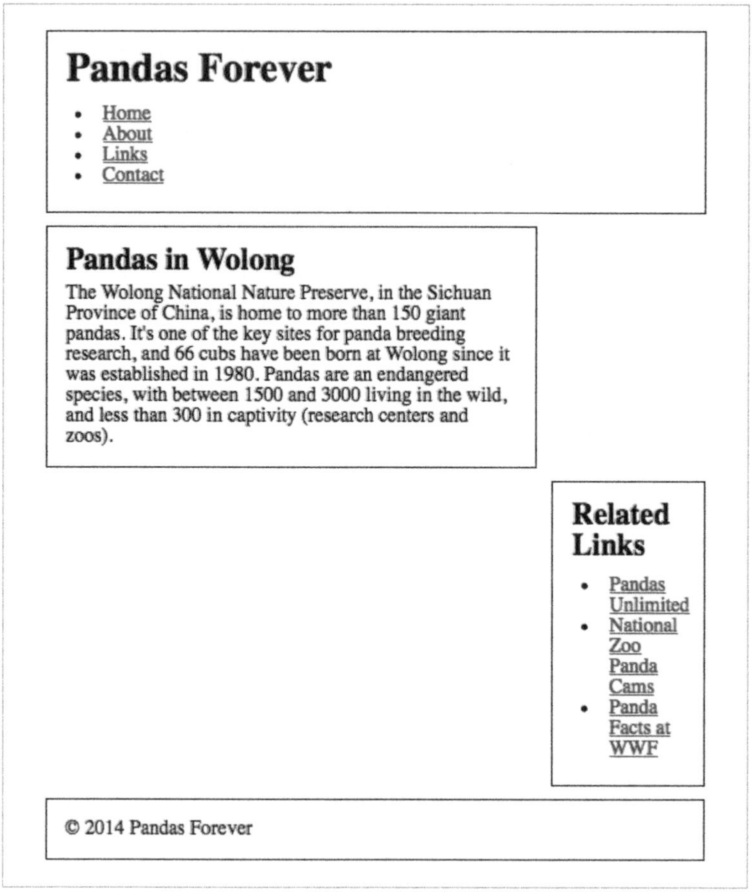

Pandas Forever

- Home
- About
- Links
- Contact

Pandas in Wolong

The Wolong National Nature Preserve, in the Sichuan Province of China, is home to more than 150 giant pandas. It's one of the key sites for panda breeding research, and 66 cubs have been born at Wolong since it was established in 1980. Pandas are an endangered species, with between 1500 and 3000 living in the wild, and less than 300 in captivity (research centers and zoos).

Related Links

- Pandas Unlimited
- National Zoo Panda Cams
- Panda Facts at WWF

© 2014 Pandas Forever

Figure 5-12. The Related Links section is below the article, not next to it as it should be.

Right now, the article has a width of 67%, plus a left margin of 5% and a right margin of 5%. The Related Links has a width of 21%, plus a left margin of 5% and a right margin of 5%. All of those numbers add up to 108%—which is why they don't all fit together going across. There should only be 2% between the two columns, not 10%.

To reduce the space between the two columns so it all fits, I'm going to give the article a right margin of 0 and give the Related Links a left margin of 0:

```
article { width: 67%; float: left; margin-right: 0; }
aside { width: 21%; float: right; margin-left: 0; }
footer { clear: both; }
```

Now everything adds up to 98%—leaving me with an extra 2%. Because the article is all the way to the left, and the Related Links is all the way to the right, the 2% of empty space is going to be the margin between them—we don't need to specify it. Now we have what you see in Figure 5-13.

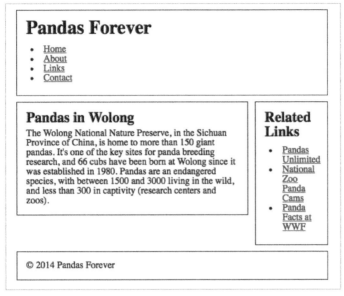

Figure 5-13. Now the Related Links section is in the correct location.

Now my layout looks good. If I decide to adjust the widths of the columns, or the margin between them, I can just change the percentages.

But I only want this layout when the viewport is 36 ems or wider. I need to use a media query to make that happen.

ADDING A MEDIA QUERY

Adding a media query here is pretty simple. I want the breakpoint to happen at 36 ems, so I'm going to tell the browser that if the viewport is a minimum width of 36 ems, it should apply those three new lines of CSS that I just came up with.

If the viewport is 36 ems or wider, the browser will apply this CSS to make a two-column layout. If it's not wider than 36 ems, it will ignore the CSS in the media query and stay with the one-column layout that we started with. You can compare the two layouts in Figure 5-14. Here's the code:

```
@media only screen and (min-width: 36em) {
    article { width: 67%; float: left; margin-right: 0; }
    aside { width: 21%; float: right; margin-left: 0; }
    footer { clear: both; }
}
```

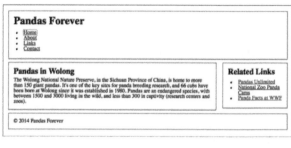

Figure 5-14. These are the two layouts we have so far, for viewport widths narrower and wider than 36 ems.

If you're trying out the code, make sure you've added the media query and try resizing your browser window from narrow to wide. At 36 ems, it will change from one layout to the other.

Setting a Maximum Width

That's great—now we have a good line length again, but as we keep making the viewport wider, again the lines will get too long, right about at 63 ems.

On a normal website, we could add a third column at this point, but with our simple site, we don't have any content for a third column.

Another possibility is to just stop the whole page layout from getting any wider at a certain point. This is a bit controversial as a design decision—users with really wide screens will be left with a lot of empty space—but in our situation, with not a lot of content on the page, we don't really have other options.

To do this, it's easiest if all the content is inside one element, so we're going to add a <div> surrounding everything on the page—just inside the <body> tags—and give the <div> an id of fullpage.

We're going to use a piece of CSS you'll learn more about in Chapter 6: `max-width`. For images in responsive design, we use it with a value of 100% to make sure the images aren't displayed larger than their containing elements.

But you can actually use `max-width` on any element, and you can give it a number instead of a percentage. We're going to take our `<div>` that surrounds the entire page and give it a style declaration of `max-width: 63em`. This means that the `<div>` will never get wider than 63 ems, no matter how wide we make the viewport:

```
#fullpage { max-width: 63em; }
```

Sure enough, if we make the browser window wider than 63 ems, the layout stops getting wider. You can see this in Figure 5-15.

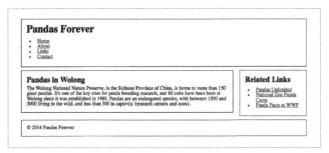

Figure 5-15. At widths wider than 63 ems, the layout stops getting wider.

One more thing—our page layout is all the way over to the left of the viewport, with all of the whitespace on the right. It would look nicer centered in the middle of the screen. To do this, we just set the margins on that `<div>` to `auto`, which means they will be equally divided on the left and right (the result is shown in Figure 5-16):

```
#fullpage { max-width: 63em; margin: auto; }
```

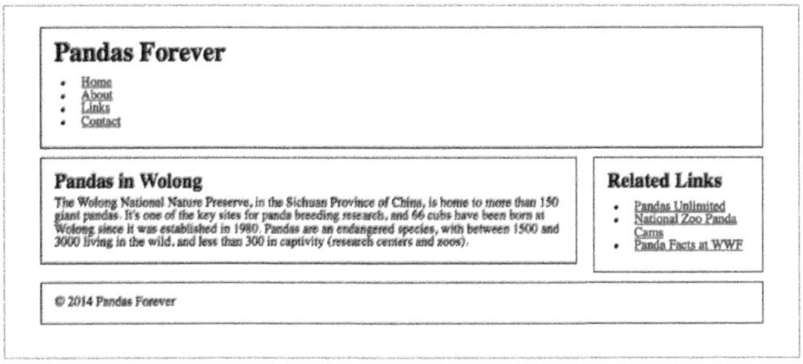

Figure 5-16. The layout is now centered on the screen.

How to Choose Breakpoints

As we learned, breakpoints can be added at any browser width. You'll probably have a general idea of where breakpoints will go as you're doing your preliminary sketches, but it's hard to know exactly where they need to go until you try out your CSS in a browser. In Chapter 7, we'll talk more about the steps of the design process.

Some designers pick their breakpoints to match the sizes of common devices such as iPhones and iPads. But doing that encourages you to focus on how your design looks at each breakpoint, where you really need to be looking at how the design looks at every viewport width through each entire design range.

Sure, you especially need to make sure your design looks good on devices that make up a big chunk of what your site's visitors are using—but your goal isn't to create a design that looks good just on those devices, it's to create a design that looks good on *all* devices, no matter what their viewport width is.

So should you not consider devices at all? No, devices are important; you just shouldn't think of them *first*. It's best to not start out thinking of how your design will look on particular devices, although you can think of it in more general terms, such as mobile phone size, tablet size, and desktop size.

After you've determined breakpoints by resizing the design in your browser, try it on a few devices to see how it looks. You can tweak the breakpoints a bit, because the numbers were based on characters per line, and that doesn't need to be precise.

For example, if the iPad width is just a few pixels from a breakpoint, you could decide to move the breakpoint a bit so that the iPad falls in a different design range—for example, getting the two-column layout instead of the one-column layout.

Remember—and this is really important, so I'm repeating it—the important thing is how the design looks across each design range, not how it looks at each breakpoint.

Summary

Media queries allow you to apply different style declarations based on features of the device the website is being viewed on. This is a key part of responsive design, allowing users to see a different layout or design of a website depending on the size of the screen.

Although powerful, media queries are actually very simple. You start with a question about the device, called an expression, and if the expression is true, the CSS inside the media query is applied. If the expression is false, the CSS inside the media query is ignored.

By using media queries, you will start with a default value for a particular style to apply to the website, but override that value with a different value depending on the width of the viewport.

Media queries can be included directly inside a stylesheet, but they can also be used to link to a separate stylesheet, in which case the entire stylesheet will be applied to the page only if the media query is true.

In responsive design, media queries are generally only used to query the width of the viewport, which is the part of the browser window that contains the web page. The viewport is variable on desktop and laptop computers, as users can change the size of the browser window. On mobile devices, the viewport width doesn't change; it's the same as the screen width.

Other media features can be queried, such as orientation, aspect ratio, and resolution, but because these features are not consistently supported by the major browsers, they are currently not often used. This will likely change in the future. Viewport width media queries are supported by all the major browsers except IE 8 and older, which require conditional comments or a polyfill to apply the correct styles.

Breakpoints are the numerical points in your media queries referring to the viewport widths at which the design will break into two variations. Design ranges are the spaces between breakpoints: the range of viewport widths at which each variation is rendered.

When adding media queries to your site, it's easiest to start from the smallest screen width first and work upward, using progressive enhancement for more capable screens and devices. Grids are used to give your layout cohesion no matter what the screen size.

When choosing breakpoints, don't pick points that match common devices, but instead make sure that common device widths fit comfortably within one of your design ranges. You can adjust your breakpoints after testing your design on various devices.

In the next chapter, Chapter 6, we'll look at how to incorporate images into responsive websites.

[6]

Images

So far you've learned how to set up your web page, add some basic styles, and use media queries to adjust the layout depending on viewport width.

But your page is going to look quite boring until you get some images on it.

You've probably heard that there's a lot of complexity around adding images to responsive websites. Images won't always be displayed at the same size, because they're flexible, so how do we make sure that we aren't wasting bandwidth by sending a huge image to a device with a small screen?

And then how do we make sure we're sending appropriate images to high-density (retina) screens?

This is one of the parts of responsive design that's still being worked out. There are a few solutions that are in common use, which we'll talk about here, but each has some drawbacks, and none of them seem like the *perfect* solution. It's likely that there will be new ideas coming along in this area in the next couple of years that may change how we handle images on responsive websites.

In the meantime: start with the basics, which we'll cover in this chapter. Optimize your images for the Web. Don't use images when stylized text can do the same job, and use other solutions like icon fonts when appropriate. Make sure your images have good alternative (alt) text so they're accessible to everybody.

When you're deciding the best way to handle responsive images on your site, look at the different options and figure out what works for you. If you don't implement a responsive image solution on your site, the site may take longer to load. That's not optimal, but it's not the end of the world as long as you don't have lots of huge images. There are other ways to reduce page weight (the combined size of all the files needed to display the page), which we'll address in Chapter 11.

Providing images to high-density screens is complicated too, but it's also not the end of the world if you aren't able to do it. Regular images will still work; they just won't be as crisp.

Most importantly, keep up with what's new in responsive images, to make sure you can take advantage of the new ideas and solutions that are likely to be coming soon.

[NOTE]

We'll be talking a lot about the *size* of an image in this chapter. In this context, we're using that word to mean the file size of the image, usually measured in kilobytes (KB). We'll refer to the height and width of an image as its *dimensions* to avoid confusion.

Ways to Display Images

When adding images to your website, there are several methods you can use, depending on the purpose of the images.

CSS ALTERNATIVES

When adding images to your site, the first thing to consider is whether you actually *need* all the images.

For example, CSS makes it possible to add borders, shadows, and gradients to buttons and other elements, like you see in Figure 6-1. Until recently, it was common to use images for this type of decorative effect. But now you can get the same look using CSS, meaning that there will be fewer images to download (and less page weight).

Figure 6-1. This button was created using CSS, not an image editor.

Additionally, by having elements such as buttons styled with CSS instead of displayed as images, you can easily change colors and other styles site-wide by changing a bit of CSS, rather than having to re-create each image. CSS-styled elements are also more responsive, as they can change dimensions without losing quality.

Not all older browsers support these CSS properties, but this small proportion of your users will still get usable buttons on the screen—they just might not have rounded corners or a shadow.

The code to create a button like that is pretty complex, but if you do a web search for "CSS button generator" you'll find numerous websites that will allow you to design a button by choosing values for all the possible properties, and then provide you with the necessary CSS that you can copy and paste into your stylesheet.

You can also display any stylized text on your site using CSS instead of an image. Pretty much anything you can do in an image editor with text is also possible in CSS—outlined text, sideways text, and so on. Take advantage of that, so you can make sure your stylized text is responsive and also accessible.

However, if the stylized text is something like a company logo that needs to always look exactly the same, it's best to use an image to make sure it comes out correctly.

CONTENT IMAGES

Content images are those that convey meaning to the user, either as part of the message of the site (such as an action photo accompanying a newspaper article), or as a navigational element (such as icons that lead the user to the website's social media pages).

Remember that not all of your users will be viewing the website in the same way. Some may be using devices that can't display the latest CSS, and some will be using screen readers that display alternative text in place of images.

For images that are part of the site content, you'll generally use the HTML <img> element. Remember with structured HTML, each element has meaning.

The `<img>` element is one of the few that has only one tag, not a starting and ending tag. It also has attributes:

```
<img src="images/norwaypine.jpg" alt="An evergreen tree
with big bushy branches.">
```

The two attributes you'll always use are the `src` attribute, which tells the browser where to find the image file, and the `alt` attribute, which provides a text alternative in case the browser is unable to display the image. We'll go into alt text in more detail shortly.

BACKGROUND IMAGES

The CSS `background-image` property allows you to add images to the page for decorative purposes, without having them be part of the content:

```
p { background-image: url(flowers.png); }
```

You shouldn't use `background-image` to add content images because they won't be visible to people using screen readers or other text-based browsers.

When you add `background-image` to the CSS for an element, the image will display as the background of that element, behind whatever is contained inside it (like the text in a paragraph). You'll see an example later in the chapter.

IMAGE SPRITES

As you'll learn in Chapter 11, each separate HTTP request that a web page makes for necessary files (CSS files, images, etc.) will add to the load time of the page. Reducing the number of requests will make your page load faster.

You can reduce the number of image *files* that need to be loaded by combining many small images into one large image, and then using CSS positioning to only display each particular piece of the image in the correct place on the page.

These combined images are called *image sprites*.

For example, Figure 6-2 is the image sprite that Apple uses to display the background for the top navigation on its website. It's various states for each button (active page, hover, etc.), combined in one image.

Figure 6-2. This image sprite is used to create many variations of the navigation on the Apple website.

The actual navigation looks like what you see in Figure 6-3, with the active page (here, "iPhone") having a different background than the other buttons. Each rectangle section of the image sprite provides a possible background image for a button, and with CSS, only one rectangle is displayed for each button.

Figure 6-3. This is how one version of the navigation created with an image sprite looks.

Of course, as we learned earlier in this chapter, buttons like this often can be displayed with pure CSS, not requiring images at all!

ICON FONTS

Icon fonts are a great solution for small graphics. An icon font set is like any other font, but the alphanumeric characters have been replaced by symbols. You can see an example of an icon font in Figure 6-4.

Figure 6-4. The IconSweets icon font (*http://iconsweets2.com/*) from Yummygum.

Icon fonts, like regular fonts, are vector-based, which means each character can be displayed at any size without any change in quality. This means they scale well, even to large dimensions and on high-density displays.

Although each character can only be one color, not multicolor, you can choose any color, just like you do for text (and also use any other CSS you like to style them, as you do for text).

You can find an icon font with pretty much any symbol you need. Usually they're based on themes. There is an icon font set with symbols of the shapes of all the world's countries. You can also find weather icons, social media icons, animals, traditional symbols—anything.

To include icon fonts in your design, use `@font-face`, just like with any other font (you'll learn how to add fonts to your site in Chapter 9).

Check out Chris Coyier's "Using Fonts for Icons..." (*http://css-tricks.com/using-fonts-for-icons/*) on CSS-Tricks for instructions on how to get started. Also make sure to read Drew Wilson's "Using Icon Fonts" (*http://pictos.cc/articles/using-icon-fonts/*) on Pictos to find out how to ensure they are accessible.

You can search the Web to find icon fonts (many of which are free), and there are even websites that allow you to create your own icon font.

Although icon fonts generally have a small file size, don't use them indiscriminately—it does add up.

Alt Text

Keep in mind that not every user visiting your website will be able to *see* the website.

Most commonly, this will be the case for users who are blind and using a screen reader. The user cannot see the image, so the screen reader reads the alt text to describe to the user what's in the image. You need to have good alt text so that these users aren't missing out on important parts of your content.

But it's not only blind users who are a potential audience for your alt text. Sometimes an image won't load because of problems with the Internet connection or the files, and in that case the user will see your alt text on the screen in the location where the image should appear.

In Figure 6-5, you can see the Amtrak website with all its images displayed, and in Figure 6-6 with all of the images replaced with alt text.

Figure 6-5. The Amtrak website with all the images in place.

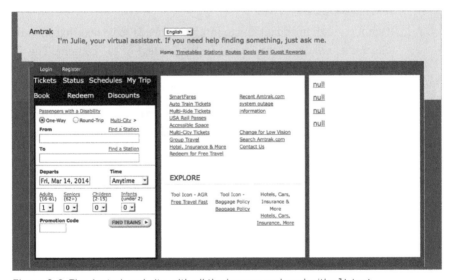

Figure 6-6. The Amtrak website with all the images replaced with alt text.

You'll notice that the content images are replaced with alt text, such as the Amtrak logo at the top left. However, the train conductor head next to the logo is not replaced, because it's decorative and does not contribute to the meaning of the content.

If it would not make sense to replace an image with alt text, use an empty set of double quotation marks for the alt attribute's value, *without a space between them*:

```
<img src="images/decorative.jpg" alt="">
```

Don't simply omit the alt attribute. If you do that, screen readers won't know whether or not the image is meant to be content, and because there is no alt text, they will read the filename to the user as the next best option.

Using empty double quotation marks will tell the screen readers to skip the image entirely.

One problem on the Amtrak site is that the promo images in the right column don't have any alt text—not even empty quotation marks—so they show up as "null."

WRITING GOOD ALT TEXT

It's not enough to add alt text to images; it needs to be text that actually tells a user what's in the image, in the context of the content. The alt text is a replacement of the information provided by the image, not just a description of the image. I'll explain the difference.

To figure out what the alt text should be for a particular image, imagine that you are reading the web page out loud to someone. When you get to the image, what would you say?

Keep in mind that the caption provides information as well, and you don't need to duplicate that information.

For example, consider the image in Figure 6-7. Let's say that the caption of the photo is "Along Highway 101 in Florida."

To choose good alt text, you'll need to consider the context of the surrounding content first.

For example, maybe this picture accompanies an informational article about hurricanes. The picture conveys the effect of a hurricane on palm trees. Your alt text might be, "A line of palm trees during a storm, with their branches all being pulled in one direction by the wind."

Figure 6-7. There could be many possible descriptions for this photo, depending on the surrounding content.

Or perhaps the picture accompanies a news article about a hurricane that went through Florida yesterday, and conveys a description of what the highway looked like during the hurricane. Your alt text might be, "Palm trees tilting in the wind, alongside a wet, deserted highway."

The same picture accompanying different content has a different meaning, and because you can't possibly describe every nuance of the photo, you need to decide what's most relevant to the context.

Even though only a few of your users will likely see this alt text, it's very necessary to those users, and you should put effort into it. It may be tempting to be overly terse and give the photo brief alt text such as "Trees." Although that does describe the image, it doesn't provide helpful information to the user.

Go into as much detail as is necessary to adequately convey the meaning of the image. However, don't make the alt text too long. It's customary to keep it under 256 characters (including spaces), but there's not actually a character limit.

You don't always need to describe the visual appearance of the image. For example, a company logo can generally be replaced by the name of the company and any additional text that appears in the logo. You don't need to describe the colors and appearance of the stylized text.

In other cases, the image may display redundant information. Say you have a page listing corporate sponsors for an event, and each list item has the company's logo next to the company name in text. If your alt text would mean that the list item would be read as "Company Name, Company Name," it would make more sense to *not* use any alt text for the logo, so "Company Name" is only read once.

If you're not sure, just imagine the page without the images, and see if your alt text helps the page make sense. Your browser or an add-on likely has an option where you can replace all the images on your page with the alt text, so you can see exactly how it turns out.

You don't need to start your alt text with "Image of…" or "Picture of…"; the screen reader will announce that it's an image before reading the alt text.

It's fairly common, but not a good practice, to use the `title` attribute to provide additional information about an image, which will "pop up" when users move the mouse cursor over the image. Doing this means the information is not available to all users (mobile users, keyboard-only users, most screen reader users). If you have information to provide to users, it needs to be in the caption so it's provided to all users.

And don't simply duplicate the alt text in the `title` field, because some screen readers will read both. For more information, see Steve Faulkner's "Using the HTML title attribute" (*http://blog.paciellogroup. com/2013/01/using-the-html-title-attribute-updated/*) on The Paciello Group website.

Image File Formats

Generally, the images you'll use on your site will be JPEG, GIF, and PNG images. Any browser can display those file types. We'll also look at SVG images; these are more flexible than the other types, but currently not all browsers can display SVG images. You can tell the file type of an image by its extension.

The differences among the file formats are important for responsive design, because the format you choose can affect the size of the image. You want to use the format that results in the lowest file size, while still producing an image that looks the way you want it to.

There are other image file types, but they don't work in all browsers, so you should avoid them. If you have an image with a different extension that you want to use on your page, you can use your image editing software to convert it to a JPEG, GIF, or PNG file.

JPEG

File extension: *.jpg* or *.jpeg*. Pronounced "jay-peg."

These are traditionally the most common type of images used on the Web. They work well for photographs and other types of images that use a large range of colors.

GIF

File extension: *.gif*. Commonly pronounced with a hard G, like "gift," but some people pronounce it with a soft G, like "jif."

This type of image is compressed (giving it a smaller file size) by reducing the number of colors used in the file. A GIF can display no more than 256 colors, which means that it generally can't be used for photos, which might have thousands of colors. Figure 6-8 shows a photo saved in GIF format. It looks pixelated because there aren't enough colors to make everything blend together.

Figure 6-8. This GIF looks pixelated because the colors are reduced.

The GIF format is best used for images with a smaller range of colors, such as logos or illustrations, rather than photos.

Unlike JPEG images, GIFs can be made to have areas that are transparent, so when the GIF is displayed on the page, the background will show through the transparent areas of the image.

Additionally, GIF images can be used for very short animation clips, by saving a number of different frames to be displayed in sequence. Although this may occasionally be useful, the file size will greatly increase. You may be able to reproduce the animation using CSS, which will have less impact on your site's performance.

Another thing to consider is that many people find moving parts on a web page to be distracting, so animated images are best avoided.

PNG

File extension: *.png*. Pronounced "ping."

There are two types of PNG images, and when you save a file as a PNG in your image editing application, you'll be asked to choose between these:

- 8-bit PNG files support only 256 colors, similar to a GIF file, but because PNGs are compressed differently, the file size might be smaller than the same image as a GIF.

- 24-bit PNG files support millions of colors, similar to a JPG file, although the compression often leads the file size to be *larger* than the same image as a JPG.

Both types of PNG files allow for transparency, like GIF files. However, the 24-bit PNG files also allow for *partial* transparency, which is when you can see the background (the web page) behind the image as a whole, not just through the empty areas of the image (this effect isn't supported by IE 6 or older). You can achieve a similar transparency effect with CSS using `opacity`.

SVG

File extension: *.svg*. Pronounced "ess-vee-gee."

SVG is a vector graphics format for images. What that means is that instead of having data for every individual pixel of the image, as other formats do, it has data in XML format that defines the various parts of the image and their relationships: lines, shapes, colors, gradients, filters, and so on. This type of image is appropriate for graphics, but not photos.

Because SVG stores the data in this way instead of pixel by pixel, it's resolution-independent. You can resize the image to any dimensions without degrading the quality, so you don't need to have separate images for different resolutions.

The only downside is that IE 8 and earlier and Android 2.3 and earlier don't support SVG images at all, so in those browsers you'll need to use JavaScript to replace the images with images in a different format. You can do this with a plug-in such as SVG Swap (*https://github.com/teleject/svg-swap*).

To learn more about using SVG images, read Chris Coyier's "Using SVG" (*http://css-tricks.com/using-svg/*) on CSS-Tricks.

Optimizing Images

One of the biggest problems with user experience on websites is performance—how long it takes the page to load and finish rendering. If it takes too long, the user will give up and go away. Worse, over a slow connection the page might not finish loading at all, no matter how long the user waits.

One of the most common culprits is images.

PIXELS AND RESOLUTION

Before we talk about optimizing images, we need to talk about *pixels*. You probably know what a pixel is. On your computer screen, it's one physical point of color (or grayscale), the smallest point the screen can display. The images you see on the screen are actually made of dots, the same as images that you see on a TV or printed on paper. There are so many of them that you generally can't see each individual dot, but zooming in, they look like what you see in Figure 6-9.

Figure 6-9. This is what the individual pixels of an image on the screen look like.

The number of pixels determines the resolution of a computer screen. For example, a 1024 × 768 monitor screen is 1,024 pixels wide by 768 high. That's considered a 15" display—12" wide by 9" high, or 15" diagonal.

Until recently, pixels were always the same size. You could tell from a screen's resolution how big it was. A 1280 × 1024 screen was physically larger than a 1024 × 768 screen.

And so that was how we designed things—in pixels, because they'd always be the same size on every screen. An image that was 300 pixels × 300 pixels would appear the same size no matter what monitor you used to view it.

But in recent years some device manufacturers realized that if they made the pixels smaller, fitting more pixels on the screen, it would make what's on the screen look more "real."

For example, an iPhone screen appears to be 320 × 480 pixels, when you look at the physical size. But the actual resolution is 640 pixels × 960 pixels—twice as many pixels in each direction.

What does this mean for that 300-pixel image that we just mentioned? Well, the iPhone screen, when displaying a web page at actual size, will *behave* as if the screen is 320 × 480 pixels—otherwise, everything would always be really tiny. So that 300-pixel image will be displayed using twice as many pixels in each direction: instead of 300 × 300, it will use 600 × 600 pixels.

So now we need to differentiate between the pixels that the iPhone pretends it has when it displays the web page (320 × 480 pixels) and the actual, physical pixels that make up the screen (640 × 960 pixels). The pretend pixels that we refer to in our designs are called *reference pixels* or *CSS pixels*, and the physical pixels on the screen are called *device pixels* or *hardware pixels*.

HIGH-DENSITY SCREENS

These newer screens like the iPhone's that have more device pixels than reference pixels are called *high-density screens*. By definition, they have a *pixel ratio* of higher than 2. The extra pixels make these screens *look* better than normal screens—with enough pixels, the human eye is unable to see the individual pixels, and it looks more "real."

Apple calls these screens *retina displays*, and you can find them on newer iPhones, iPads, and MacBook Pros. For example, an iPhone 3 has a resolution of 320 × 480. The iPhone 4 is the same physical size, but has a resolution of 640 × 960, which is twice as many pixels in each direction (four times as many total).

The difference between device pixels and reference pixels can be pretty confusing, which is one reason why we're moving toward using relative units like ems and percentages in web design—so we don't have to rely on what the screen is calling a pixel (which could change in future devices), but instead use measurements that will be the same on every screen.

Different devices represent pixels differently, and that's all still being worked out.

If you want to learn more, read Scott Kellum's "A Pixel Identity Crisis" (*http://alistapart.com/article/a-pixel-identity-crisis*) on *A List Apart*.

The issue with high-density screens is that if you send normal images to these screens, the screens will display the images at the expected dimensions, but because they are filling a space with four times as many physical pixels as if they were displayed on a non-high-density screen, they will often look pixelated or blurry.

The optimal solution is to provide an image with twice the dimensions. For example, instead of a 200 × 200 image, provide a 400 × 400 image, but display it in the same 200 × 200 (reference pixel) space. On high-density screens, it will look the same size, but it will appear very sharp.

But now that we're trying to provide different images for high-density screens, we have images with greater file sizes that take more time to load. You don't want users with non-high-density screens to have to waste bandwidth on these larger images. We'll address this later in the chapter when we talk about responsive images—how to use different images depending on whether the screen is high density.

If you're using sets of two equivalent images, the convention has been to add "@2x" on the end of the filename to designate which images are for high-density screens. For example, your files may be named *tree.jpg* and *tree@2x.jpg*.

Additional images don't have to always be 2x, because high-density screens can have various pixel densities; sometimes it's ideal to create both 1.5x and 2x images for screens with different resolutions, although it may not always be necessary and can just create an extra level of complication.

You can use various solutions involving JavaScript or CSS to switch out images so that high-density screens get high-density images. To learn more, read Edward Cant's *Menacing Cloud* blog post, "Optimising for High Pixel Density Displays" (*http://menacingcloud.com/?c=highPixelDensityDisplays*).

If you don't have the skills or resources to add separate high-density images to your site, you have two options.

First, you can use a high-density version for all screens, and just make sure it's sized correctly. The downside to this is that the image will be much larger and take longer to load. If your site doesn't have very many images, this may be an acceptable solution.

The second option is to stick with the regular-density versions of your images. They will still display on high-density screens, but may look slightly blurry. Check out how your site looks on a high-density screen to determine if that's acceptable to you.

Of course, you can decide between one option and the other for each particular image on your site—you don't have to do the same thing for all of them.

COMPRESSING IMAGES

Compressing your image files is a way to decrease their size and help your images load faster.

In your image editing application, you can start with finding an option to save your image as low, medium, or high quality (look for an option like "Save for Web" or "Export"). Try saving your image at different quality levels to see how the file size changes. Some images will look blurry or pixelated at lower quality, and not acceptable to use on your site. But other images will still look good at a lower quality setting, allowing you to use smaller-sized files.

Changing the image file type may also decrease the file size. Try saving your image as a JPEG, GIF, or PNG to see if that makes a difference. Again, make sure it doesn't noticeably decrease the quality.

Applications like Photoshop give you the option to see different versions of your image next to each other before saving, and compare file size and file type on the screen.

Try to use the version of your image with the smallest possible file size that still looks good. Make sure you test it on different device screens, as that can make a difference in the appearance.

Also try tools like Smush.it (*http://www.smushit.com/ysmush.it/*) from the Yahoo! Developer Network, a web-based tool that can optimize images without changing the visual quality.

To learn more about how to optimize your images for the Web, read Christopher Schmitt's *Designing Web & Mobile Graphics: Fundamental Concepts for Web and Interactive Projects* (New Riders).

[NOTE]

Even though you're compressing images to optimize them for the Web, you need to keep the original, high-resolution image files in case you need them someday. One trick for keeping track of the original files is to simply upload them to the same directory in your website as the optimized images you're using on the site. Even though the high-res versions won't actually be used on the site, if someone else needs to use the files in the future, they'll know where to find them.

Storage is cheap, so your cost in keeping them there will be minimal. Give the original files similar names that make it clear they're originals so you'll know which is which, such as *flowers_original.psd*.

ACTUAL DIMENSIONS

If you don't use HTML or CSS to tell the browser what dimensions to make the image, the browser will by default display it at full size. These are the dimensions you saved it as in your image editing program—let's say 300 × 400 pixels.

Sometimes this is fine, but sometimes you want your image to be smaller than its actual dimensions, depending on the width of the viewport. You can use CSS to make it smaller.

However, you never want to have your image display *larger* than its actual dimensions, because it will end up being blurry. Luckily the browser will never do that, unless you purposely specify it in your CSS. Figures 6-10 and 6-11 compare the difference between an image at its actual dimensions, and an image displayed larger than its actual dimensions.

Figure 6-10. Image at its actual dimensions.

Figure 6-11. Image made larger than its actual dimensions.

With responsive design, your image might be resized for different screen widths, so you always want to start out with an image file that's the largest dimensions you'd want your image to be at any viewport width, and go from there.

However, you don't want your website to download an image file that's much larger than the one you need for a particular screen size—we'll address that issue later in the chapter.

Content Images

When adding content images to your website, you'll be using the `<img>` element. In the next few sections, we'll look at how to add content images to your page, get them in the right place, and make sure they're the right size.

THE <IMG> ELEMENT

The <img> element is an inline element. In the following code, it is between two block elements, the <h2> and a <p>, so it's stacked between those elements, as you see in Figure 6-12:

```
<h2>Pandas in Wolong</h2>

<img src="images/pandaphoto.jpg" alt="A panda eating
bamboo.">

<p>The Wolong National Nature Reserve, in the Sichuan
Province of China ...
```

Pandas Forever

- Home
- About
- Links
- Contact

Pandas in Wolong

The Wolong National Nature Preserve, in the Sichuan Province of China, is home to more than 150 giant pandas. It's one of the key sites for panda breeding research, and 66 cubs have been born at Wolong since it was established in 1980. Pandas are an endangered species, with between 1500 and 3000 living in the wild, and less than 300 in captivity (research centers and zoos).

The Wolong Nature Reserve covers around 200,000 hectares (772 square miles) in the Ming Shan mountain range, in the ABA Tibetan Autonomous Region, near the Tibetan Plateau. Elevations in the reserve range from 1555 to 4600 meters (4,000 to 11,000 ft).

The Wolong Panda Center was devestated during the May 2008 earthquake, and the main road to the center was impassable after the earthquake. Five staff members and one captive panda died in the earthquake. The pandas at the center were temporarily relocated to another panda center in China, until a rebuilt Wolong Panda Center opened in 2012, in another area of the reserve. The new center integrates scientific research, scientific research with captive breeding and also creates opportunities for introducing pandas into the wild.

Related Links

- Pandas Unlimited
- National Zoo Panda Cams
- Panda Facts at WWF

© 2014 Pandas Forever

Figure 6-12. The website with a photo of a panda added in the main content section.

The `<img>` element is a little different from other elements we've looked at so far, in that it doesn't have opening and closing tags with content between them, as heading and paragraph elements do. Instead, it has only one tag, and uses the `src` and `alt` attributes to determine what to display on the page. Both of those attributes are required.

The `src` attribute simply is a link to your image file, either as a relative link if your image file is part of the same website (*images/pandaphoto.jpg*) or an absolute link to another website (*http://www.example.com/pandaphoto.jpg*).

We already discussed the `alt` attribute, which tells the browser what to display when the image is unavailable.

ADDING AN IMAGE

Right now we're just going to look at our layout at the widest viewport width. There's a big empty space next to the photo that we want to do something about.

You've seen enough websites, magazines, and newspapers to know that the text usually will wrap around the picture to fill all that whitespace. This is where the **float** property, which we discussed in Chapter 4, comes in.

We'll give the image a **float: left** so the element will be positioned all the way to the left and the following elements will "float" around it to fill any available space, as in Figure 6-13:

```
article img { float: left; }
```

You could also float the image to the right, as in Figure 6-14:

```
article img { float: right; }
```

And then you may need to add a little padding to make it look right, as in Figure 6-15:

```
article img { float: right; padding-left: 3%; padding-
bottom: 10px; }
```

Pandas Forever

- Home
- About
- Links
- Contact

Pandas in Wolong

The Wolong National Nature Preserve, in the Sichuan Province of China, is home to more than 150 giant pandas. It's one of the key sites for panda breeding research, and 66 cubs have been born at Wolong since it was established in 1980. Pandas are an endangered species, with between 1500 and 3000 living in the wild, and less than 300 in captivity (research centers and zoos).

The Wolong Nature Reserve covers around 200,000 hectares (772 square miles) in the Ming Shan mountain range, in the ABA Tibetan Autonomous Region, near the Tibetan Plateau. Elevations in the reserve range from 1555 to 4600 meters (4,000 to 11,000 ft).

The Wolong Panda Center was devestated during the May 2008 earthquake, and the main road to the center was impassable after the earthquake. Five staff members and one captive panda died in the earthquake. The pandas at the center were temporarily relocated to another panda center in China, until a rebuilt Wolong Panda Center opened in 2012, in another area of the reserve. The new center integrates scientific research, scientific research with captive breeding and also creates opportunities for introducing pandas into the wild.

Related Links

- Pandas Unlimited
- National Zoo Panda Cams
- Panda Facts at WWF

© 2014 Pandas Forever

Figure 6-13. The photo floated to the left in the main content section.

Pandas Forever

- Home
- About
- Links
- Contact

Pandas in Wolong

The Wolong National Nature Preserve, in the Sichuan Province of China, is home to more than 150 giant pandas. It's one of the key sites for panda breeding research, and 66 cubs have been born at Wolong since it was established in 1980. Pandas are an endangered species, with between 1500 and 3000 living in the wild, and less than 300 in captivity (research centers and zoos).

The Wolong Nature Reserve covers around 200,000 hectares (772 square miles) in the Ming Shan mountain range, in the ABA Tibetan Autonomous Region, near the Tibetan Plateau. Elevations in the reserve range from 1555 to 4600 meters (4,000 to 11,000 ft).

The Wolong Panda Center was devestated during the May 2008 earthquake, and the main road to the center was impassable after the earthquake. Five staff members and one captive panda died in the earthquake. The pandas at the center were temporarily relocated to another panda center in China, until a rebuilt Wolong Panda Center opened in 2012, in another area of the reserve. The new center integrates scientific research, scientific research with captive breeding and also creates opportunities for introducing pandas into the wild.

Related Links

- Pandas Unlimited
- National Zoo Panda Cams
- Panda Facts at WWF

© 2014 Pandas Forever

Figure 6-14. The photo is floated to the right in the main content section.

Figure 6-15. Adding padding around the floated image.

FLEXIBLE IMAGE DIMENSIONS

The image is displayed at full size, because we didn't use CSS to change its dimensions. At our maximum page width, that works well—the image is large enough to see a lot of detail, and there's still plenty of room for the text to flow around it.

But if we make the browser window narrower, it gets to a point where the text is kind of cramped around the image, as in Figure 6-16.

As the viewport gets smaller, it makes sense for the image to get smaller, so it's not taking up so much of the screen real estate. We can do this by giving the image a width of 50%, which means it is half the width of the containing element:

```
article img { width: 50%; }
```

As you see in Figure 6-17, the image is a nice size on the screen at a range of widths, heading down to 36 ems, where the layout is going to switch to one column (we'll look at that shortly).

Figure 6-16. There's enough room for the image at a wider page width, but as the screen gets narrower, it gets crowded.

Figure 6-17. As the screen width gets narrower, the image gets smaller.

On a larger screen, you can take advantage of the available space to show the image at a large size. On smaller screens, the image is still a good size, but it doesn't overwhelm the other content.

[NOTE]

It's possible to give an image an exact width and height using HTML, and this used to be the common way to code images (e.g., `<img src="image.jpg" alt="alt text" width="400" height="200">`). However, if you use HTML to give images a size, you can't make them responsive. So, avoid doing this, and if you need to size images, do it with CSS instead.

MEDIA QUERIES

When the screen gets narrower and passes our breakpoint of 36 ems, the layout changes to one column. The image now takes up half of the single column, and at 36 ems and slightly smaller, it's still a good size.

But as you continue to decrease the width of the viewport, as in Figure 6-18, the image gets really small—you can't see the details as well, and it just feels like it should be larger.

Pandas Forever

- Home
- About
- Links
- Contact

Pandas in Wolong

The Wolong National Nature Preserve, in the Sichuan Province of China, is home to more than 150 giant pandas. It's one of the key sites for panda breeding research, and 66 cubs have been born at Wolong since it was established in 1980. Pandas are an endangered species, with between 1500 and 3000 living in the wild, and less than 300 in captivity (research centers and zoos).

The Wolong Nature Reserve covers around 200,000 hectares (772 square miles) in the Ming Shan mountain range, in the ABA Tibetan Autonomous Region, near the Tibetan Plateau. Elevations in the reserve range from 1555 to 4600 meters (4,000 to 11,000 ft).

The Wolong Panda Center was devastated during the May 2008 earthquake, and the main road to the center was impassable after the earthquake. Five staff members and one captive panda died in the earthquake. The pandas at the center were temporarily relocated to another pandas center in China, until a rebuilt Wolong Panda Center opened in 2012, in another area of the reserve. The new center integrates scientific research,

Pandas Forever

- Home
- About
- Links
- Contact

Pandas in Wolong

The Wolong National Nature Preserve, in the Sichuan Province of China, is home to more than 150 giant pandas. It's one of the key sites for panda breeding research, and 66 cubs have been born at Wolong since it was established in 1980. Pandas are an endangered species, with between 1500 and 3000 living in the wild, and less than 300 in captivity (research centers and zoos).

The Wolong Nature Reserve covers around 200,000 hectares (772 square miles) in the Ming Shan mountain range, in the ABA Tibetan Autonomous Region, near the Tibetan Plateau. Elevations in the reserve range from 1555 to 4600 meters (4,000 to 11,000 ft).

The Wolong Panda Center was devastated during the May 2008 earthquake, and the

Figure 6-18. At narrower screen widths, the image gets too small to see the details.

Fixing this is pretty simple—we can just add a media query so that at this viewport width (or narrower) the photo takes up the entire width of the column, rather than just half. We'll need to add a breakpoint at about 28 ems.

This time we're going from wide to narrow, so we need to use `max-width` instead of `min-width` in the media query.

We'll give the image a width of `auto`, which means it will display at its natural size, which is 300 pixels wide. To override the styles that we've already added, we need to stop it from floating to the right by adding `float: none` to the styles, and remove the left padding that we used when it had text wrapping around it:

```
@media only screen and (max-width: 28em) {
    article img { width: auto; float: none; padding-left:
    0; }
}
```

Now we get what you see in Figure 6-19.

Figure 6-19. For narrow screens, the image will fill the full width of the screen without text wrapping around it.

You might be wondering why we've gone from wide to narrow when adding this image, instead of narrow to wide as we've done previously. Really, we could have gone in either direction. When adding an image to a design it's sometimes easier to go wide to narrow, simply because the size of your image has a hard stop at its actual width (300 pixels, in this case).

You can certainly mix `min-width` and `max-width` media queries in your stylesheets. The problem is that now our default style for this image (without any media queries) is for wider screens, so small screens that can't understand media queries will get our wide-screen image instead of our narrow-screen image.

Don't worry, though; even if you add media queries going in both directions, you can easily flip some of them around so they all go the same way (it tends to be less confusing if all the media queries on a site go in the same direction).

For example, these styles that we used in the earlier example have the default for wider screens, and a media query to add styles for narrower screens:

```
article img { float: right; padding-left: 3%; padding-
bottom: 10px; }
@media only screen and (max-width: 28em) {
    article img { width: auto; float: none; padding-left:
    0; }
}
```

Flipping that around, you get this:

```
article img { }
@media only screen and (min-width: 28em) {
    article img { float: right; padding-left: 3%;
    padding-bottom: 10px; }
}
```

But hold on—why aren't there any styles for article img on the first line, for the narrow-screen styles? Because all the styles we used in our example for the narrower design range—width: auto; float: none; padding-left: 0;—were used to change properties back to the default values.

If we start with the defaults, we don't need to declare them. (Taking this further, of course, the entire article img { } line is unnecessary, because there are no styles in it.)

MAXIMUM WIDTH

Using max-width on your website is one of the keys to making responsive design work correctly, and it's actually super easy. Here's an example of how it works.

Our photo looks good right at our breakpoint of 28 ems, but of course we need to look at the entire design range, down to our minimum of 320 pixels. Unfortunately, we have a problem, as you see in Figure 6-20.

Once we get down to about 22 ems, the image is wider than the column! Not only does the image go outside the border of the column, but its edge is cut off because it goes outside the browser window.

Luckily, this is an easy problem to fix.

Figure 6-20. At this width, the image is too wide for the container.

We don't want to simply give the image a set percentage size, because we want it to be as large as it can be, up to its actual size of 300 pixels.

Instead, we can use a really handy property, max-width. You'll remember that we used this property in Chapter 5 to tell our two-column layout to stop getting wider at a certain viewport width. In that example, we set the value in ems.

For this image, we're going to give it a value of max-width: 100%. By using 100%, we're telling the browser that the image should never be displayed at a width that is greater than the width of its containing element—in this case, the <article> that it's inside of:

```
article img { max-width: 100%; }
```

You can see in Figure 6-21 that although the image at its actual size doesn't quite fill the column at 28 ems on the left, as we make the window narrower, the image gets narrower to fit inside the column (it will also stay inside the element's padding).

Figure 6-21. With `max-width:100%`, the image is never wider than the container.

If you've read up much on responsive design, you've probably heard that `max-width` is part of the three main tenets of responsive design. And it is definitely important—without `max-width`, responsive sites wouldn't work, because you'd often run into this issue of images that don't fit where they're supposed to.

But here's a little secret: because `max-width` for images is so critical to your responsive website, you can simply apply it to the entire website. That is, you can apply `max-width:100%` to *all* of your images by adding the following code near the top of your stylesheet (just below the reset code is a good place):

```
img { max-width: 100%; }
```

Once you've done that, you don't have to think about it again; it's done!

Although you don't *need* `max-width: 100%` on all of the images on your site, there's no harm in having it apply to all the other images, because the only thing it does is make sure images aren't larger than their containers. It doesn't affect anything else having to do with the size of the image. In the rare instances where you don't want `max-width: 100%` to apply to a particular image, you can simply add CSS to override it for that particular image.

TELLING STORIES WITH PHOTOS

When choosing photos to place on your site, make sure that the images are interesting and actually convey the personality of your site.

It's tempting to use purchased stock photos—and while many of these are great photos, they are often not chosen with care and look over-posed, which makes it obvious that they are stock photos. This makes your site look bland.

If you have a restaurant website, don't use a stock photo of a random person eating a random hamburger. Use actual photos of your restaurant and its food. Make sure they are good-quality photos—it may be worth it to hire a professional photographer.

Most importantly, use captions as much as you can. The story of a photo is not always apparent from the photo itself. A photo of your busy restaurant is nice, but it's even more effective with a caption reading, "The restaurant on a busy Saturday night. We often fill up early with the theater crowd, so don't forget to make a reservation so you don't have to wait."

Background Images

Not all images are part of the content. You'll also have images that are decorative, that add to the design of the site without adding any meaning.

You can add images that that are part of the style rather than the content using the CSS property background-image.

Don't add content images with background-image, because they won't be visible to people using screen readers or other text-based browsers.

(An exception: there are actually ways you can display a CSS image and then provide alternate text with HTML that's hidden from the visible website, but it's hacky and difficult, and there are few circumstances where it's a good design choice.)

ADDING BACKGROUND IMAGES

Let's say we want to add a background image to the header of our example website.

Again, we're going to start at the widest screen width. When our design is at its maximum, the header is approximately 900 pixels wide, accounting for margins, so we need to make the banner image at least that wide. The header area on our page appears about 140 pixels high, but it could be taller depending on the size of the fonts, so we need to make the banner image tall enough so that the header will definitely be covered (see Figure 6-22).

Figure 6-22. The background.

Adding the background image to the header is simple. You can see the results in Figure 6-23:

```
header { background-image: url(images/pandabanner.png);
}
```

You'll notice that the image in the banner is lighter than an actual photo would be. This is called *opacity*, or *transparency*. In this case, I wanted the photo to be light so that it wouldn't be difficult to read the text that's on top of it.

You can use CSS to adjust the opacity of a content image using the **opacity** property, but to do so on a background image isn't all that easy. So instead, I changed the opacity of the photo in an image editing application before uploading it to the site.

Figure 6-23. The background image added to the header.

ALIGNMENT

If you make the browser window narrower to see how the banner looks, you'll notice that the panda that was more or less centered in the banner is now off to one side, as seen in Figure 6-24.

This is because the banner image is aligned to the left (by default), and the right side of the banner is cut off because it doesn't fit in the element.

Unlike content images, the background-image is applied as a style to an element, so it will never go outside the bounds of the element (you simply won't see the excess areas of the image). Thus, there's no need for max-width.

By default, background images are aligned to the top left. You can use the background-position property along with two values to align the image horizontally (along the x-axis) and vertically (along the y-axis).

Figure 6-24. At a narrower screen width, the banner image is no longer centered.

In our case, we want to center the image but keep it at the top, as in Figure 6-25. We can do this as follows:

```
header { background-image: url(images/pandabanner.png);
background-position: center top; }
```

Figure 6-25. Using background position, the image can be centered.

You can also use percentages or fixed measurements such as pixels to align a background image.

Responsive Images

One big topic of discussion in responsive web design is responsive images. How do we provide images with appropriate dimensions to large screens, taking advantage of the screen space, but not waste bandwidth by sending those huge images to devices with small screens? And how do we serve crisp-looking images to high-resolution screens, but not send those larger files to devices with lower-resolution screens that don't need them?

If we have multiple image files of different sizes for different screens, we want to make sure devices are only downloading the one they need, not all of them.

A lot of possible solutions have been thrown around, and while we'll look at some of the more popular solutions here, none of them are perfect. It's likely that there will be a lot more discussion on this issue during the next few years, and it's definitely possible that other responsive image solutions will come about.

One of the major issues with the current solutions is that they're all fairly complex. A lot of web content is created by people who are not developers, and who use content management systems (CMSs) to edit their websites. WYSIWYG (what you see is what you get) editors allow the website editor to add an image by clicking a button and choosing a file—for example, adding a photo within a blog post.

Although some of these solutions could be integrated into a CMS, website editors would have little control over choosing the best image sizes (and likely not have the knowledge to do so).

Even for developers, if a responsive image technique is too complicated, many of them will simply avoid it and continue to use the straightforward `<img>` element.

Creating multiple images to switch out is also not future-friendly. We are choosing image dimensions and resolutions based on the screen sizes of today, but they may be very different in the future.

PROPOSED CLIENT-SIDE SOLUTIONS

Ideally, there would be a way to switch out images based on device capabilities, using HTML and/or CSS, that would be supported by all the browsers.

And this is the goal that the W3C's Responsive Images Community Group (*http://responsiveimages.org*) is working toward.

Unfortunately, its work is still in progress. There are two potential responsive image solutions, the <picture> element and the srcset attribute, but neither has been implemented by all the major browsers and neither is part of the HTML specification yet.

It is likely that one or both of these solutions will become part of a future HTML specification, so we'll go over them briefly here so you can get a sense of how they are intended to work (although you won't be able to use <picture> or srcset on your website yet).

Later in the chapter, we'll address other solutions that can currently be used.

srcset

The srcset attribute to the <img> element will allow you to specify and upload multiple versions (different files) of the same image, and the browser will only download the particular file it needs, instead of all of them.

Currently, the src attribute to <img> allows you to specify one image file; the srcset attribute would allow you to specify multiple files, separated by commas. Each image file would be described by the viewport size or pixel density it should be used for. The browser would then choose the most appropriate image, and download and display that image.

Let's consider an example:

```
<img src="images/flower.jpg" alt="a flower" srcset="
images/flower-HD.jpg 2x, images/flower-small.jpg 600w,
images/flower-small-HD.jpg 600w 2x">
```

In this example, the default image is *flower.jpg*. For high-density screens (a pixel density of 2 or greater), *flower-HD.jpg* will be used instead. For narrow screens, less than 600 pixels wide, *flower-small.jpg* will be used. For screens that are both less than 600 pixels wide *and* high density, *flower-small-HD.jpg* will be used.

The image can be replaced on the fly, if the device's conditions change. For example, if you rotate a tablet screen so that the viewport width changes, the browser will check if it needs to download a different image from the srcset.

Note that you can specify images by maximum viewport width (as in the 600w in this example), which has the same effect as a max-width media query (*if the viewport is a maximum of 600 pixels wide, use this image*). Unfortunately, srcset can be used only with maximum widths, not minimum widths.

Older browsers that do not support srcset will simply ignore the other options and use the default image in the src attribute.

<picture>

As with srcset, the <picture> element would allow you to specify and upload multiple versions of the same image, and the browser would only download the particular file it needs, instead of all of them:

```
<picture>
<source media="(min-width: 45em)" src="images/flower-
large.jpg">
<source media="(min-width: 18em)" src="images/flower-
medium.jpg">
<source src="flower-small.jpg">
<img src="images/flower-small.jpg" alt="a flower">
</picture>
```

You can see in this example that the media attribute uses very similar syntax to a CSS media query. You can query by either min-width or max-width.

For viewports of 45 ems or wider, the browser will use the first <source>, *flower-large.jpg*. For viewports of 18 ems or wider, but less than 45 ems, the browser will use *flower-medium.jpg*. And for all other viewports (less than 18 ems), the browser will use the third <source>, which doesn't have a media query, *flower-small.jpg*.

You'll notice that by ending with the default, this goes in the opposite order of how we use media queries in CSS, where we start with the default value and follow it with media queries.

Any browsers that don't support the <picture> element will ignore it and use the fallback <img> element, which is located *inside* the <picture> element.

You can also combine the `<picture>` element and the `srcset` attribute if you want to use both viewport size media queries and versions with different resolutions:

```
<picture>
<source media="(min-width: 45em)" srcset="flower-large.
jpg 1x, flower-large-hd.jpg 2x">
<source media="(min-width: 18em)" srcset="flower-med.jpg
1x, flower-med-hd.jpg 2x">
<source srcset="flower-small.jpg 1x, flower-small-hd.jpg
2x">
<img src="flower-small.jpg" alt="a flower">
</picture>
```

OTHER SOLUTIONS

Other responsive image solutions are available, but they are mainly *polyfills*. A polyfill is a piece of code that replicates newer HTML/CSS features in older browsers. Some of these solutions replicate the behavior of the proposed `<picture>` and `srcset`. The downside of using a polyfill is that it will add additional code to your site.

None of these solutions is perfect for every circumstance, so you'll need to understand the pros and cons of each, and when they should be used. If you need to choose between responsive image solutions, you can refer to Chris Coyier's "Which responsive images solution should you use?" (*http://css-tricks.com/which-responsive-images-solution-should-you-use/*) on CSS-Tricks, where he compares many of the solutions.

Picturefill

Although you can't actually use the `<picture>` element yet (because it hasn't been implemented by the browsers), Scott Jehl has created a polyfill called Picturefill (*https://github.com/scottjehl/picturefill*) that essentially does the same thing using JavaScript.

To use Picturefill, visit the website and follow the instructions. You will need to add the *picturefill.js* file to your website.

The code for Picturefill uses similar syntax to the `<picture>` element:

```
<span data-picture data-alt="a flower">
<span data-src="images/flower-small.jpg"></span>
<span data-src="images/flower-medium.jpg"
data-media="(min-width: 18em)"></span>
<span data-src="images/flower-large.jpg"
data-media="(min-width: 45em)"></span>
<noscript><img src="images/flower-small.jpg" alt="a
flower"></noscript>
</span>
```

The Picturefill JavaScript uses the `<span>` element to create an `<img>` element in the appropriate size for the viewport. Inside the `<noscript>` element is a fallback for non-JavaScript browsers.

You can also use Picturefill to give the browser image options based on resolution, for high-density screens.

Adaptive Images

Adaptive Images is another polyfill for responsive images. This one is a server-side solution, which means that the server hosting the website does some of the work—it's not all up to the HTML and CSS.

It works differently than the responsive image solutions described previously, as you only need to create one version of your image—at full size. Adaptive Images detects the size of the user's screen (not viewport), and creates and serves a resized version of each image at an appropriate width for that screen.

To use this polyfill, your server needs to be running Apache and PHP, so Adaptive Images doesn't work for every website. But as long as you have those on your server (and they are very common), you can easily add Adaptive Images to any website, as it doesn't require you to change your HTML for images at all—you just use the regular `<img>` element.

Because you don't have to change your HTML, this will likely be the best solution for adding responsive images to existing websites, where it's not feasible to go back and change the code of legacy content.

To install Adaptive Images on your website, download the files from the Adaptive Images website (*http://adaptive-images.com*), then follow the setup instructions, including editing the *.htaccess* file on your website and adding some JavaScript to your page `<head>`.

You then choose and set the breakpoints (viewport widths) at which you want your image dimensions to change. Because you're uploading the *largest* version of your image, the breakpoints are the widths at which your image will be made smaller. (Note that breakpoints have to be set in pixels, not in the ems that we've used for the earlier examples in this book.)

So, if your breakpoints are set to 800 pixels and 400 pixels, and you upload an image that's 1,000 pixels wide, it will be resized to two versions: 800 pixels wide and 400 pixels wide (and of course, the height of the image will be adjusted accordingly).

As your web page is loading, when it encounters an `<img>` element, it requests the image from the server. The Adaptive Images code looks at the width of the user's screen, and picks the smallest image that's at least as wide as the screen. So, if the screen is 320 pixels wide, it will pick the 400-pixel image (based on the breakpoints in the previous paragraph); if the screen is 700 pixels wide, it will pick the 800-pixel image.

If you upload an image that's only 500 pixels wide—because that's the widest you need it to be on the screen—it will only be resized for the 400-pixel breakpoint. Images are never made larger.

When an image is requested, the server automatically creates a file at the requested dimensions. It then caches the image to save it for the next request, so only the first user visiting the site in any breakpoint range will have a slight delay while the extra image is being created.

One downside of this polyfill is it only resizes images based on the screen size, not the dimensions at which the image is going to be displayed. So images that aren't displayed at the full screen width are less likely to get a scaled-down version, even when one would be appropriate.

This polyfill needs JavaScript to work. In browsers without JavaScript, Adaptive Images will simply not run; the browsers will display the original, full-sized images in the `<img>` elements.

Adaptive Images is licensed under Creative Commons, so it's free for you to use with attribution to the author, Matt Wilcox. There are also plug-ins available for WordPress and Drupal.

HiSRC

HiSRC (*https://github.com/teleject/hisrc*) is a jQuery plug-in from Chris Schmitt that allows images to be replaced based on network speed and screen resolution.

The browser will first load a low-resolution "mobile first" version of each image. It will check the speed of the connection via JavaScript, and if the device has mobile bandwidth such as 3G, it will keep the low-res version of the image in place. If there's more bandwidth available, it will download a higher-resolution version and replace the original low-res image with the new image file. If it also detects that the screen is high density, it will download and replace the image with an appropriate version.

To use HiSRC, you will need to add jQuery to your site and upload and link to the HiSRC JavaScript file. You will also need to make and upload the three versions of each image.

The HTML is fairly simple. You will need a `<div>` with the appropriate class, and the `<img>` element will have extra attributes to specify the three image files:

```
<div class="hisrc">
<img src="images/flower-mobile.png" data-1x="images/
flower-400x200.png" data-2x="images/flower-800x400.png">
</div>
```

[NOTE]

You don't have to use HiSRC for all the images on your site. If you don't want to use it for a particular image, just use the `<img>` element without the extra `<div>`. Another JavaScript plug-in that provides responsive images is Foresight.js (*https://github.com/adamdbradley/foresight.js*).

Third-party services

Several companies offer responsive image services that will automatically resize your images to fit the screen width. As an example, we'll look at Sencha.io SRC (*http://www.sencha.com/learn/how-to-use-src-sencha-io/*). This third-party service is free for small websites.

[NOTE]

Other third-party services that provide responsive images include ReSRC (*http://www.resrc.it*), Thumbr.io (*http://www.thumbr.io*), and Responsive.io (*https://responsive.io*). Pricing is generally based on either the number of images or total GB per month.

The way it works is by detecting what brand and model the device is, and then using that information to determine the screen size. It scales the images to the width of the device screen, and also holds the images in the cache for 30 minutes so subsequent requests by the same device will be faster.

All you have to do is add the Sencha URL, *http://src.sencha.io/,* into the src of your image.

For example, if this is your `<img>` element:

```
<img src="http://www.example.com/images/butterfly.jpg"
alt="butterfly">
```

you would add in the Sencha URL like this (note that you also must use a full URL for your image, like *http://www.example.com/images/butterfly.jpg,* rather than a relative link like *images/butterfly.jpg*):

```
<img src="http://src.sencha.io/http://www.example.com/
images/butterfly.jpg" alt="butterfly">
```

The image will be resized to the width of the device screen. This means that if the image is actually being displayed on the screen at a percentage of the width, the image file will be bigger than it needs to be.

If you want to have the image resized to a specific size, you can do that by adding either the width and height as part of the URL, as in the following example, or just the width (it will automatically constrain the height):

```
<img src="http://src.sencha.io/400/200/http://www.
example.com/images/butterfly.jpg" alt="butterfly">
```

Even more useful: you can use percentages. If you want an image to be resized, and you know that it never takes up more than 50% of the screen width in your design, this code will resize it to whatever 50% of the device's screen width is:

```
<img src="http://src.sencha.io/x50/http://www.example.
com/images/butterfly.jpg" alt="butterfly">
```

Or you could do 50% of the width, and 25% of the height:

```
<img src="http://src.sencha.io/x50/x25/http://www.
example.com/images/butterfly.jpg" alt="butterfly">
```

Sencha can do a whole lot of other things, including reducing the image size by a given amount of pixels, using formulas that are combinations of any of the above, and changing file formats.

Keep in mind that when you use any third-party service, you're relying on that service to render parts of your site. There's always the remote possibility that a service like Sencha could suddenly cease to exist, without warning—which would essentially break your website. More likely, there may be times when the third-party site is temporarily down, or slow, and this will affect the performance of your site.

If you don't want to rely on a third-party solution, and if you have a very large site that makes the effort worthwhile, you could build a similar system on your own server.

BREAKPOINTS

Some of these responsive image solutions require choosing one or more breakpoints—the viewport widths at which the images change from one file to the other. How do you choose where those breakpoints are?

If your responsive images use art direction (displaying a different crop of the image, rather than just a different resolution of the same image), you probably will need to have your image breakpoints at the same widths as your layout breakpoints.

But if you're using the same image at different resolutions, it doesn't depend on your layout at all. Instead, you should switch to a different image at the point where the file that's being downloaded is unnecessarily large.

If you're using Picturefill (as we'll do in the next example) or any other solution that allows you to set breakpoints individually for each image, you'll have to do a little bit of work to make the best choices for each image.

Start by determining the *smallest* and *largest* dimensions that the image will be on the screen, so you know what your limits are. Determine the file size's for each of those two images, and then you're going to decide on the breakpoints in between.

It's kind of arbitrary how far apart the breakpoints are. If you have a lot of images on each page of your site, you may want to have the breakpoints closer together, to waste the least amount of bandwidth. Of course, that means creating more image files—you'll need one for each size variation of an image.

Or, if you have only a few images on each page of your site, you might not think it's worth doing this extra work at all just to save a few KB.

A good place to start is to aim for a gap of 20 KB between images. Try resizing your image to various dimensions, check the file size, and pick spots at which the file size is about 20 KB less than that of the previous image file.

For example, if your image is displayed in your design at widths between 320 pixels and 960 pixels, you might end up with a list of images like that in Table 6-1.

TABLE 6-1. Example of possible image breakpoints

DIMENSIONS	FILE SIZE
960 × 720	108 KB
780 × 585	85 KB
600 × 450	63 KB
500 × 375	43 KB
320 × 240	19 KB

To tell the images apart, you might want to include the width in the filename, like *panda960.jpg*.

Next, you'll need to set media queries for each of these file sizes. If the image is something like a banner that will always be displayed at the full width of the viewport, it's easy: match the breakpoints to the image widths.

You'll start with the largest image as your default. If the browser doesn't have JavaScript, it will only be able to display the default image. You want the largest image as the default so it will work on any screen size.

So, for the widest screens, we're displaying *panda960.jpg*, which is 960 pixels wide (we already determined that's the widest the image will ever be displayed). That image will either be displayed at 960 pixels, or scaled to a smaller size.

For the first media query we're saying that if the viewport is 780 pixels wide or less, the browser should use *panda780.jpg* instead. That image will either be displayed at 780 pixels, or scaled to a smaller size. Images will never be made larger than their actual size.

Notice that for this example we're using pixels instead of ems, because we're matching images that are sized in pixels:

```
<span data-picture data-alt="A panda eating bamboo.">
    <span data-src="images/panda960.jpg"></span>
    <span data-src="images/panda780.jpg"
    data-media="(max-width: 780px)"></span>
    <span data-src="images/panda600.jpg"
    data-media="(max-width: 600px)"></span>
    <span data-src="images/panda500.jpg"
    data-media="(max-width: 500px)"></span>
    <span data-src="images/panda320.jpg"
    data-media="(max-width: 320px)"></span>
    <noscript><img src="images/panda320.jpg" alt="a
    flower"></noscript>
</span>
```

Keep in mind that when we created the five different versions of this file, aiming for about a 20 KB difference in size, that only applied to this particular image. If you did the same for another image, you might have a different number of variations, and their widths would be different. So, optimizing your images in this way to waste the least amount of bandwidth would clearly involve a lot of manual work.

Another option would be to just choose a few breakpoints and resize *all* of your images to those breakpoints. You would still have to create variations of each image, but you wouldn't have to spend time calculating file sizes and determining the best breakpoints for each image. The downside is that you wouldn't save as much bandwidth as you would if you calculated sizes for each image.

For more details about how to choose image breakpoints, read Jason Grigsby's "Sensible jumps in responsive image file sizes" (*http://blog. cloudfour.com/sensible-jumps-in-responsive-image-file-sizes/*) on the Cloud Four Blog.

Summary

Images are a key part of both your site's content and its design.

The images you use on your website can be JPEG, GIF, PNG, or SVG files. The file types you should use depend on what kinds of images you have. Make each file as small as possible to reduce the amount of time it takes to download.

When displaying images on your site, first determine if you actually need the images, or if you can replace the effect using CSS. Use the `<img>` element for content images, and CSS `background-image` for decorative images. Icon sprites and icon fonts can help you lower the bandwidth required for your images.

Images need to be flexible on responsive websites. Use `max-width` to make sure they aren't too large for their containing elements. You can float images in your layout to get text to wrap around them.

Content images need to have alt text so that their messages are still available if the images can't be viewed. Make sure your alt text provides the same information as the image, which depends on context.

High-density screens need images of a higher resolution, but you should avoid having every device download these files if they don't need them. You can use various methods to have the browser only download the images that it needs.

The `<picture>` element allows you to specify different images depending on viewport width, but it hasn't been implemented by the browsers yet. One option you can use now is the Picturefill polyfill; others include Adaptive Images and third-party services such as Sencha.io.

Choose breakpoints for switching out images based on when the file size of the image being downloaded is unnecessarily large.

The area of responsive images is still evolving, so make sure to keep up with what's happening so you can take advantage of new ideas and solutions.

Now that we've touched on all the major pieces that you need to put together a website, in Chapter 7 we're going to talk about the process of creating responsive websites.

Part III

Working Responsively

[7]

Responsive Workflow

It's one thing to understand all the pieces of a responsive website. It's another thing altogether to be able to create one.

In this chapter, we'll look at the process for creating a responsive design, starting with user research and content strategy, then designing in text, sketching, and creating responsive prototypes.

We'll look at style tiles and other new approaches to design that provide alternatives to creating unresponsive, fixed-size designs in tools like Photoshop.

And at the end of the chapter, we'll finish up by looking at how to sell responsive design—both to clients and to coworkers—and how to adjust your approach to working with clients when you're doing a responsive project.

If you want to delve deeper into how to adjust your workflow to produce responsive websites, check out Stephen Hay's book *Responsive Design Workflow* (*http://responsivedesignworkflow.com*).

Strategy and Planning

Before you even start thinking about the design of a website, you need to step back for a moment and think about the goals of the website.

Unless it's the rare occasion when you're just making a site for fun or practice, your goal isn't to build a website, it's to solve a problem: how to communicate with customers, how to sell products online, and so forth.

The website is the tool you're creating to solve the problem.

You should know from the start what the goals are for the website or project, whether from your own communication with the client or stakeholders, or from information passed on from a project manager or other staff. "Our company needs a website" isn't a goal. Dig a bit deeper and find out who the company is trying to communicate with, and what it hopes the website will accomplish.

Creating a website, whether it's responsive or not, is not straightforward. There are a lot of creative decisions made during the process, starting with what content is included on the site, where the content goes, and what paths users will take through the site. If you know the goals of the site, you'll make better decisions during the design process.

USER RESEARCH

At the start of the project, you'll likely be doing user research and developing personas, scenarios, and other resources to guide you in the site design process.

For the most part, none of this work is specific to responsive design, so we won't go into details here. There are a lot of great resources out there, in case you want to learn more: in particular, check out *Communicating Design: Developing Web Site Documentation for Design and Planning, Second Edition* (*http://communicatingdesign.com*) by Dan Brown, which will tell you how to create much of the documentation you need during the web design process, such as personas, flow charts, wireframes, competitive reviews, and usability reports.

One warning, though, particular to responsive design: as you're developing personas, resist the temptation to make them correspond with device types. You aren't creating a website for a "mobile user" and a "desktop user," you're creating a site for users who each may be using different devices at different times to access the website.

CONTENT

Content is the most important part of any website. You should address content first during the design process, rather than trying to piece it into a finished visual design at the end.

In Chapter 2, we looked at how to create a content strategy for your site and discussed starting the design process with a content audit. We also talked about how to create content that will work well across screen sizes.

Information architecture

Once you've decided what content you need on your site, the next step is to organize and label it, and develop a structure for the site. This part of the process is called *information architecture* (IA).

The general IA principles you'd use for any website still apply to responsive sites, but you need to make sure that the site architecture will work on small screens, where there may not be room for a large or detailed navigation.

Also remember that your site architecture will not be set in stone, so the IA and design need to be flexible enough to accommodate future changes, as organizational or project needs require. If you don't leave room for changes, you may end up feeling like any new content added after the site launch needs to be shoehorned into existing boxes, where it may not belong.

Content outline

As you start organizing the content that will go on the new site, your first step should be creating a simple high-level outline of the content areas. This will be reflected in the main navigation of the website.

For example, Figure 7-1 is a screenshot showing the main navigation on Mule Design's website. This is followed by a simple content outline.

Figure 7-1. The Mule Design website has a straightforward main navigation.

- Home
- About (Who We Are)
    - Individual Bio #1
    - Individual Bio #2
    - Etc.
- Services (What We Do)
- Portfolio (Our Work)
    - Client #1
    - Client #2
    - Etc.
- Blog (Our Blog)
    - Blog Entry #1
    - Blog Entry #2
    - Etc.
- Contact (Hire Us)

The top-level content areas are pretty much the same as what you'd find on many design agency websites: Home, About, Services, Portfolio, Blog, and Contact. You'll notice that the text on the website is different from what's in the outline: "Who We Are" instead of "About."

As you are first creating a content outline, it's best to use general terms like "About" to give you an idea of where the content fits in, rather than deciding on the specific wording for your page titles or navigation. Otherwise you'll get too hung up on things like whether the terms fit well in the navigation, if they have similar lengths, and so on.

As you continue with compiling or developing the content for the site, you'll be able to add more detail to each section.

Just as with your content inventory, you don't need to list every individual item (like blog posts, or products on an ecommerce site); just get the categories and the main content pieces down.

Content Before Layout

Once you have worked through a content strategy and created an information architecture, you can start thinking about what the content will look like on the screen.

The content is the most important part of the website, so you're going to build your design around the content, not the other way around.

The best way to get started is to create an unstyled web page containing all your content. This shuld include all the page components, marked up with semantic HTML (appropriate heading levels, etc.).

Doing this *before* you start the visual work of sketches and wireframes or prototypes allows you to think about the role that each piece of content will play on the page, before you get distracted by how it will look.

COMPONENTS

First, determine what pieces of content will go on a page. Some examples may include the site logo, a search box, the main navigation, the body content, and the footer.

You need to think of these as separate pieces of content in this part of the design process, so that you can move them around on the page as you create a prototype.

For example, it's common to think of the page "header" as a solid unit, containing the site logo, search box, navigation, and so on. But you need to step outside the box, so to speak, because not all of these items will necessarily stay in the "header" area as you design responsively.

Some examples of the site-wide components that you might include:

- Logo
- Search box
- Primary navigation
- Secondary navigation
- Informational links
- Copyright notice
- Ad(s)
- Social media links
- Login link

And depending on the type of page, you may have components like:

- Title
- Body content
- Secondary content
- Synopsis
- Author
- Date
- Pull quote(s)

DESIGNING IN TEXT

Next, take all the content elements you need on your page and mark them up with basic, structured HTML. We looked at how to do this in Chapter 3. For example, in Figures 7-2 and 7-3, you can see our example web page from that chapter, before we added any CSS.

Remember that for a responsive website, the first design is no design; that is, the first design you should create is what a user will see if his browser or device is unable to render the CSS and JavaScript.

Figure 7-2. This is our website on a desktop monitor with no CSS applied.

Figure 7-3. This is our website on an iPhone with no CSS applied.

With just this basic code, you already have a functional web page that is mobile-ready, responsive, and accessible. By starting out your design this way, you're making sure that your web page will be functional for all users.

It's much easier to start with a page that's accessible to everyone, rather than trying to add in accessibility and compatibility later.

LINEAR DESIGN

As you're adding the structured text to your page, you're going to create what's called a *linear design*.

Linear design is a pretty simple idea. Imagine someone is reading your web page from start to finish—all of it. What order would you want them to read in? Your HTML should be in that order.

This seems pretty basic, but traditionally it's been common to do a visual design first, then write code to accommodate the design, and then fit content into the spaces. This often leads to the actual HTML being in a strange order.

But with small mobile devices, everything will pretty much be displayed in one column, so users will read it in a linear order anyway.

By starting with a linear design for your unstyled text, you're starting off with something that will work on narrow screens, and also that will work in browsers that can't display your styles.

CONTENT HIERARCHY

You need to make some decisions at this point. What parts of the content are most important?

The most important content should come first on the page. Imagine someone is reading your page from top to bottom. Likely you'll have the site's title and/or logo at the top of the page, so that when users arrive on the page, they'll know where they are. The page title will also need to be near the top, so users know what the page is about.

Keep in mind you aren't making final design decisions yet, so don't stress out over getting everything right. You can always make changes later.

You also want to avoid thinking of your content in terms of layout at this point, because with responsive design it won't always be in the same place. You may be used to placing certain elements in a sidebar, but some screen sizes may not have room for a sidebar, so those elements will have to go above or below the main content. Focus your thinking on the hierarchy of the content.

Thinking About Layout

Once you know what's going to go on each page, you'll start working out what each page will look like. You'll need to think about how the design will look on screens of various sizes.

Before you move on to formal wireframes or prototypes, you may want to start by making rough sketches.

SKETCHING

Stephen Hay, in his book *Responsive Design Workflow* (*http://responsivedesignworkflow.com*), calls sketching "thinking on a surface." You can do small sketches, with few details, to try many ideas quickly. Later, when you have your ideas more fleshed out, you can move on to more detailed sketches.

Start by thinking about how the site will look on various sizes of screen, from small mobile phones to huge monitors.

Don't worry if you can't "draw." You're only drawing shapes and lines, and it doesn't even matter if the lines are straight.

Make notes on what works and what doesn't work, so you can incorporate those thoughts into the design later. Your preliminary sketches are not meant to be deliverables for the client; they're just a design tool. You can share the most helpful sketches with your team members—or not. It's up to you.

Think of the various screen sizes—mobile phone, small tablet, larger tablet, and so on—and make rectangles of those approximate sizes to draw your layout ideas in. But don't use a ruler to measure the rectangles—you're not aiming toward specific devices for the design breakpoints, you're just looking at general device categories.

You can draw on paper, or you may find it easier to visualize a device screen by drawing directly on the device with a stylus, as in Figure 7-4. A good iPad app for sketching is Paper (*http://www.fiftythree.com/paper*).

Figure 7-4. Preliminary sketches can be drawn directly on a device screen with a stylus (photo credit: Baldiri, *http://www.flickr.com/photos/baldiri/5734993652*).

START SMALL

Whether you're starting with sketches or prototypes, it's best to use a small-screen-first approach. Start with the design for the smallest screen size, and work your way up to the widest screen size. We'll talk in Chapter 8 about how to determine the range of screen sizes you should design for, but essentially the smallest screen size is going to be a mobile phone–sized screen.

Why not go from large to small? After all, the desktop-sized design is going to be more detailed, so wouldn't it be easier to get it out of the way first?

Actually, it's quite the opposite. I like to use this metaphor to explain: imagine you live in an apartment, and you have the opportunity to move into a much larger house. There will be plenty of room for your furniture and belongings, and even extra space to add some new pictures on the walls and other decorations.

Then imagine moving from a house into a small apartment. Everything is squished together, you have boxes piled against the walls because there's no room to unpack them, and even then you have to get rid of half your furniture.

Now imagine doing that with a website. Trying to fit everything from a desktop-sized screen onto a small screen is incredibly difficult.

It's much easier to start with the small screen, because then you'll end up only using what you can actually fit into the design. It will force you to pay more attention to your content and what is actually necessary, rather than just sticking everything in there because there's room.

The same thing goes if you live in a small apartment: you only own what you have room for, yet somehow you manage to fit in everything you need. If you live in a larger house where there's plenty of extra room, though, you'll tend to accumulate lots of extra belongings that you don't really need and never use.

However, there are times when starting your design with the desktop-sized screen may be a better option, such as when you're doing a redesign of an existing website and you have to use the existing fixed-width design as part of the responsive design. If you already have a desktop-sized design, and it needs to stay like it is, starting there might be more effective.

Keep in mind too that starting with the design for small screens first doesn't mean you can't be thinking about the larger screens as you go along. Sometimes it's helpful to move back and forth, at least during the preliminary process.

MOBILE FIRST

You've probably heard the term "mobile first," and you may be wondering if it's the same thing as "small-screen first." Although the concepts have some overlap, they aren't exactly the same.

"Mobile first," a term popularized by Luke Wroblewski in his book *Mobile First* (*http://www.abookapart.com/products/mobile-first*), is an approach to creating websites and web apps in which your design prioritizes users who are using mobile devices and how those users interact with the site. It requires that you think first about the constraints and capabilities of mobile devices. And the word "first" in that context means considering mobile to be more important than nonmobile.

Making sure your site works well on touchscreens is important, and in Chapter 8 we'll talk about devices and address topics such as touch-target sizes. But as you're designing a responsive site, it's best to be as flexible as possible with regard to devices, aiming to design a device-agnostic site that will work well on any type of device.

There isn't such a fine line between mobile and nonmobile devices anymore. You can buy a desktop computer that has a touchscreen. You can hook a monitor and keyboard up to your mobile phone and use it as a "computer." The lines will only continue to blur.

So when I use the phrase "small-screen first" in this book, I'm referring only to the process of designing a responsive layout and design for a website. And I don't use the word "first" to mean that small screens are more important, but rather in a chronological sense—you are designing for small screens before you design for larger screens.

All the screen sizes are equally important, and even though you are starting with the smallest screen, you'll probably end up spending more time on how the design looks on wider screens.

Prototypes

Once you have a rough idea of your layout, you can start putting it together.

WIREFRAMES VERSUS PROTOTYPES

Before you dive into the visual design, you need to start with a good backbone of the site layout and how it's going to work, and where things go on the screen.

There are two different ways to visualize the site layout. Traditionally, web design has used *wireframes*, which are static drawings of what a page looks like.

But with responsive design, you don't just have one design; you have a design that changes depending on the width of the screen. So, it's becoming more common to use *responsive prototypes*, which are basically wireframes built in responsive HTML. They can be viewed on various screens to see how the design changes with the viewport width.

WIREFRAMES

Traditionally, the next step in the web design process would be creating wireframes.

Wireframes for a website are a model of where the individual components should go on the page. An example is shown in Figure 7-5. You can see the general shape of things, but a wireframe specifically leaves out the visual details, which will come later.

For a fixed-width website, a wireframe lays out the exact locations of the different page components: header, navigation, search box, columns, and so on.

But for a responsive site, you don't have just one location for each component, as the layout changes across viewport widths. So, rather than creating formal documents that are not a true representation of a responsive website, you'll likely find it's more effective to create responsive prototypes (sometimes referred to as responsive wireframes).

RESPONSIVE PROTOTYPES

A *prototype* (also a term used in industrial design and other fields) is a model that not only demonstrates how something will look, but also how it will work.

A prototype is not necessarily produced by the same method as the final product. For example, when a new car has been designed, often a prototype is made and sent to car shows to get consumer feedback, before a decision is made as to whether the car should actually be manufactured. These prototypes are individually manufactured in research labs, not made with the usual factory assembly line process, and they may not even be drivable.

Similarly, your responsive prototype doesn't need to be coded in the same way that the actual website will be coded, and interactive elements don't need to work. You might build a prototype with HTML, or use a prototyping application (we'll look at a few of those in a bit).

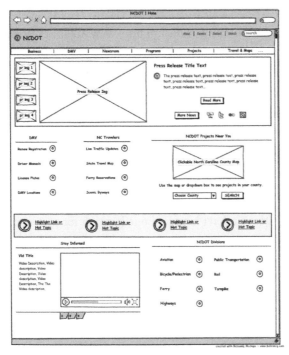

Figure 7-5. A detailed wireframe for a fixed-width website (photo credit: After Victory, *http://www.flickr.com/photos/aftervictory/5097418313/*).

A responsive prototype is a "real" web page, in that you can view it in a browser, but it's just the basic layout, with a similar look to a wireframe. In fact, it is essentially the same thing as a wireframe, with the difference being that the layout is responsive, so that you can resize your browser window or look at the prototype on different devices to see how the layout changes.

Prototypes may be at any depth of fidelity: anywhere from minimal detail to very close to the actual end product. A car prototype may look like a real car but be just for visual show, lacking an engine and the rest of what's under the hood. Or it may be a working car, but only meant to travel at low speed for demonstrations, lacking safety features that would make it highway-ready.

The same thing applies with a website prototype. Generally, you'll start out early in the process with a low-fidelity prototype, and as you get further along, it will be more in-depth.

WHAT'S IN A PROTOTYPE?

Your prototype should show the basics of the layout, and how the site layout responds to changes in viewport width.

Although you can continue to make changes to the layout later in the process after you've started working on the visual design, it's easier to get a lot of the layout decisions taken care of now, when you can focus only on the layout.

Although you will likely have prototypes for a few different types of pages (e.g., front page, interior page), don't attempt to connect them so you can click from one to the next as if they were part of the actual website. That just adds complexity, when you should only be focused on layout. Later on in the process you may want to make *interactive prototypes* that can be used to test how the site actually works (such as a checkout process), but for now your prototypes should be only visual, not interactive.

START WITH THE BASICS

The first responsive prototypes you create will just give a rough idea of content placement and content hierarchy on the page at the various viewport widths. Eventually, you'll move on to higher-fidelity prototypes.

You don't want to be thinking about details such as typefaces or colors here, just the layout. Choose a simple sans-serif font for everything, and use borders and shades of gray to separate various items on the page. This will help you focus on the layout. If you make your responsive prototype look too realistic, clients may have trouble understanding that it isn't the "real" website.

If you're doing responsive prototypes, start out from the beginning testing them on different devices, in a range of device categories, so that any issues can be addressed early.

As you start with low-fi prototypes, you can either use placeholders for content, or use actual content. The benefit of using actual content is that you can get an idea of how it will fit in the layout. For example, if you have the words "Example Page Title" at the top of the page, they may fit fine where you want the title, but later when you have to plug in an actual page title that's 10 words long instead of 3—it may not fit.

Also, when you're creating prototypes, don't just think about how an ideal page on your website would look. Make sure your prototypes can handle the edge cases: the most complicated pages on your site.

HOW MANY PAGE LAYOUTS TO CREATE

As you start looking at actual pages on the site, you need to decide which pages, or page categories, to create layouts for.

Because parts of the design will look the same on most pages or on every page (e.g., the header and navigation are likely the same on every page), you'll only need to create layouts for a few types of pages.

Go through your content outline and figure out the types of pages you have, based on content.

For example, on a newspaper website, some types of pages might be:

- The home page, which will be unique
- Article pages, each containing one article
- Category pages (e.g., a "Local" section with links to the current articles in that category)
- Photo gallery pages, which are freestanding pages similar to articles, but contain primarily photos instead of text
- Informational pages, such as a "Privacy Policy"

You can see these types of layouts from *The Washington Post* website in Figure 7-6.

There will be elements that are consistent throughout all the pages. For example, every page on the site will probably have the same header, navigation, and search box at the top—but not necessarily. In Figure 7-6, the navigation bar is the same on every page type except the front page, which omits the logo for "The Washington Post" on the left side of the bar.

Think about how each page can be divided into components, which are self-contained pieces of content that can be moved around the page, or replicated on other pages.

Figure 7-6. Six of the different layouts used on *The Washington Post* website.

Some page types will be mostly similar to other types. For example, the article pages and the information pages just described will probably be very similar, as they both contain mostly text. However, the article pages will need to have a place for metadata such as author and date, whereas the informational pages will not.

You'll do one or more layouts during the design process, for each of the different page types. Generally, two to five page types are common. These should be the most complicated layouts, because the simpler layouts can often be derived from those. For example, you would not need to create a separate prototype for the informational page, because it's just an article page with some of the components removed.

It's tempting to do the front page first, because it's what feels like the "face" of the website. But it's often easier to start with the most straightforward interior pages and then, when you have a solid layout for those, move on to the more complex home page.

FRAMEWORKS

To make the prototyping process quicker, you may want to use a *framework*. A framework is a downloadable set of HTML and CSS that contains all the elements needed to make a basic website. You can create a responsive HTML prototype in an hour or two by starting with a framework, rather than having to start from scratch. Frameworks can also be used as the basic code for actual websites.

With a framework, the included CSS adds basic style to the HTML elements. Thus, your paragraphs, headings, lists, buttons, and form fields all look good (but basic) from the start, without you having to write CSS to style them. The framework will also include instructions on how to use the CSS classes to add responsive layout to your page elements, including columns and navigation.

Even if you only have a basic knowledge of HTML and CSS, you can easily use a framework to create a responsive prototype fairly quickly, like the ones in Figure 7-7. Using a framework isn't a substitute for knowing how the code works when creating an actual website, but during the prototyping process, it means that design team members will be able to create or work on responsive HTML prototypes—they don't need to be developers to be able to use frameworks and modify the code as needed.

 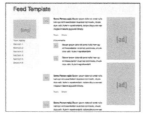 

Figure 7-7. These example prototypes were all created using the Foundation responsive framework.

Foundation by ZURB (*http://foundation.zurb.com*), as you can see in the example prototypes, is a great place to start. It has a small-screen-first, 12-column flexible grid, with semantic markup. Bootstrap (*http://getbootstrap.com*) is another commonly used framework. You can also search the Web for "responsive framework" and find dozens of other options. They are all different, so check a selection out to find the framework that best meets your needs.

PROTOTYPING TOOLS

If you don't want to create a prototype in HTML, there are several tools that you can use to create responsive prototypes—both desktop and online applications.

However, for the most part, these tools will not create true responsive prototypes that can be viewed at any screen size. Instead, they will let you create several separate static wireframes at different screen sizes.

Some responsive prototyping tools include:

- Balsamiq (*http://balsamiq.com/*)
- Froont (*http://www.froont.com/*)
- HotGloo (*http://www.hotgloo.com/responsive-prototype-tool*), as pictured in Figure 7-8

Also check out Balsamiq's article "Responsive Design with Mockups" (*http://support.balsamiq.com/customer/portal/articles/615901-responsive-design-with-mockups*) for some tips on getting started.

Visual Design

Moving on from the prototype, the next step is creating a visual design for the website. This is where you add colors, typography, and branding elements. Once again, this needs to happen a little differently than with a fixed-width site.

Traditionally, the design would be presented to clients or stakeholders in one or more Photoshop comps (a flat visual representation of what the site will look like), to show the front page and interior pages of the site. However, with a responsive site, you don't want to show them just one static view of the page.

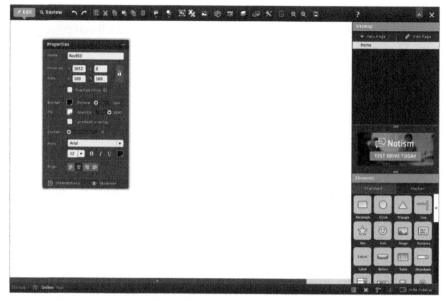

Figure 7-8. The HotGloo online prototyping application.

It's best to involve clients earlier in the process by showing them the responsive prototypes. This will help make sure they have a clear understanding of what a responsive site is, throughout the process. When you get to the visual design part of the process, there are ways to present visual design elements other than those Photoshop comps.

STYLE TILES

If we aren't going to show clients a pixel-perfect design comp, how do we bridge the gap from prototypes to a fully designed site? Style tiles are one place you can start.

Designer Samantha Warren came up with the idea of Style Tiles (*http://styletil.es*) as a "design deliverable consisting of fonts, colors and interface elements that communicate the essence of a visual brand for the web."

Warren explains that creating style tiles is similar to the process used by interior designers when designing a room in a house. The interior designer doesn't just come up with three different room designs off the bat. First, the designer works with the client to decide on colors, textures, and materials; design options are then based on those choices.

You can see an example of style tiles in Figure 7-9.

Figure 7-9. The three style tiles were used to get to the final design used on The Examiner website, shown in the fourth image.

Using style tiles helps you get the core design elements worked out before committing to a full design.

Start out by listening to the client, and asking questions—all the things that you normally do during requirements gathering. Try in particular to get an idea of the visual look and feel that the client wants from the site. Adjectives are good. Additionally, make sure to find out if there are existing branding or style guidelines that need to follow.

When creating style tiles, you can either use an image-editing tool like Photoshop, or work directly in the browser. Either way, you can iterate as much as needed to come to an agreement. It's a lot easier to iterate now than later. But don't feel like you *can't* make style changes later— sometimes you don't know the full effect of design decisions until you see them on the live site design.

TESTING AND ADJUSTING

The responsive process requires continual testing as you go along. As
soon as you have an HTML prototype, you should be testing it on different devices to see what happens. If a layout that seemed good in theory
ends up not working on particular screen sizes, it's better to discover
the problem early on, rather than trying to make adjustments to an
almost-finished site.

We'll go into the how-to of testing in more detail in Chapter 8.

STYLE GUIDE

A *style guide* collects and documents all the design decisions that have
been made for the site. What typefaces are used, and where? What are
the correct font sizes? What do buttons look like?

It can be as basic or as detailed as needed for the project, and it serves two
purposes. First, the style guide helps you make sure you're consistent
during the development process. If submit buttons are always supposed
to be blue, why does a particular form have a green submit button?

Sometimes inconsistencies happen because we don't notice mistakes
in our code, and sometimes because design decisions are made for a
particular page without anyone realizing that those particular decisions have already been made for the site as a whole. A website will have
a much better feel if there is visual consistency throughout the site.

The second purpose is that the style guide documents design decisions
for whoever will be managing the site in the future, and helps maintain a website's design identity over time, as staff members change.
Whoever designed the site is probably familiar with which typefaces
go where and why, but when the client's internal web staff has to add a
new feature later, will they know which typeface to use?

Style guides have been used in print design for many years, and are sometimes called style manuals or branding guidelines. Often, a company will have a general style manual that addresses things like logo usage. A website style guide should start there and go into more detail.

Besides just listing the design elements (typefaces, colors, etc.), it's helpful to actually show them, as in Figure 7-10, so it's easy to see at a glance what they look like. You can also specify the particular CSS that's used to create specific effects.

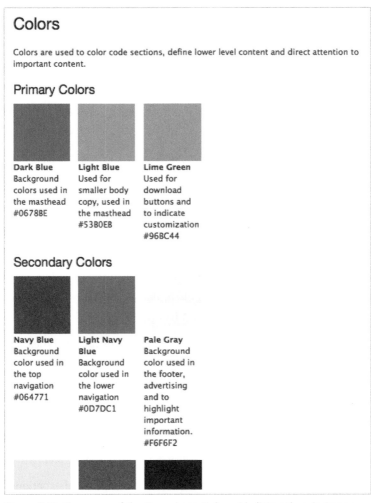

Figure 7-10. One page of the Drupal.org style guide lists colors (primary colors, secondary colors, and message colors); each entry gives the color name, hex value, and its use (e.g., Dark Blue, #0678BE, Background colors used in the masthead).

The style guide doesn't have to only include visual style; it can also include content style and coding standards (or those can be in separate style guides).

Although it's common to create a style guide as a document in Word or some other text application, it can often be easier to create it in HTML, which allows you to more accurately show how styles look on the screen. Otherwise, you could include screenshots of examples.

Here are some examples of things you may wish to include in a style guide:

- Typography

- Colors and textures

- Layout system/grid

- Styles for HTML elements such as list items, form elements, or blockquotes

- Appropriate markup (Is <h1> the site title or the page title?)

- Logo usage

- Voice

- General styles like punctuation and word usage, if not using a commercial style guide like *The AP Stylebook* or *The Chicago Manual of Style*

A good place to start is the Style Guide Boilerplate (*http://brettjankord. com/projects/style-guide-boilerplate/*) from Brett Jankord.

Here are some examples of good web style guides of various types:

- Starbucks.com (*http://www.starbucks.com/static/reference/style-guide/*) (style guide)

- South Tees Hospitals NHS Foundation Trust (*http://www.south-tees.nhs.uk/style-guide/*) (style guide)

- Drupal.org (*http://drupal.org/coding-standards*) (coding standards)

- BBC's digital services (*http://www.bbc.co.uk/gel*) (global experience language)

- Paul Robert Lloyd (*http://www.paulrobertlloyd.com/about/style-guide/*) (markup style guide)

Responsive Design Tools

What tools should you be using when designing websites?

Keep in mind that the right tool is going to be the one that works for you, to get you to the end product. There is no *right* answer, and the clients don't care, they just want a website.

ADOBE PHOTOSHOP

Photoshop has traditionally been the most common tool for designing websites. However, a Photoshop comp is just, in essence, a picture of a website. If your goal were to make a website that looks exactly the same in every browser—and that was the goal, for many years—a picture would work. But now that we're trying to make a website that will look different depending on the viewport width, a picture of a website is not as helpful.

You still may want to use Photoshop for some parts of the process, though, such as designing specific page elements or image assets.

> **[NOTE]**
>
> If you are using Photoshop, make it work better for your responsive process. Check out Dan Rose's "Repurposing Photoshop For The Web" (*http:// www.smashingmagazine.com/2013/04/22/repurposing-photoshop/*) on *Smashing Magazine*.

ADOBE INDESIGN

A lot of designers have found that Adobe InDesign works much better for responsive design. (Photoshop was never meant to be a web design tool. Photoshop was meant to be used for *photos*, and InDesign for *design*. Makes sense, doesn't it?)

InDesign has specific features that help you to build responsive layouts, such as grids, styles, includes, and liquid page rules. Figure 7-11 shows the liquid layout option, which allows you to create layouts for multiple device sizes.

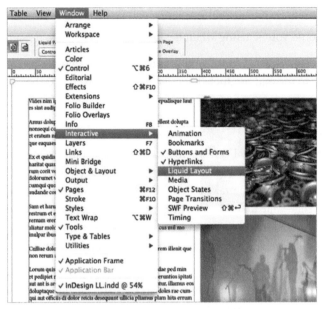

Figure 7-11. The liquid layout option in Adobe InDesign.

ADOBE EDGE REFLOW

Edge Reflow is a new design tool from Adobe that allows you to create responsive designs with media queries, and export the HTML and CSS of your design to hand off to developers. It's not meant to create production-ready code, but rather to create responsive layouts for various screen sizes, and enable designers "to share their responsive design intent."

It's kind of like creating comps, except they're responsive.

Using Edge Reflow, the designer creates responsive layouts based on grid columns, and adds CSS effects like fonts or drop shadows. But the application's interface is purely design, with no access to the actual HTML and CSS except for exporting. You can see what the Edge Reflow interface looks like in Figure 7-12.

Figure 7-12. Adobe Edge Reflow.

ADOBE DREAMWEAVER

Adobe Dreamweaver is still around. It recently added something called Fluid Grid Layout, which allows you to create responsive layouts.

Unfortunately, when creating a website in Dreamweaver, you can only specify three layouts, as you can see in Figure 7-13, rather than being able to add media queries for different components of the site at the most appropriate breakpoints.

Within each layout, you can choose the number of columns you'd like, and add and move elements within the grid. The resulting CSS uses percentage widths and floats, so the layouts can adapt to different screen sizes.

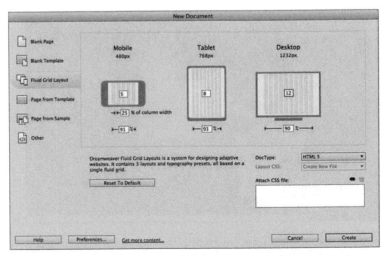

Figure 7-13. The Dreamweaver interface lets you set up three layouts for a website.

THE BROWSER

Although those are all useful tools, many designers find it easier to skip the image editors and design directly in the browser.

By starting in the browser, you can be sure that what you're designing won't end up looking different when it's in the browser.

I've been a client many times, working with many different agencies, and it never fails that even for static websites, the actual website looks fairly different from the Photoshop comps. Fonts render differently in a browser, and things don't align the way they're supposed to. Developers try to replicate the Photoshop design, but they're using a totally different tool, so it's not all that simple. So why put in so much effort making something look "perfect," when it's not actually going to look the same in the end product?

By designing in the browser, you can make your design responsive to start, so there's no question about how the site is supposed to look across screen sizes.

The code produced by the designer doesn't need to be the same code that ends up being turned into the actual website, so don't worry if it's not perfect. But it can be a good starting place to save time later, especially if it's properly structured HTML.

There are also disadvantages to designing in the browser. You have less control over directly manipulating objects, such as lines and shapes. If there are graphic elements on the page, they have to be produced separately.

Designers who aren't designing in the browser should be working closely with developers during the design process, to understand how their designs will be rendered on various screen sizes. They should at least have a basic understanding of how HTML and CSS work, and how the code for responsive design, such as media queries, works in particular.

If you're designing in the browser, you can create pages using the text editor that comes with your computer, such as TextEdit on Mac OS or Notepad on Microsoft Windows. Or you can use a code editor such as Sublime Text (*http://www.sublimetext.com*), which has an interface particularly suited to writing various flavors of code.

Selling Responsive Design

If you're reading this book, you might already be sold on the idea of responsive design, but it's likely that you'll still need to sell it to others.

This might be a matter of convincing your coworkers that your company should consider responsive design for a website redesign. Or, if you work at an agency, it might involve convincing clients that this is the best option for their websites.

Whatever your role, you'll probably be working with people who haven't heard of responsive design, or don't really get what it is.

In this section, you'll look at how to sell the idea of responsive design to your clients, coworkers, and other stakeholders.

WHY BOTHER WITH RESPONSIVE DESIGN?

Several months ago, I was chatting about responsive design with two people who work at a small web shop. One of them was a developer, and he was really excited about the idea of being able to create websites that will work on any device. Their agency hadn't done any responsive design projects yet, but he was trying to learn all he could.

The other person in the conversation was a salesperson at the web shop. I asked him if they had been trying to sell responsive design to potential customers, and he said no. They were going to continue selling their customers separate desktop and mobile websites.

The reason: the sales team felt like customers would be willing to pay more if they were getting two websites instead of one.

That may be true, but besides being a bit unethical, it's just not a good business practice. For many websites, responsive design is the best option if you want a website that's going to be usable for years into the future. There are some situations where a separate mobile site might be a better option—but that shouldn't be your default option without considering responsive design.

Not even letting your clients know that responsive design is an option means that they are likely to get websites that they're unhappy with shortly after launch, when they realize that they don't work on all devices and aren't flexible enough to keep up with changes to the web landscape.

If you actually want your company to make money, your goal shouldn't be keeping your customers satisfied only until their last checks have cleared. If you're providing them with websites that will meet their needs for a few years, that will translate into repeat business and referrals.

If your agency is resisting responsive design because it's *too hard* or because you think you'll make more money selling separate mobile sites, you should think about whether the websites you're selling today will result in happy customers that will help you grow your business in the future. What's more, being able to produce well-designed responsive websites will give you a competitive advantage, because not everybody knows how yet.

EDUCATING YOUR CLIENTS

It's your responsibility to educate your clients and potential clients on what comprises a good website.

They will come to you with ideas, but not always good ones. Don't just do everything they ask for; take their ideas and make them into something better, using your own skills and knowledge. *That's what they're paying you for.*

Clients will frequently just say that they want a "mobile site" or "mobile app," and they think they must have a separate website in order to have it work on mobile. They may not know that there are other options.

If clients come to you and say they just want a website, you can educate them on what the options are, including responsive design. If they don't know much about how websites work, they probably won't even know that responsive design exists, and even if they do, they may have misconceptions about how it works.

This is your opportunity to let them know that responsive design may be a better option for them, so they can have just one site rather than multiple sites to maintain, and so that site will work on all devices, not just certain sizes of screens.

Your job is to determine what the best solution is for each client's problem, and sell them that solution. If they've never heard of responsive design, but you think that's what they should do with their website, you need to both help them understand what responsive design is and convince them that it's the best way to solve their problem.

EMPHASIZING RESPONSIVE

Keep in mind that your end goal isn't just producing a great responsive website that meets business goals and user needs; it's producing that website and *making sure the client is happy with it.*

If you create the greatest website in the world, but the client is unhappy because it's not what they thought they'd be getting, you have a problem.

You need to make sure that clients understand what's going on throughout the entire process. Remind them at each point in the process that you're creating a responsive site, and what that means. Show them the design on various devices so they grasp what happens to the layout on different screen sizes.

If you get to the end of the process for a responsive site and you find out the client is confused because the website looks different on his phone than on his computer (yes, I've heard of that happening), then you weren't communicating the idea of responsive design well enough.

Responsive design is a new idea to people. Don't assume they get it the first time you explain it. Show them. Make sure they understand.

RESPONSIVE DESIGN IS NOT ALWAYS THE BEST OPTION

Keep in mind that responsive design isn't always going to be the answer. Most of the time it's a good solution, but here are some reasons why it might not be:

- The team working on the project doesn't have enough experience with responsive design to do it well (but make sure you get experience, so you can implement it in the next project).

- The client doesn't have enough money for the additional cost of a responsive website (but make sure they know a responsive design will likely save them money in the long run).

- The site is for a short-term project, such as an upcoming event, and you can focus on specific devices and don't need to worry about future device compatibility.

COST

Here's a question you'll hear a lot from clients: how much does a responsive site cost?

They want a concrete answer. Is it 25% more than a fixed-width site? Is it twice as much? Is it X dollars more?

Unfortunately, there isn't one answer to that question. What goes into creating a responsive site varies, just as what goes into creating any website varies. You'll certainly find that out if you ask multiple agencies for a quote on the same website project.

Designing a responsive site almost definitely costs more than designing a fixed-width site in the same circumstances. There is more work to do: instead of one size layout, you have to create a layout that varies across screen sizes, so at minimum that means adding media queries.

But it really depends on how complex the site is. A few media queries might be enough, or there may be design elements that require additional attention.

It depends, too, on how responsive the clients want the site to be. You can delve pretty far into the details, for example, making font sizes vary slightly depending on the screen width to take best advantage of the space. Although that may make the site look and function better, it's not *necessary* for a responsive site.

Does it cost *more*? Yes, but they're not paying more for the same end result. A responsive site is going to work on more devices, meaning that they'll increase their potential user base. A responsive site is going to last longer, so extra money spent is an investment in the future.

Something to keep in mind is that if your team members who are creating the website are new to responsive design, you're certainly going to be spending extra time learning and trying things out as you go along. It may take you extra tries to get something to work right, and you may have to do research to find the best way to accomplish something. This will take extra staff time, and you need to plan ahead for this. Generally this isn't a cost you can pass on to the client.

Working with Clients

As I explained earlier, the term "client" doesn't just refer to agency clients; it includes internal clients for in-house web staff, and other stakeholders on a project. So even if you don't work at an agency or freelance, this section applies to you.

Your clients or stakeholders will generally come to the table with pre-existing expectations of what they want. They'll ask for a website, but what they really need is their problem solved. And you need to help them figure out what the ideal solution is, by first asking questions:

- What kind of content do they want to put on the website?

- Who is the audience for this content? Do they have analytics to back this up?

- How often will the website be updated, and by whom?

- What problems do they have with the existing site that they want to avoid in the new site?

The more you learn, the better end result you can give them.

DELIVERABLES

Deliverables for a responsive website may end up being a lot different from what you're used to for a fixed-width website, such as wireframes and comp revisions.

You'll still have deliverables, such as content structure, responsive prototypes, and style tiles, but because you're changing the way you think about the process, you also need to change the way you think about the deliverables.

To start out, your job when designing a website isn't to create deliverables, it's to design a website. Deliverables are just pieces of that process that help make sure the project is on track.

Maybe you've worked on projects where there's an initial requirements-gathering meeting with a client, and then the very next thing that happens after your team has worked on the design for a while is that there's a meeting to show the client your proposed designs. The client has no idea of what's been worked on in the meantime; a few designs to choose from are just "revealed." They get to pick one design from the options, and that's what they're stuck with for the rest of the process.

Although this is dramatic and exciting, it often doesn't lead to the clients getting a product they're happy with, because they were excluded from the design process. It's better for clients to share their opinions as the project proceeds.

On a responsive site, you can't treat deliverables as end products the way you may be used to doing, because there needs to be more flexibility in the process. Deliverables are working documentation of an iterative process; they aren't set in stone.

You don't want to get into a situation where interim design documents are "approved" by the client (i.e., the high-level stakeholder holding the purse strings), and then, when it is discovered later that something different would work better, the client won't allow the change because the previous work has already been "approved" by the higher-ups and they don't want to go back to them and say that the previous decisions were wrong. Nothing should be locked in during the process.

To produce a product that clients are truly happy with, you need to realize that they are a part of the design team. Allow them to be part of the process from the beginning, and make decisions collaboratively.

Of course, allowing changes throughout the process doesn't mean you should let the client request changes to the scope of the project without adding to the cost. By making the high-level decisions early on, and narrowing it down from there, you should be able to stay on track to come up with a final design that pleases the client.

And keep in mind that not all project documents are deliverables. Document your team's work as you go along, so everybody is clear on where the project is going and what needs to happen to get there. Working documents don't need to be shared with the client.

[NOTE]

Need some help in creating your project documents? Check out Dan Brown's book *Communicating Design: Developing Web Site Documentation for Design and Planning, Second Edition* (*http://communicatingdesign.com*). He'll show you how to create site maps, flow charts, wireframes, personas, and more.

PRESENTATION

If you're working as part of a team, and you meet with the client to show them the in-progress design, all the people who worked on the design (visual designers, UX designers, etc.) should be present so they are able to get any feedback firsthand. You don't want changes being filtered through a project manager who may not understand what's going on.

Although having responsive prototypes is nice because you can show the client how the site is responsive at different viewport widths, you need to retain control of the presentation. During the early parts of the process, use your own computer: you don't want the clients using their phones/devices yet if all the bugs haven't been worked out.

You may want to simply show screenshots early in the process, so that you can focus on the way the site looks between major breakpoints, and not on the behavior or interaction of the site.

Start by showing the small screen first. Explain that this layout will be what users see on small devices like mobile phones, as well as some older browsers and devices with fewer capabilities. Then move on to larger screen widths.

Also, make sure that early meetings focus on big issues and not little details. You want a font size that works with the layout, not a layout built around the client wanting *this exact font size*.

Keep the discussion on track, but make sure you're going slowly enough that the client can actually look at everything.

Remember to show the client the design progress frequently enough that there aren't any big surprises. You want to avoid what's called "the big reveal," where you show the design all at once.

When you move to showing a live prototype and demonstrating how the layout changes when the size of the viewport changes, make sure the client understands that resizing a browser window isn't the same as actually looking at the site on different actual devices. If there aren't a variety of devices available at the meeting, bring screenshots.

Make sure that the client knows that anything about the design can be changed—and should be, if it doesn't look like the best solution. They should feel free to offer feedback at any point. Clients with a fresh eye will often see bugs or issues that your team hasn't even noticed.

[NOTE]

Need a way to add annotations to HTML-based prototypes? Check out Metaframe (*https://github.com/elliance/metaframe/*) from Elliance, which allows you to use a simple CSS class to add numbered notes on top of your page design.

Summary

In this chapter, we looked at why you should start off with user research and a content strategy before creating a visual design for a website.

We looked at the steps in the design process, starting with sketching design ideas and thinking from a small-screen-first perspective. We talked about prototypes, and how responsive prototypes differ from traditional wireframes.

We looked at using style tiles to come up with a look and feel for a website, and what tools you can use to design for responsive websites.

Finally, we talked about selling responsive design to clients or to coworkers, and how to work with clients on responsive projects to make sure they have a clear understanding of what they will be getting.

In the next chapter, Chapter 8, we'll be looking at the user experience of responsive sites, and how mobile devices need to change the way you think about design.

[8]

Mobile and Beyond

There are two things you need to give a lot of thought to when you're creating a responsive website: users and devices. In this chapter, we'll discuss both extensively.

First, we'll look at what the user experience is and why it's important. Next, we'll discuss design strategies for making sure your site works well and looks good on as many devices as possible.

Following that, we'll go over the types of devices that are currently available, and some of the device qualities that are important design considerations, such as touch and screen size. We'll also talk about how to make sure your site is accessible to users with disabilities.

Finally, we'll talk about testing your responsive website—what devices you should support and test your site on, how you can get access to those devices, and what kinds of testing you can do without actual devices.

User Experience

When you're making a website, your job isn't just to make it look nice; it's to make something that can be used for its intended purpose, and that works well.

Your ecommerce site can have the most beautiful product pages ever, but if the user has trouble getting through the checkout process and decides to go to another website, it's all for naught.

User experience has always been a significant part of web design, but for a long time we didn't have to put too much effort into it, because all users had a very similar experience—they were all on a desktop or laptop computer, with a similar-sized monitor, using a keyboard and mouse or perhaps a touchpad to navigate. We were designing on the same types of devices, so it was easy to predict how other users would experience the site.

But now everything is different. Not only do screen sizes range from teeny-tiny to ginormous, but we also interact with websites in a wide variety of ways, from touchpads to voice controls.

We've also stopped thinking of the Internet as something we *experience*. It used to be we would sit down at a desk, turn on our computers, and "go online." But now the Internet is always with us. We can pull our phones out of our pockets anytime and anywhere, for quick interactions, long interactions, distracted interactions. We can pull the Internet up on our TVs or our game consoles, or even interact with web browsers on multiple devices simultaneously.

Remember that responsive design is not about designing for mobile. These days we tend to focus on mobile because we're used to designing for non-mobile, and that's natural. There's a lot to learn and get used to. But there are plenty of people still sitting at desks behind monitors, so you can't make sites that are optimized for mobile but feel awkward when you have a keyboard and monitor in front of you.

Before you make a responsive site, you need to know about the devices it will be viewed on, and how users interact with those devices. Your goal is to have a site that will work on the wide range of currently available devices and that is also future-friendly, able to accommodate devices that haven't been invented yet.

USERS COME FIRST

Before we even get to talking about mobile devices, we need to talk some more about users. After all, users are the most important part of the equation when you're making a website.

With the novelty of all the new types of mobile devices on the market and the new things that are possible in HTML5 and CSS3, it's easy to get caught up in the excitement and spend time and effort developing exciting websites that show off all the things you can do.

But keep in mind that the purpose of a website isn't to be as technologically impressive as possible. Learning to design and develop a website is not just about writing the code that renders the website. It's about creating an experience for the people who will be using the website.

As much as all of us who work on the Web are talking about responsive design, making responsive sites, and thinking about responsive design, we need to remember that the average website user has no idea what responsive design is. And there's no reason for him to.

All users want is a website that works well on the device they are using *at that moment*—which may not be the same device they are using at other times during the day. They don't want to think about what device they're using; they just want to have a website that works.

Users aren't thinking about the fact that they're using a mobile phone to visit a website on the way to work, a desktop computer during their lunch break, and a tablet when they're browsing the Web while watching TV late at night. And it shouldn't matter to them. They should just get a website that works, no matter which device they use to access it.

So when you're designing a responsive site, keep in mind that your goal isn't to create a *responsive* site, but rather to create a *site that works well for users*; responsive design is the tool you will use to create that site.

Users don't care what's under the hood. They just want a website that is going to give them the content and functionality that they want, with a minimum amount of fuss to get to where they want to go.

And always remember, it's up to the user what device she wants to use, not up to you. You can decide what types of devices you want to support, but if your site doesn't work on the device the user wants to use, you'll lose that customer.

THE MYTH OF THE MOBILE USER

When the iPhone first came out and we started designing websites to work on mobile phones, there was this "myth of the mobile user" that came about: the idea that any person using a mobile device was "out and about," on the go, in a hurry to get somewhere, in a hurry to get information. That typical mobile phone user didn't want to browse the Web, he just wanted to get quick information, like a restaurant address or whether his flight was on time.

And at that point, the myth was probably true. It was hard to access websites on a smartphone. There weren't yet responsive sites or even many mobile sites, so what you had was a tiny site you had to zoom in and out on to read anything. Users probably didn't use their mobile phones to access websites unless they absolutely had to, and saved their web browsing for their home or office computers, where it was much easier.

But then websites started to change to accommodate mobile phones, and it got easier to do things on your phone. And then tablets came along, which were mobile, but not really, because a lot of them only worked on WiFi so you weren't really *mobile* when you were using them.

And now people use their mobile phones all the time, whether they're out of the house or sitting on the sofa at home with a laptop a couple of feet away, because it's just easier to reach for the phone.

More and more people are relying on mobile devices as their primary or only way of accessing the Internet, so you can't keep assuming that users only want to look up restaurant addresses or flight times. People want to do everything on their mobile devices that they could do on their desktop computers—that is, as long as you let them.

DESIGNING FOR CONTEXT

Although we shouldn't assume that users of particular devices only want certain content or interactions, we *can* determine that particular parts of the site are used more often on certain devices, and make sure that content is very easy to access.

For example, we can't assume that mobile device users only need certain content, because they aren't necessarily "on the run" and looking for "on the run content." However, they are *sometimes* "on the run." And because it's more difficult to navigate a website on a mobile phone using your fingers than it is to navigate a desktop site with a keyboard and mouse, we should make sure it's easy for mobile users to get to the important things.

In Figure 8-1, a responsive website from Kiwi Bank in Australia, the narrow-width design has a few key links and pieces of information at the top. The login link is first—which is also prominent on the wider site, at the top right.

Following that, you see "Find a Branch," the bank's main phone number, and the bank's opening hours. These are all things that some mobile users will want to get to easily and quickly when they're in a hurry, so they are right there.

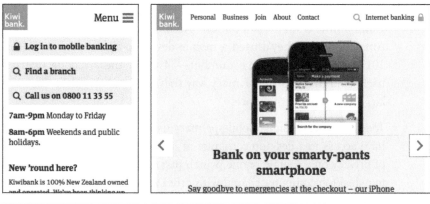

Figure 8-1. Using media queries, you can change what content is most prominent on the screen depending on viewport width.

But you don't see "Find a Branch," the phone number, or the hours when you look at the wider version of the site. They're still there—you just have to click on "Contact Us" to get to them. A desktop user is likely not in so much of a hurry, so she won't mind a couple of extra clicks, which are easier to make when you have a mouse.

The mobile user still gets everything that you see on the wider design—he just needs to scroll down on the narrow-width site to get to the navigation and all the content. A mobile user looking for interest rate comparisons is probably not in as much of a hurry as a mobile device user who needs the branch hours, so he won't mind the extra scrolling.

MOBILE-ONLY USERS

If you're reading this book, it's likely you have a job where you spend a good part of your day in front of a desktop or laptop computer. You can browse on the Internet whenever you want. It's easy to forget not everybody has that desk job experience. People who work in service jobs, for example, generally don't spend their work time in front of a computer. Some of them have computers at home, but some don't. And some that do have computers just prefer to use mobile devices.

The rise of smartphones means that more and more people are going online from mobile devices. According to Pew Internet, 57% of Americans said they'd used a mobile device to access the Internet in 2013. A surprisingly large number—34%—of these mobile Internet users said that was the primary way they accessed the Web.[1] This is a large and growing audience.

Teens are increasingly mobile-primary users. Although many of them have access to a desktop computer at home, they have a greater sense of privacy on a mobile phone, which just belongs to them, as opposed to a desktop computer shared with other family members, where they may get little privacy. They also aren't sitting in front of a computer all day like many office workers. Teens may not be a big part of your target audience, but as they grow into adults, they will continue to be comfortable using their phones for a majority of their web browsing.

So what does this mean? Your website has to work on all devices. You can't assume that if something is too "complicated" for a small screen, you can just ignore the issue because users will switch to a larger screen for that activity. Not all of them will.

And don't think that just telling users they need to switch to a desktop browser is enough. It's not up to you what devices users choose; it's up to them.

It may not be possible to make everything easy to use on a small screen, but at least don't make things *not* usable. Unless, that is, you are willing to lose a portion of your users or customers.

MULTI-DEVICE USAGE

One thing to consider as you're making a responsive design that works across screen sizes is that any given user may visit your site from different devices at different times.

Although you'll use responsive design to change how the website is displayed at different screen widths, you want to make sure that the experience *feels* the same even on different screen sizes. Users should

---

1 For the full report, see Maeve Duggan and Aaron Smith, "Cell Internet Use 2013," Pew Research Internet Project, September 16, 2013 (*http://www.pewinternet.org/2013/09/16/cell-internet-use-2013/*).

be able to go to the site on different devices and not be unsure if it's the same website. The color scheme, imagery, and fonts should be similar, no matter what device they are using.

Something like the navigation may be displayed very differently depending on screen size, but the same options should be available, using the same information architecture to organize them in the navigation.

Device-Agnostic Design

Before you start designing responsive websites, you should know where your website will be viewed. The answer is: anywhere.

There are an incredible number of devices available these days, and even if we start talking about all of them, we don't know what devices are going to be invented next.

What do they have in common?

Most of them have a screen, but not all of them. Some users who are blind or visually impaired access the Web using a screen reader. Cars have Internet capabilities and can read you your email or the headlines; how long before you can surf the Web by listening to it in your car?

People use a wide range of input devices to access the Web. On a desktop, you'll probably use a keyboard and mouse. On a laptop, the mouse is replaced with a trackpad. On a mobile phone or tablet, you're using a touchscreen. On older mobile phones, you might be using little arrow keys.

The point here is that you can't design for specific types of devices, because there are so many different types of devices out there, going far beyond what we think of as a standard mobile device. And there's no way to predict what will be invented—which might be something that most of us couldn't have even imagined.

Device-agnostic design means creating a design that is meant to work no matter what type of device is being used. You're not designing for mobile, and you're not designing for desktop; you're designing for the Web—wherever it happens to be viewed.

Focusing on Mobile First

We talked a bit in the previous chapter about *mobile first*, which is the idea of creating a design that prioritizes users who are using mobile devices, and how those users interact with the site.

When you're creating a device-agnostic design, this is the best way to start—not because the user experience on mobile devices is more important than the user experience on desktops or anything else, but because mobile devices have more constraints, and it's more difficult to create a good user experience when you have limited screen space and a less familiar method of user interaction (touch).

We already talked about designing for small screens first, in Chapter 5. But the idea of mobile first goes beyond that, to focus on how users interact with the site and the device. Touch is the biggest complication. A layout that can be easily navigated with a mouse may be much harder to use when you're poking at a small piece of glass with your large finger.

Later in this chapter we'll talk about some of the issues specific to mobile, such as touchscreens and device capabilities. And in Chapter 11, we'll talk about performance, another issue that generally applies to mobile, but where improvements will have an effect on all devices.

Do What You Can

Responsive design is not an all-or-nothing approach. Although ideally you would create a brand-new, fully responsive site from scratch for every project, in reality you'll often be working with existing sites, and modifying or redesigning them to be responsive.

If you're working with legacy code, or if you have limited resources, it's not always possible to make a site fully responsive. But partially responsive is better than not responsive at all.

For example, Amazon's website is not fully responsive, as only some elements are flexible, and only across wider screen widths (there's a separate mobile site for phone-size screens).

Page elements have a fixed width, as you see in Figure 8-2, where the right edge of the page is cut off in a narrower browser window.

Figure 8-2. The right edge of the page is cut off in a narrower browser window.

But as the viewport width increases, as in Figure 8-3, the whitespace between elements expands, so that the page continues to fill the entire width of the screen.

Figure 8-3. On a wider screen, the whitespace between the elements expands.

At a wide enough viewport width, where there's enough room, the "Shop by Department" subnavigation menu changes from a drop-down link to a fully visible navigation, as in Figure 8-4. And as the viewport gets even wider, again the whitespace increases to fill the page, as in Figure 8-5.

Figure 8-4. In a wide enough viewport, the "Shop by Department" menu changes from a drop-down link to a fully visible navigation.

Figure 8-5. The whitespace continues to increase to fill the page.

On tablets, the desktop site is simply shrunk down to fit the viewport width exactly, as in Figure 8-6 (as any fixed-width site would be by default), although that means the text is fairly small and hard to read in the portrait view.

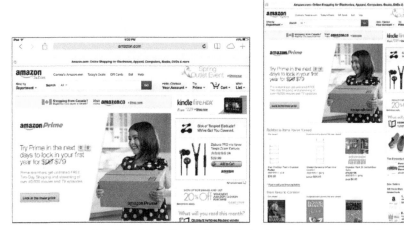

Figure 8-6. On tablets, the desktop site is shrunk down to fit the viewport width.

It's not a responsive site, but it accommodates different screen sizes to some extent. This is an example of a little responsiveness being better than no responsiveness.

Types of Devices

There are tons of different types of devices that can access the Web—everything from the familiar interface of an iPhone to tablets of all sizes, laptops, desktops, game consoles, even refrigerators.

We'll briefly go over the types of devices and differences among them, and then through the rest of the chapter talk about what you need to consider as you design responsive sites that can work on any device and any size screen.

MOBILE PHONES

As early as the mid-1990s, phones were available that could access the Web—although it was only text-based web browsing, a far cry from what we enjoy today. Web access on phones became more common through the early 2000s, although it was still only a limited version of the Web.

A smartphone, such as the iPhone, is really a miniature computer, with a mobile operating system that allows the user to install apps.

Feature phones, on the other hand, are not very much like your computer. These are the phones that people used a lot before the iPhone came out. They can access the Web, but when you view websites, they look nothing like they do on a monitor screen. Feature phones have fewer capabilities than smartphones and often don't have a touchscreen, and you may have to navigate using a little button like in Figure 8-7.

But feature phones have not been replaced by smartphones. In the United States, 58% of adults own smartphones, while 32% own feature phones.[2] Some countries have much higher rates of smartphone penetration, such as the United Arab Emirates and South Korea, which are at about 73%, while other countries, such as those in sub-Saharan Africa, have many more feature phones than smartphones.[3]

---

2 For the full report, see Susannah Fox and Lee Rainie, "The Web at 25 in the U.S.," Pew Research Internet Project, February 27, 2014 (*http://www.pewinternet.org/2014/02/27/the-web-at-25-in-the-u-s/*).

3 For more information, see Google's Our Mobile Planet (*http://think.withgoogle.com/mobileplanet/en/*).

Figure 8-7. Example of a feature phone (photo credit: Rodrigo Senna, *http://www.flickr.com/photos/negativz/38422354/*).

Part of responsive design is making sure that your site will *work* on any device, not just adapt to the screen size. As we talked about in Chapter 3, by starting with good HTML and using progressive enhancement to add CSS and JavaScript for devices that support them, you can make sure your site is usable on the most basic feature phones.

If your site has a lot of complex interactivity, it may not be possible to have your whole website work well on every device, down to the oldest browsers and devices, but do what you can.

For example, perhaps you can't make a restaurant website's online ordering work on the oldest phones, but you should be able to make the page with the restaurant's address and phone number work on pretty much every device, without a lot of extra effort.

TABLETS

Tablets have become increasingly common in recent years. They've been around for many years, but didn't become popular until the release of the iPad in 2010. The iPad is by far the most popular tablet, with other brands like Amazon's Kindle Fire trailing far behind.

Tablets are mostly very similar to modern smartphones, generally using the same operating systems, like iOS and Android, and allowing for the installation of apps.

Many tablets only have web access via WiFi, not by cellular networks, so they aren't technically classified as mobile devices. But that really doesn't matter. The lines are so blurred that it's no longer helpful to stick everything into categories of either mobile or nonmobile. It's more of a vague continuum, with phones on one end (mostly mobile) and desktop computers on the other (mostly not mobile).

Ereaders are devices that are meant to be used primarily for reading downloaded books, but many of them now include web browsers and are marketed more as a tablet (like the Kindle Fire). Some ereaders, such as more basic versions of the Kindle, have built-in browsers with limited functionality but use e-ink instead of a traditional screen, so everything appears in grayscale.

OTHER DEVICES

Many game consoles now have built-in web browsers, allowing you to access the Web on the screen connected to your console.

Some of them have very primitive browsers, meaning that what you see on the screen may not be exactly what the designer intended. But as with feature phones, as long as the site starts with good HTML and then adds CSS and JavaScript as progressive enhancement, it should be usable on these devices as well.

You never know where a web browser is going to show up. For example, WiFi-enabled refrigerators have been available for several years (it's kind of like having a small tablet embedded on the front of your fridge). Currently, they have a limited operating system that only supports certain apps, but I imagine it won't be too long before you have a full web browser in front of you in the kitchen.

There are also now watches with browsers, browsers in cars, and Google Glass, which puts a browser directly in front of your eyes. These all have very different interfaces, and you can't plan for all the possible devices that might exist in the next few years. But luckily, that's where responsive design comes in. Your goal is to design a site that's future-friendly, that will work on any screen size and any device, no matter the capabilities.

DESKTOP AND LAPTOP COMPUTERS

Until a few years ago, our access to the Web was limited to desktop and laptop computers. This is the setup all of us are probably most familiar with:

- A large screen

- Input using a keyboard and a mouse, touchpad, or trackball

- Desktops used at a desk, usually sitting, with little ability to change position

- Laptops used at a desk, or on your lap while sitting, or sometimes when lying down

- Nearly always using a wired connection or WiFi

We often think of these devices as having fast connections, but that's not always true. Many home Internet connections are not all that fast, and laptops are often used in hotels, coffee shops, or other locations with slow WiFi. Some people in rural areas don't have access to broadband, and use satellite Internet to connect.

Touch

Other than screen size, one of the key differences between smartphones and traditional computers is the input method.

Desktop and laptop computers have traditionally used keyboards in conjunction with pointing devices such as a mouse or trackpad, and we're used to designing sites that can be easily used with those devices. Touch is a little more difficult to design for, and requires some additional attention to make sure the user experience is good.

There are things you can do to make your site work better on touchscreens—and these changes won't detract from the experience on non-touch screens.

But don't think that touch is something you only need to think about for phones and tablets. Now, many desktop computers are coming out with monitors that have touchscreens (even my mom bought one from QVC, the cable shopping channel). So it's best to assume that every size screen *could* be touch-enabled.

And if you design for touch, everything will definitely work well with a mouse, while the opposite is not the case.

> **[NOTE]**
>
> Designing a good user experience for touch can be difficult. If you'd like to delve deeper into this area, check out Josh Clark's *Tapworthy: Designing Great iPhone Apps* (*http://shop.oreilly.com/product/0636920001133.do*). Even though the book focuses on app design, most of the concepts are relevant to website design.

CAPACITIVE TOUCH

Since the advent of the iPhone, the primary input method on smartphones has been a *capacitive* touchscreen.

Capacitive means that the screen works by measuring electrical charges conducted through anything touching the screen, such as a fingertip. The human body conducts electricity, but not all objects do, which is why touching a smartphone screen with something like a pen or a gloved finger has no effect. However, you can buy special styluses made of conductive material, or even gloves with conductive threads on the fingertips.

Older devices were sometimes made with *resistive* touchscreens, which have two thin layers that come together when the user presses on the outer surface with a fingertip or stylus. The screen is able to determine the precise location of the pressure. One disadvantage of this type of screen is that some amount of pressure is required, and the screens will often not register when a touch is too light. The screens are also more prone to damage.

MULTI-TOUCH

Although phones with touch interfaces had been around for years by the time the iPhone was introduced in 2007, the iPhone was one of the first with a *multi-touch* interface, which allows the screen to recognize more than one point of contact simultaneously. This allowed for much more complex interaction with the screen, such as the *pinch-to-zoom* motion.

GESTURES

Modern smartphones use *gestures* as a way to interact with the screen's content, giving users a "hidden" way to use the interface, so less of the valuable screen real estate has to be taken up with controls.

The pinch-to-zoom gesture is one of the most common, allowing an intuitive way to zoom in and out on things like maps. If you were viewing the same map on a laptop/desktop, you would see a slider with plus and minus buttons taking up part of the screen.

Some gestures, such as zooming in and out on a web page, are built into the browser or OS. Others, such as swiping sideways to go to the next image in a slideshow, have to be added to a web page using JavaScript.

Although you could skip that step and require users to tap or click arrows to navigate a slideshow, adding in gesture support can make a site much easier to use on touchscreens. Adding functionality for devices that support it, where it would enhance the experience, is a key part of responsive web design.

You can find several JavaScript plug-ins to add swipe behavior, such as TouchSwipe (*http://labs.rampinteractive.co.uk/touchSwipe/demos/*) or Swipe (*https://github.com/thebird/Swipe*).

JAVASCRIPT EVENTS

Touch events is a phrase used in the context of JavaScript to describe any interaction the user makes with the screen, whether it's a simple tap or a multi-finger movement. There are three basic touch events, touchstart, touchmove, and touchend, which can be used to define pretty much any interaction.

In addition, a touchscreen device will recognize JavaScript events that were designed for a mouse, such as click.

Hover

The hover event is a bit tricky on touchscreens—obviously, you can't just hover your fingertip over an element.

hover is used quite a bit on websites to change the visibility of elements via CSS (hide or display), such as a drop-down menu that appears when you hover over a link in a menu bar.

Most touchscreens automatically accommodate this by changing the element's behavior to double tap. That means the first tap on the element acts as a hover and changes the visibility of the element, and the second tap selects the link. However, this is awkward, and you should avoid using hover.

Of course, you could use a media query to have a different type of navigation appear on smaller screens (see Chapter 10), but now many desktop computers have touchscreens, so you need to assume that any size screen could be a touchscreen.

Touch delay

You may have noticed that mobile apps sometimes seem to be much faster than websites you view on a mobile phone. One issue that contributes to this is actually built into how JavaScript works on touch devices.

JavaScript does its best to replicate mouse events, from onClick (clicking with the mouse) to touch events. So if the browser is expecting an onClick on an element, it knows that a tap is a click—but with a twist. The browser will wait and see if you tap again, making it a double tap instead of a single tap (the double tap is a way to zoom in on a web page). That is, after you tap, the browser waits 300 ms (.3 seconds) to make sure you're not going to tap again before it goes ahead with the click event.

A third of a second doesn't seem like much, but to the user the difference can be very noticeable, because it means that things don't seem to happen "right away" when they tap.

Luckily, at least one browser maker has realized this is an issue and is starting to fix it. A beta version of Chrome for Android removes the 300 ms delay, but only for sites where the viewport element has the attribute content="width=device-width"—that is, responsive websites. The user can no longer double-click to zoom in, but zooming isn't needed so much on responsive sites, and the user can still pinch-to-zoom.

It's not clear if other browser manufacturers will follow in this direction, but in the meantime, there are JavaScript plug-ins you can use to remove the 300 ms delay on your site. Check out FastClick (*https://github.com/ftlabs/fastclick*) from FT Labs or Touche.js (*http://benhowdle.im/touche/*) from Ben Howdle.

TOUCH TARGET SIZE

For people using touchscreens to access your site, one of the biggest usability issues is *touch target* size (i.e., the size of the link or other element they need to select by tapping).

When using a mouse to click a link this isn't nearly as important, because (for most users) it's easy to get the cursor to exactly the right spot to click on a link or other element. But for users touching a screen, keep in mind that a finger is a lot bigger than a cursor, and if everything on the screen is really small, it's hard to hit the right spot.

If a target is all by itself, that's not a big deal, but if targets are very close together it's easy to accidentally hit the wrong one, sending you to a page you don't want to visit, or taking an action that you don't want to take.

You'll notice that when using a touchscreen, users actually tend to use the pads of their fingers (where the fingerprint is), not the fingertip (the very end of the finger). That can actually be a pretty wide area, depending on the person.

If a user is trying to hit a very small target he may sometimes use the fingertip instead of the finger pad to be more accurate, but this will slow the user down and make him work harder, which you don't want to do.

The average index finger is 1.6–2 cm (.6–.8 inches) in width, according to a study by the MIT Touch Lab. That converts to about 45–57 pixels. Luckily, smartphones are pretty smart when it comes to taps, and even though your finger might be touching many pixels on the screen, it can usually figure out what you were trying to tap. But if the target is too small, your success level will go way down.

Phone manufacturers actually have guidelines in place for how large an element should be so that users can easily select it on touchscreens. Apple's iPhone Human Interface Guidelines recommend that your touch target be at least 44 × 44 pixels. Microsoft Windows Phone recommends 34 pixels wide, with a minimum of 26 pixels. Nokia suggests your target should be at least 28 × 28 pixels.

That's a lot of variation, so what numbers do you use? If targets are right next to each other, I recommend making them at least 44 pixels wide if at all possible.

As you're testing your site on various mobile devices, make sure to check if links are easy to select on the touchscreens. And keep in mind that other people may not have fingers as limber as yours—some people have larger fingers, and older users may have more difficulty tapping precise points on the screen.

Increasing touch target size

You can use CSS to increase the size of touch targets. One way is to make sure any space around a link is *padding* rather than a *margin*. You'll need to go back to the box model you learned about in Chapter 3, which explains the difference between padding and margins.

Consider this list of links in Figure 8-8. The links are close together and likely are difficult to hit with your finger, depending on the text size. I've outlined each link so you can see which part is the clickable/tappable area.

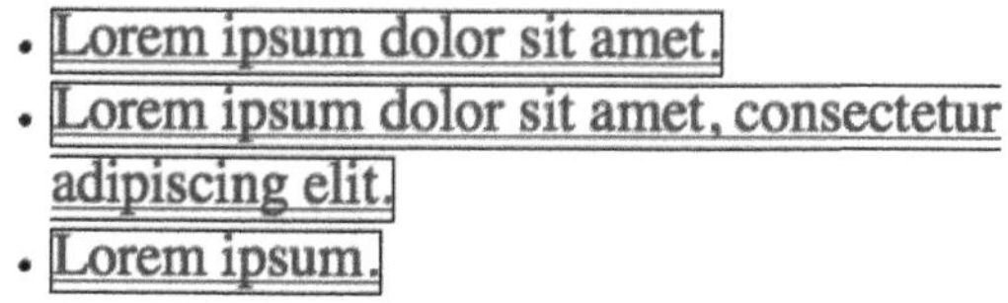

Figure 8-8. A list without styling has the links very close together.

How can we improve this? To start, you can make each link **display: block**, which will make the **<a>** element a box that extends to the full width of the containing element, as in Figure 8-9, rather than stopping at the end of the last word:

```
ul a { display: block; }
```

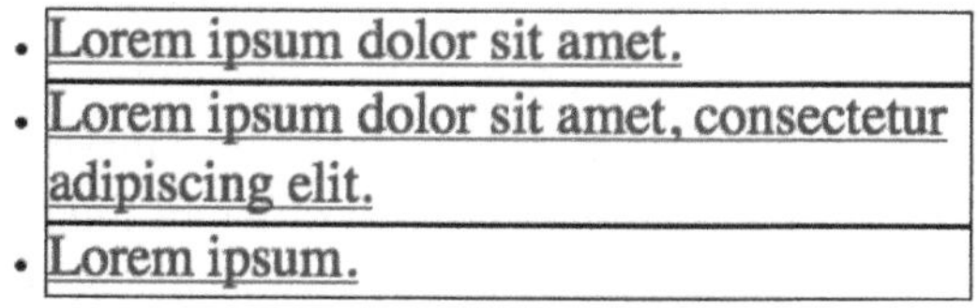

Figure 8-9. Making each link block instead of inline makes the touch target boxes extend to the full width of the containing element.

To increase the touchable area, you can also increase the padding (not margin) of each <a>, which increases the touch target size in whichever directions you choose, as you see in Figure 8-10:

```
ul a { display: block; padding: 3px 5px; }
```

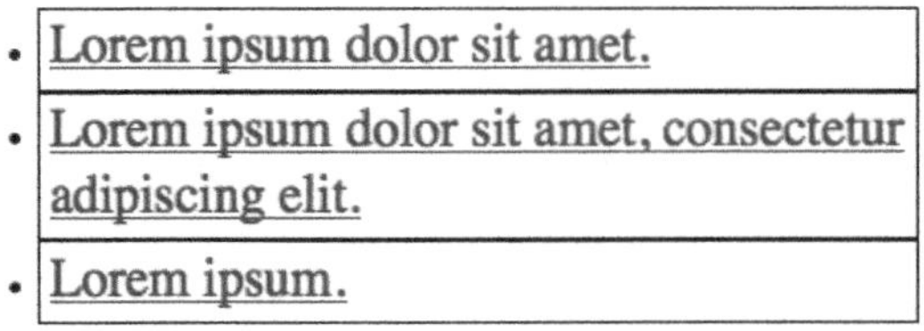

- Lorem ipsum dolor sit amet.
- Lorem ipsum dolor sit amet, consectetur adipiscing elit.
- Lorem ipsum.

Figure 8-10. Adding padding increases the touch target size in any or all directions.

Don't apply the padding to the <li>, or that will leave empty, non-tappable space between the links, as in Figure 8-11:

```
li { padding: 3px 5px; }
```

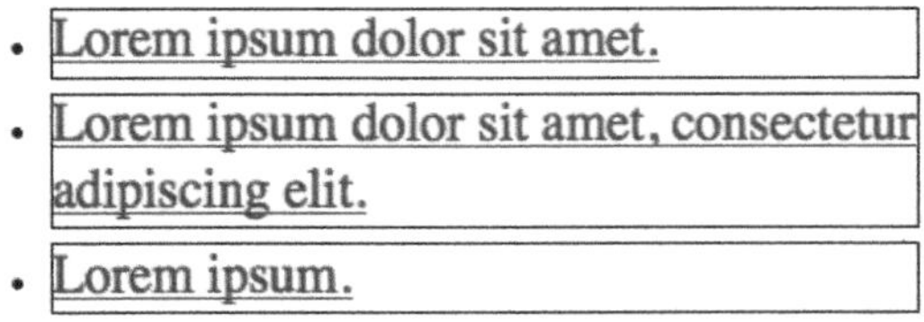

- Lorem ipsum dolor sit amet.
- Lorem ipsum dolor sit amet, consectetur adipiscing elit.
- Lorem ipsum.

Figure 8-11. If you use padding on the list items, that leaves empty space between the links and makes the touch targets smaller.

You should make use of all the available space; there's no need for empty spaces to separate the links. Mouse users will click directly on the links, so there won't be any confusion.

For links inside blocks of text like paragraphs, it's a little trickier. By making sure there is enough space between the lines, you can keep links a bit further apart (we'll look at how to do this with line-height in Chapter 9). Try not to have adjacent words be different links. Not only does that make them harder to click, but on touchscreens the users may not be able to tell there are multiple links, because they are not able to hover and see their targets.

Additionally, keep in mind this is going to be tricky for the smallest screens, where there's not a lot of available space. If you need to make your touch targets smaller than you'd like for small screens, you can use media queries to change the target size for different screen sizes. In the preceding example, if your padding of 3 pixels and 5 pixels just won't fit on a small screen, you can use media queries to give slightly less padding for the narrow screens and more ample padding for tablet size or wider.

NAVIGATION LOCATION

While the navigation on websites and desktop applications has naturally evolved to appear at the top of the screen, with key elements like the home button or search box in the top corners, this layout is really only optimal if you're using a mouse to get to the targets. With touch-screens, we enter a whole new usability world.

You know from using apps on a smartphone that navigation on apps often appears at the bottom of the screen, making it easier to hit those buttons with your thumb if you're holding the phone in one hand.

It's not just phones—with pretty much any touchscreen, it's easiest to touch the part of the screen that's closest to your hand. Even on a desktop touchscreen, it's physically easier and less fatiguing for users to touch elements near the bottom of the screen.

And not only does placing controls at the bottom of the screen make them easier to reach, but it also has a bonus effect: your fingers (or your arms, with a desktop touch monitor) aren't blocking the rest of the screen, so you can still see it.

This is a difficult topic, so we'll touch on it only a bit in this book. In Chapter 10, we'll look at an example of a website with navigation at the bottom of the screen. Although this adjustment to the standard user interface isn't often used, it's bound to become more common as web usage moves further away from traditional keyboard and mouse devices.

If you'd like to learn more about the idea of optimizing navigation for touchscreens, check out Josh Clark's blog post, "New Rule: Every Desktop Design Has To Go Finger-Friendly" (*http://globalmoxie.com/ blog/desktop-touch-design.shtml*) or Luke Wroblewski's "Responsive Navigation: Optimizing for Touch Across Devices" (*http://www.lukew. com/ff/entry.asp?1649*).

Screen Size

When doing responsive design, a primary consideration is making sure that websites can be viewed on any size screen.

It used to be that you could categorize devices by screen size, and design for a few set sizes: mobile phone, tablet, laptop, wide screen. But now, devices no longer fit easily into such categories, because they come in pretty much any width imaginable.

Smartphones start out with a screen size of around 3 inches (diagonal), with many in the range of 4 or 5 inches. Currently, one of the largest phones is the Galaxy Mega, with a 6.3 inch screen. Yes, it looks gigantically huge when you hold it up to your ear, but many people use their phones primarily for Internet access, not for actually *talking* to people (and anyway, you can always use your headset to make calls).

The iPad mini, on the small end of the tablet range, has a screen size of 7.9 inches, not that much bigger than the largest phone. Many tablets fall within the range of 7 to 10 inches, with the iPad at 9.7 inches.

Touch-enabled Ultrabooks range from 11.6 to 13.3 inches, and touch-screen desktop monitors take off from there—I found one as large as 55 inches for sale online, although I'm sure the $5,000+ price tag doesn't make it all that popular.

So, when you're creating a responsive website, you need to create a design that works on *every* possible screen size. A few years ago, creating layouts for those four set device sizes worked decently, because nearly every phone was an iPhone and nearly every tablet was an iPad. But now that screens come in all sizes, focusing only on small ranges of sizes means you're leaving out a lot of users.

ROTATE

A common problem with mobile apps—and less so with mobile websites—is that they don't rotate.

A website should rotate to be usable in either the vertical or horizontal screen orientation. Sure, it's nice to be able to design for one orientation, but an issue we have is pull-out keyboards, as you see in Figure 8-12.

Figure 8-12. For phones with a pull-out keyboard, the site must be usable in the horizontal orientation.

On phones with a pull-out keyboard, apps and websites can only be viewed in horizontal orientation (unless you don't need to use the keyboard).

It's also frustrating to users to tell them a website isn't available when they're holding their devices in their preferred orientation, such as in Figure 8-13. Again, remember that it's up to the users to choose their devices and how they hold them; it's up to you to make the site responsive to accommodate the users.

Figure 8-13. Some sites require that they be viewed in a particular orientation.

Accessibility (Universal Design)

Universal design is the concept that resources should be usable by the widest possible spectrum of users, rather than just the average user.

This encompasses the idea of *accessibility*, which primarily means making sure your website is usable by users with physical and cognitive disabilities. But you also want to make sure your website is easily usable by older users, people for whom your website is not in their first language, and those using outdated or nontraditional equipment to access the site.

But the word *universal* implies *everyone*, and indeed if you make your website more accessible for users with disabilities, you're making it generally more accessible for everyone.

We've addressed accessibility throughout the book, and it should definitely be a consideration throughout the web design process. But for now we'll talk about the various types of access that you need to pay attention to, and some major points to think about.

[NOTE]

There's much more to accessibility than we have space to cover in this book. To learn more about accessibility, check out *Just Ask: Integrating Accessibility Throughout Design* (*http://www.uiaccess.com/JustAsk/*) by Shawn Lawton Henry, which is available to read online for free, or Katie Cunningham's *Accessibility Handbook* (*http://shop.oreilly.com/product/0636920024514.do*).

VISUAL

Because most of us think of using a computer or mobile device as primarily a *visual* experience, it stands to reason that one of the main impediments to using a computer or mobile device is not being able to see the screen, or not being able to see it well enough.

Screen readers

As an example, users who are blind access the Web using software called a screen reader, which reads the text that's on the computer screen out loud to them.

Using correct, semantic HTML (which you should do anyway) is the first step for making your site accessible. If you've used semantic HTML to code your site, correctly tagging elements like headings, navigation, and forms, it will be much easier for the user to navigate the site—even without being able to see what it looks like!

We've already mentioned screen readers several times in this book, and in other chapters we talk about a few things you need to do to make sure your site is accessible to users who are accessing it with a screen reader.

To get a better idea of how a blind person would hear a web page being read out loud, download the Fangs Screen Reader Emulator (*https://addons.mozilla.org/en-us/firefox/addon/fangs-screen-reader-emulator/*), an add-on for the Firefox browser from Peter Krantz.

[NOTE]

Want to hear what it's really like to use a screen reader? Check out the blog post "Things I learned by pretending to be blind for a week" (*http://blog.silktide.com/2013/01/things-learned-pretending-to-be-blind-for-a-week/*), where David Ball, who is not blind, tells about the week he spent browsing websites with a blindfold and a screen reader to see what it's like.

Text size

Although blind users will comprise a very small part of the audience for most websites, a much larger number of users will be low-vision. The technical definition for this is someone who can't read a newspaper at a normal viewing distance, even with corrective lenses. For the purpose of this book, I'll make it a little broader and we'll define it as anyone who has trouble reading a computer screen while browsing the Web.

And this includes more people than you think.

Vision naturally worsens as we age. In particular, visual acuity (sharpness of vision) for things that are up close starts to decrease around age 40 (hence why a lot of older people use reading glasses).

This means that many users—especially, but not only, older users—tend to have trouble seeing what's on their computer screens. Walk through any office where there are older workers, and you'll see some of them are squinting at the screen, leaning in, trying to read type that's too small.

So that's something to think about when you create websites: make sure everything is of a size that is easy to read—not just for you, but for most users. We'll talk about this more in Chapter 9.

Also make sure that your code doesn't do anything that would keep users from adjusting the size of text on the page—for example, using the user-scalable=no attribute on the meta viewport tag, which we talked about in Chapter 3.

Color contrast

The color of the text on your website has a significant effect on its legibility.

Black text on a white background is straightforward and classic, but you may want to get a little more interesting.

However, you need to keep in mind that people visiting your site may have difficulty reading text if there isn't enough contrast between the background color and the foreground color. This will include users with low vision, including many older users, and also users who are color-blind. Even for someone with perfect vision, low contrast can be a problem when trying to read on a tiny mobile phone screen with light glaring on it.

Keep in mind that the visual design of your site is meant to sit on top of your content, not overwhelm it.

The Web Content Accessibility Guidelines (WCAG) recommends that the contrast ratio of text color to background color is at least 4.5 to 1. For large text, such as headlines, the contrast ratio needs to be only 3 to 1, because it is easier to read large text with less contrast. For more information on this, see "Understanding WCAG 2.0 - Contrast (Minimum)" (*http://www.w3.org/TR/UNDERSTANDING-WCAG20/visual-audio-contrast-contrast.html*), from the W3C.

You generally won't be able to tell if the contrast is acceptable just by looking, but you can use an online tool such as the Color Contrast Checker (*http://webaim.org/resources/contrastchecker/*) from WebAIM to check if there is enough contrast between two colors. You simply enter the hex codes of the two colors, and it will tell you the contrast ratio and whether it passes or fails for both normal and large text.

Another tool is Color Contrast Check (*http://snook.ca/technical/colour_contrast/colour.html*) from Jonathan Snook. After entering the numbers, it lets you play around with sliders to adjust the RGB settings, hue, saturation, and value of the colors, to see how you can get to a set of colors that passes.

To check everything on your website all at once, use CheckMyColours (*http://www.checkmycolours.com*) from Giovanni Scala. It will test every single element on a web page and give you a list of which colors pass and which fail.

Even gray can be a problem. It's trendy for text to be gray instead of black—it looks more elegant—but it's often hard to read.

The text in Figure 8-14 is pure black (#000000), and two shades of gray (#777777 and #AAAAAA). Both of the grays fail the contrast test.

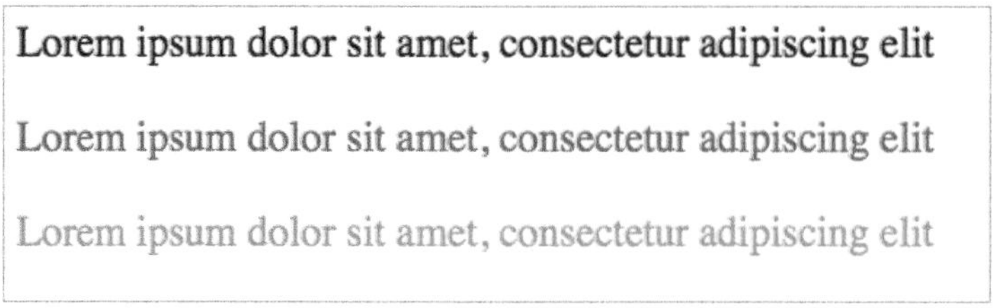

> Lorem ipsum dolor sit amet, consectetur adipiscing elit
>
> Lorem ipsum dolor sit amet, consectetur adipiscing elit
>
> Lorem ipsum dolor sit amet, consectetur adipiscing elit

Figure 8-14. The two shades of gray text fail the contrast test.

Color blindness

Another thing to think about when using color on a website is making sure you're not creating problems for color-blind users.

People who are color-blind don't just see everything in shades of gray; that type of color blindness is very rare. Rather, there are certain colors that are not distinguishable. For example, the most common type of color blindness is red–green, in which shades of red and shades of green look similar.

This means that looking at a stoplight, the red light and the green light look like similar colors. But color-blind people can still drive, because they know that the red light is always at the top and green at the bottom, even if they look the same. In that case, position is used to convey meaning, as a backup to the meaning conveyed by color.

You need to do the same thing for your website. Use color for visual decoration as you wish, but if you're using color to convey meaning, you need to include an alternate method.

For example, you might have a chart that uses red and green to note which features are available in a comparison of products. You could, at the same time, use Xs and checkmarks to convey the same information. The color will look compelling—perhaps showing at a glance that your product has far more green checkmarks than the competitor's product—but someone who can't interpret the colors will still be able to use the Xs and checkmarks to understand the chart.

When color is a key part of the website content, you need to provide enough information so that the user can make accurate choices.

For example, an online shopping site that sells shirts should make sure to label the colors, rather than just providing colored squares to demonstrate the color options. Also, use accurate color names. One popular clothing website lists color names such as "sugar coral" and "cloudburst." Although they make the clothes sound intriguing, those meaningless names certainly won't help customers who can't distinguish the colors on the screen.

To learn more about how color blindness affects website users, with a lot of great examples of how to make sure your site is compliant, see Geri Coady's blog post "Colour Accessibility" (*http://www.24ways. org/2012/colour-accessibility/*) on 24 Ways.

AUDIO

Most of the Web is visual, but there are also bits that are audible, such as videos and audio clips. For users who are deaf or hard of hearing, this information needs to be presented in a different format to be accessible.

Videos should have captions whenever possible. Unfortunately, although creating videos requires very little technical skill (pretty much anybody can do it), captioning is quite a bit more difficult. If you aren't able to caption videos, providing a transcription is an alternate option. It's not as good, because the user can't match the visual images with the words at the same time, but it's better than nothing.

Audio clips should, of course, have a transcription.

This doesn't only help users who can't hear the content. Other users may just prefer to read rather than listen (it's faster), or perhaps they are in a loud location where it would be hard to hear the content, or a quiet location like a library where they can't play the audio out loud and they don't have headphones.

INPUT METHODS

Although users with visual disabilities are the most obvious category of people who use assistive devices to access the Web, there are also people who have no trouble with vision, but who can't physically use a keyboard and/or mouse in the same way that most of us do.

Keyboard only

Some users are able to use a keyboard, but are physically unable to use a pointing device like a mouse. This might be due to something as common as carpal tunnel syndrome.

Blind users also fall into this category, because they can use a keyboard by feel, but can't use a pointing device because they aren't able to see where the pointer is on the screen.

And some power users just prefer to use a keyboard instead of a mouse because it's faster than switching back and forth.

By default, HTML makes web pages fairly accessible to keyboard-only users. But you need to make sure you don't do things that take away this accessibility.

Keyboard-only users navigate through the elements on a screen by using the Tab key. It takes them from one selectable element to the next (form fields, links, etc.), and the selected element is visually highlighted when they are on it. Try going to a website and hitting Tab several times—you'll see that each link on the page is surrounded by a dotted line when it is selected. If you hit the Enter key, it's the same thing as clicking that selected link.

The tab sequence will follow the same order as your HTML, which is another good reason to make sure your HTML is written in a logical order.

For users who are navigating by keyboard and *can't* see the screen, elements need to be labeled clearly. For example, a link should describe what is behind it, rather than using a generic "click here."

Speech recognition software

Users who can't interact with a keyboard at all might use speech recognition software, which allows them to speak commands to the computer.

Generally, if you make your site accessible for keyboard-only users, it will also be accessible for speech recognition users. But an additional consideration is making sure that form fields and links have unique labels, allowing the voice user to easily select them.

COGNITIVE DISABILITIES

People with cognitive disabilities are an often-ignored portion of a website's user base.

Providing clear and simple language, which we talk about in Chapter 2, is a great start to making your website more accessible to these users. This also helps users for which your website is in a language other than their native language.

You can also help users by having consistent design patterns throughout the site, such as using the same navigation options on each page. If you redesign a website, some users will have to "relearn" how to use the site—it's not simply a matter of finding where different things have moved to.

Another issue is animated graphics, which can be distracting for users with dyslexia or ADHD. It's best not to have anything on a web page animated by default, and make sure you don't use animated GIFs to communicate information, as some users use browser settings to turn off animations entirely.

Deciding Which Devices to Support

The tricky part of responsive design isn't just designing for different screen sizes. After all, you can easily design and test media queries just by changing the size of your browser window. The difficult part is making sure your site works on the widest possible variety of devices. Just because your website looks good when you resize your browser window doesn't mean that issues won't crop up on certain devices. Besides the fact that browsers don't all support the same features, every device and browser has little quirks.

When you start a project, you need to decide which devices you will support with the site design. This doesn't mean that these are the only devices the site will work on; it just means that those are the only devices you are agreeing to test to make sure the site works.

While responsive sites are designed to work on any size or type of device, there are occasional quirks that might make something go wrong, and you can't realistically test on *every* device out there. So, you need to select a list of devices and browsers to test on that are generally representative of the common devices, operating systems, browsers, and viewport sizes.

Here's an example of a list of devices and browsers you might include in the project plan for a website:

- Computers running Microsoft Windows 7 and newer
  - Internet Explorer 9 and newer
  - Latest releases of Firefox, Safari, and Chrome
- Computers running Mac OS X 10.7 Lion and newer
  - Latest releases of Firefox, Safari, and Chrome
- Tablets and smartphones running Android 4.0 Ice Cream Sandwich and newer
  - Chrome on Nexus 7 tablet
  - Chrome on LG and Motorola smartphones
- iOS 6.0 on iPhone 3GS
  - Mobile Safari
- iOS 7.0 on iPhone 4s and 5, iPad 2, and iPad mini
  - Mobile Safari
  - Chrome for iOS

The exact devices on your list will depend on the needs of the project. For example, the preceding list doesn't include Blackberry or Windows Phone devices. The stats for your existing site might tell you that you have a very low number of visitors using Blackberries, so you may decide it's not worth your time to include those devices. But keep in mind that if the existing site doesn't work well on certain mobile devices, statistics may mean that users with those devices are just avoiding your site, while they might turn into regular users if the site worked correctly for them.

You should also find out what particular device each of your stakeholders uses, and make sure you're testing on that device, even if it's obscure. No matter what devices are on the list, your stakeholders are going to expect that the site will work on their own phones.

Why Use Real Devices for Testing

Just because you are planning to support a list of particular devices, it doesn't mean you have to actually own all those devices. You can use online emulators and simulators to see how the site will look on various devices (more on that in the next section).

However, although using an emulator from your desktop browser will let you see how the site looks on various devices, it won't give you a feel for the user experience of the site. For example, are your touch targets large enough? Is it easy to move between sections of content? Does the site load quickly enough on a slow mobile connection?

If you can't obtain all the actual devices you want to test, at the very minimum you should test on an iPhone, an Android phone, an iPad, and a 7" tablet (either an iPad Mini or an Android device). That's in addition to the major browsers on both Mac OS and Microsoft Windows.

DEVICE LABS

If the world was perfect, every company that makes websites would have a *device lab*, a collection of a wide range of mobile devices that designers and developers could use to test the websites they're working on. But unless you work at a large company with a big equipment budget, you're probably not that lucky.

You can probably ask around and come up with at least a few coworkers who will let you borrow their phones, but they're likely to have similar devices, and you probably won't find all the device types you want to test on.

The open device labs that have started cropping up in the past few years are one solution. An *open device lab* is a place where you can find a collection of mobile devices that are available for the community to use. Some device labs are owned by web agencies or other companies that have generously made their labs open to the public; others are community organizations or nonprofits that rely on donated resources.

There are open device labs in cities around the world, although most are located in major cities of Europe and the United States. You can find a list of device labs on OpenDeviceLab.com (*http://opendevicelab.com*).

What you will find in a device lab will vary. Some labs may only have a few devices, while others may have several in a wide range of operating systems and form factors (physical interfaces). Some device labs charge a small fee for access, but many are free.

BUYING DEVICES

Although it sounds expensive to buy devices to use for testing, there are ways to get some of them cheaply.

Having to pay for a cellular plan to go along with each phone can be prohibitively expensive, but many phones can be used on WiFi without having to pay for a cellular plan. This is generally adequate for testing purposes, although it won't allow you to test performance over a mobile connection.

You can get many older phones used off of eBay, Craigslist, or other sale websites, or even ask friends and coworkers. Not all mobile providers have a way to "trade in" your old phone when getting a new one, so people tend to just stick their old phones in a box in the closet, as it just doesn't seem right to throw away that once-expensive piece of equipment.

You probably already have, or can easily borrow, both an iPhone and an Android phone; it's worth having a 7" tablet and a 10" tablet on hand for testing too, so you can get a feel for actually using a website on that size screen, as opposed to just viewing it on an emulator.

Testing

A key to successful responsive design, as we've mentioned throughout the book, is testing your site on various devices. Besides using actual devices, there are other ways to test your site to make sure it will work correctly on the widest range of devices.

VALIDATORS

One of the first things you should do to test your site is validate your code. This can catch code errors right off the bat, and save you a lot of time troubleshooting things that don't display correctly.

Validation tools are built into web developer add-ons for major browsers, or you can use an online service to validate your code, such as the W3C Markup Validation Service (*http://validator.w3.org*) (for HTML) and the W3C CSS Validation Service (*http://jigsaw.w3.org/css-validator*).

BROWSER RESIZING

As you're designing or coding a responsive website, you'll certainly be resizing your browser window to see how the design looks at different viewport widths. Although this is useful—and where you should start—it's not necessarily going to give you an accurate picture of what the site will look like on actual devices.

However, browser window resizing gives you an advantage you don't get on mobile devices: you get to see how the design looks at every possible viewport width, not just the widths of whichever devices you test on. And no matter how many devices you test on, you're not going to be seeing every possible device width, so the browser window may be the only place you can see some weird layout quirk that happens only between 643 and 647 pixels.

Browser tools

When you start your testing in the browser, there are a few tools you can use to make the job a little easier.

Although changing the window size gives you an idea of how the design looks across all viewport widths, you'll also find it useful to see the site in the exact size of common devices.

In Firefox, this is easy; there's a built-in tool. Go to Tools → Web Developer → Responsive Design View, shown in Figure 8-15. After loading a page, you can use a drop-down menu to choose among several different preset screen sizes, and there's even a button to allow you to take a screenshot of the web page.

In Safari, there's an extension called Resize (*http://resizesafari.com/*) that lets you resize your browser window to configurable preset sizes.

For Chrome, try the Windows Resizer (*https://chrome.google.com/web store/detail/window-resizer/kkelicaakdanhinjdeammmilcgefonfh*).

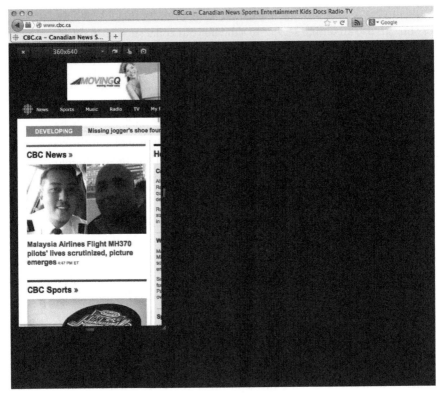

Figure 8-15. Responsive Design View in Firefox.

BROWSERS AND OPERATING SYSTEMS

A few years ago, we only had to test our websites on two operating systems (Mac OS and Microsoft Windows) and a handful of browsers (Firefox, IE, Safari, and maybe Opera).

Now, however, there are several mobile operating systems and many mobile browsers to consider as well. Here's a list of the major mobile operating systems and the default browser for each:

- iOS (iPhone, iPad): Safari
- Android: Chrome (newer devices) or Android Browser (older devices)
- Windows Phone: Internet Explorer Mobile
- Blackberry: Blackberry Browser

For each operating system, you should test on the most recent version of the OS, and if possible also test the previous major release, especially for iOS and Android.

You may also wish to test the Symbian OS that runs on Nokia devices; it was the most popular OS worldwide until 2010, and many Symbian phones are still in use. Several open source mobile operating systems are also available, including Firefox OS, Sailfish OS, and Ubuntu Touch OS.

The Kindle Fire runs Fire OS, which is a custom version of Android.

Every mobile phone comes with a default browser, such as the ones just listed, and many users don't even realize that they have the option to install other browsers on their phones, just as they would on a desktop computer. Besides the default browsers already listed, you may want to test:

- Dolphin Browser (Android, iOS)
- Chrome (Android, iOS)
- Firefox for Mobile (Android)
- Opera Mini (Android, iOS, Blackberry, other device types)
- Opera Mobile (Android, other device types)

And don't forget about desktop computers. In addition to testing on both Microsoft Windows and Mac OS X, make sure to test on all the major browsers:

- Chrome (Mac OS X, Microsoft Windows)
- Firefox (Mac OS X, Microsoft Windows)
- Internet Explorer (Microsoft Windows)
- Opera (Mac OS X, Microsoft Windows)
- Safari (Mac OS X, Microsoft Windows)

EMULATORS AND SIMULATORS

If you don't actually have a particular device, you can still test on that device by using a mobile emulator or simulator, which will allow you to use your desktop monitor to view what your site would look like on a particular device.

The difference between an emulator and a simulator is that the former will show you how the device would behave, while the latter only shows you what the device's screen would look like.

Many of the mobile operating systems and manufacturers have emulators or simulators you can download; check out Maximiliano Firtman's "Mobile Emulators & Simulators: The Ultimate Guide" (*http://www.mobilexweb.com/emulators*) for an extensive list.

However, rather than having to download a lot of different software, you may find it easier to use a browser-based tool that will allow you to test many devices or operating systems at once.

Two of the most popular and comprehensive are BrowserStack (*http://www.browserstack.com*) and Cross Browser Testing (*http://crossbrowsertesting.com*). These have a monthly fee based on users or usage. You can find many others, some free, by searching the Web.

ASSISTIVE TECHNOLOGY

Don't forget that some users will be coming to your site using assistive technology, such as screen readers.

To make sure these users are able to access your site, you should test in at least one screen reader. If you don't have the budget to buy any of the popular commercial software options, there are several free options available.

Mac OS X has a screen reader built into the operating system: Voiceover for OS X (*http://www.apple.com/accessibility/osx/voiceover/*).

You may also wish to try the Fangs Screen Reader Emulator (*https://addons.mozilla.org/en-US/firefox/addon/fangs-screen-reader-emulator/*), an add-on for Firefox.

Even before testing in a screen reader, you can start by viewing your site without the images—replacing them with the alt text—to see if the site still makes sense. Web developer add-ons for the major browsers will give you this option.

Summary

When creating a responsive website, you need to give a lot of thought to both your users and the devices they might be using. Although responsive design is not only about designing for mobile, it's natural to focus more on mobile because it's a less familiar medium, and because there are so many new capabilities and limitations to consider with mobile devices. Just don't forget to make sure your design works well on desktop screens as well.

You shouldn't design for particular devices, but rather create a design that will work well across all devices. By focusing on mobile first, it's easier to make sure everything works well on the mobile interface.

Responsive design is not an all-or-nothing approach. If you don't have the resources to make your site fully responsive, you can make it partially responsive, which is better than not responsive at all.

There are many different types of devices that can access the Web, from mobile phones and tablets to desktops, as well as other devices like ereaders and watches. Touch is one of the biggest changes now that we are designing for mobile devices. Make sure that your touch target sizes are large enough, and that JavaScript events work correctly on touchscreens.

You also need to make sure your site is universally accessible. There are a lot of details to consider, such as making sure that color-blind users won't miss any important information that your site conveys with color.

Deciding which devices to support with your site will depend on your resources. It's best to use real devices for testing, but if you can't, there are other tools like simulators and emulators.

Now that you've been thinking about your users and the devices they are using, we'll jump back into design. In the next chapter, we'll look at typography for responsive websites.

Part IV

Designing Responsive Websites

[9]

Typography

Websites are about communication, about getting information to people. Although some of the information is conveyed through images, most of it is conveyed through text.

Because the words on a web page are so important to being able to communicate your message effectively, you want to make sure text is easy to read and visually appealing.

Your goal is not just to make the text look good and fit in with the overall site design, but to create the best possible user experience for the user who is reading the text.

When creating website designs, we tend to want to control the visual appearance of text too much, thinking of it as a static thing, like the text on a magazine page. We try to control exactly how the text flows around other items on a page, and exactly how the words look next to each other.

To some extent, we can do this, but as we make our websites responsive, we lose some of the control over the text. Instead, we need to style text in such a way that it will look good however the design and layout change—and even if our content is displayed somewhere other than on the web page we designed.

In this chapter, we'll learn the basics of how to add fonts to a website. Then we'll look at how to size text, and what units of measurement are most appropriate for responsive sites. Then we'll learn how line length affects readability, and add media queries to an example site to see how to keep the line length within the recommended range no matter what the viewport width is. Last, we'll look at a few more details about typography, such as whitespace and when you should adjust the typeface based on screen size.

Start with HTML

When you're thinking about how your text is going to look on the screen, the first thing you'll probably think of is CSS—setting a font size, a typeface, colors, and so on.

But in reality, styling your type needs to start out with HTML. Remember that users who are reading your text might not be seeing it styled with the CSS from your website. They may be on a device that doesn't display CSS correctly or at all, or they might be using an RSS reader, or a service like Instapaper that strips out all the styles. Or users may be hearing the text read out loud by a screen reader.

In case the CSS isn't available to the user, your text needs to be marked up with the correct HTML, as we talked about earlier in the book. If the CSS isn't available, the browser will use default styles for HTML elements like `<h1>` and `<strong>` to make sure the user still gets text that is readable and usable.

Typefaces

The choice of typeface is one of the most important visual elements of a website. Typeface influences the tone of the message, which in turn can affect how the message is interpreted.

Additionally, choosing the right typeface will impact whether the content on your site is easy to read. Using the wrong typeface may make it difficult for your message to get across.

Your website will likely use more than one typeface. It's all right to use multiple typefaces as long as they look good together and there isn't so much visual variation that it distracts from the message.

Generally, a simple, easy-to-read typeface is selected for the body copy (paragraphs and such). Your goal with that is to make the type as easy to read as possible.

When choosing among possible body copy typefaces, try them out on a few different devices, at the font size that you plan to use. View a long passage of text, not just a few words. Is it easy to read?

For headings, you have more leeway. Heading text will be at a larger size, so the typeface can have more detail and personality.

Try out some sample headings, using text you might actually use on your site. The width of text varies by typeface, even at the same size, so think about whether the typeface you're choosing will take up too much horizontal space on the page. A narrower typeface might keep your headings from wrapping onto multiple lines.

There's a lot more that goes into choosing typefaces that look good on the screen and work well together—far too much to address in this book. To learn more, try these resources:

- "On Web Typography" (*http://alistapart.com/article/on-web-typography*) by Jason Santa Maria on *A List Apart*

- "The Elements of Typographic Style Applied to the Web" (*http://webtypography.net/toc/*) by Richard Rutter

---

[NOTE]

Although the words *font* and *typeface* are often used interchangeably, they actually have different meanings. A typeface is a set of designed letters, numbers, and symbols, like Helvetica or Times New Roman.

The word *font*, on the other hand, actually refers to the electronic file on your computer or website that produces the letters on the screen. You can think of it like the difference between a song and an MP3.

CHOOSE YOUR TYPEFACE FIRST

Later in this chapter we'll be looking at how to adjust different properties of the text, such as `font-size` and `line-length`, to make it easier to read.

But before you can start looking at those properties, you first need to decide which typeface(s) you'll be using on your site. Although you'll be able to choose the size that type is displayed in, different typefaces will vary slightly in how much space they take up on the screen.

For example, in Figure 9-1 you can see the same text in 10 different typefaces, but in the exact same `font-size`. Because the actual size of the characters varies slightly, you can see that the line length will be different depending on which typeface you choose. If you design your site for optimal line lengths and then change the typeface, your line lengths will change and you'll have to start over!

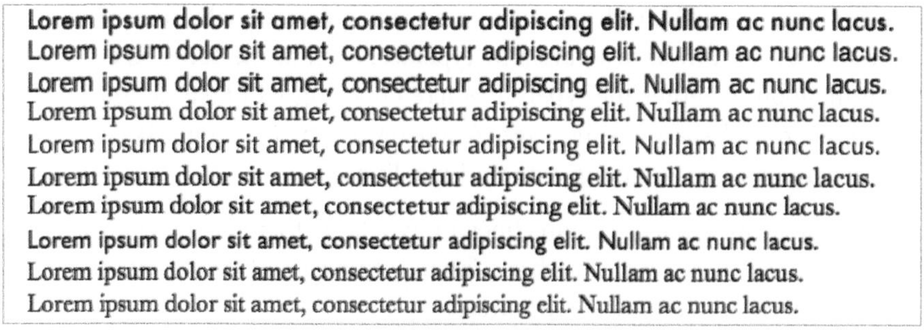

> Lorem ipsum dolor sit amet, consectetur adipiscing elit. Nullam ac nunc lacus.
> Lorem ipsum dolor sit amet, consectetur adipiscing elit. Nullam ac nunc lacus.
> Lorem ipsum dolor sit amet, consectetur adipiscing elit. Nullam ac nunc lacus.
> Lorem ipsum dolor sit amet, consectetur adipiscing elit. Nullam ac nunc lacus.
> Lorem ipsum dolor sit amet, consectetur adipiscing elit. Nullam ac nunc lacus.
> Lorem ipsum dolor sit amet, consectetur adipiscing elit. Nullam ac nunc lacus.
> Lorem ipsum dolor sit amet, consectetur adipiscing elit. Nullam ac nunc lacus.
> Lorem ipsum dolor sit amet, consectetur adipiscing elit. Nullam ac nunc lacus.
> Lorem ipsum dolor sit amet, consectetur adipiscing elit. Nullam ac nunc lacus.
> Lorem ipsum dolor sit amet, consectetur adipiscing elit. Nullam ac nunc lacus.

Figure 9-1. Different fonts in the same size don't take up the same amount of horizontal space.

Thousands of fonts are available for you to use on your website, and later in this chapter you'll learn where to find free and not-free fonts, and how to use them on your site.

Using Fonts

It used to be that the only fonts you could use on a website were the ones that were already installed on the user's computer. Other than a very few that were consistent across operating systems, you had no way to know which fonts the user had, so your choices were very limited.

With CSS3, we have the ability to embed fonts in a website. What that means is your site can link to a file that contains all the information needed to display a given font. When the user views your website, her device will be able to display any font that you link to (as well as the default fonts installed on the user's device).

Font files can either be hosted on your own server along with other website assets (remember, fonts are digital files), or you can use a *font service*, which is a website that lets you link to the font files on its servers.

Web fonts may look slightly different across devices, so as usual, test on different devices.

WELL-DESIGNED FONTS

Now that everything is electronic, it's easy to obtain fonts to use on your website, and there seem to be millions of them out there. There are even tons of free fonts, but you need to beware that you often get what you pay for.

Typefaces are designed by people called *type designers*. Designing a typeface is difficult and tedious work. It's not as straightforward as just creating the design for each letter.

Making individual letters is not actually the most difficult part. The tricky part is making the letters fit together well in blocks of text, because the spacing between letters (*kerning*) needs to vary depending on what the letters are.

If you are using a poorly made font, you will notice the difference once the letters are put together into words and sentences. The spacing between them will not look right.

When purchasing fonts, make sure that you can first view sample blocks of text on your screen. Don't rely on an A–Z display of characters to determine if the font will work for you.

SELF-HOSTED FONTS

Hosting your own web fonts is not difficult.

You can buy fonts, or find free fonts, using some of the following websites (make sure to specifically look at their sections on web fonts, because they may also offer font downloads for use on a computer, and that's not what you need):

Font Squirrel (http://www.fontsquirrel.com)
All fonts are free, including for commercial use.

MyFonts (http://www.myfonts.com/info/webfonts/)
Offers more than 60,000 fonts, with pricing based on pageviews.

Fonts.com (http://www.fonts.com/web-fonts/self-hosting)
Subscription pricing based on pageviews.

The font file you'll download will typically be a ZIP file. Unzip it and you'll see that the contents include font files in several formats, and typically also a text file of the license.

Upload the files to your site. Later in this chapter, in "Linking to Font Files," you'll learn how to apply them to the text on your site using CSS.

FONT SERVICES

Using a font service is generally easier than hosting fonts yourself. Although there are some free fonts, you'll typically pay a subscription fee, monthly or annually, for the use of fonts. Fees might be based on the number of fonts (typefaces) you use, the number of users on your company account with the font service, or the amount of bandwidth that your website uses to download the fonts over a period of time.

Through an online interface, you'll choose the font or fonts you need for your site, selecting from various options and settings. Then you'll be given the CSS and/or JavaScript that you will need to add to your site. Once you've included that code, you simply add the name of the font to any `font-family` declarations in your styles where you wish to use that font.

These are some of the current popular font services, all of which have an option that allows you to test the fonts for free on your site with limited pageviews or for a limited time. Subscription pricing is based on pageviews and the number of sites you use the fonts on, and starts as low as a few dollars per year—with the exception of Google Web Fonts, which is free:

Google Web Fonts (http://www.google.com/webfonts)
>   Free, with more than 600 font families available. All the fonts are open source and can be used however you want, including for commercial projects.

Font Deck (http://fontdeck.com)
>   Annual fee for each font used.

Fonts.com (http://www.fonts.com/web-fonts)
>   Subscription pricing allows use of 20,000 different fonts.

Typekit (https://typekit.com)
>   Subscription pricing allows use of thousands of fonts.

Web Ink (http://www.webink.com)
>   Subscription pricing allows use of thousands of fonts.

Webtype (http://www.webtype.com)
>   Annual fee for each font used.

Another service that may be of use to you when testing fonts:

Typecast (http://typecast.com)

Allows you to easily test and compare fonts in your browser, for a monthly fee. Free 14-day trial.

LINKING TO FONT FILES

Whether you're hosting your own font files, or using a service, you need to let your CSS know that the fonts are available to be used on your website. To do this, you'll be using the @font-face property. This is a separate step before you can use the fonts to style elements on your site.

If you're using a font service, the service will provide you with the code to use, but it will typically be similar to what you see here.

If you've downloaded files to host yourself, you'll probably also be provided with code to use, and you'll just need to change the directory in the URL. First upload the files to the selected directory on your website so they are available for linking.

Your code might look something like the following. Add this code at or near the top of your first stylesheet, as it needs to be downloaded before you start styling text with the font:

```
@font-face {
    font-family: WebFontName;
    src: url('WebFontName.otf');
}
```

A few key things to note here:

- The font-family you specify here is what you will refer to the font as elsewhere in your stylesheets. In theory, you can call it anything you want, but it's generally easiest to give it the same name as the actual font name.

- If the font-family is multiple words, it needs to be in single quotation marks (i.e., 'Web Font Name').

- Make sure the URL to the font file has the correct path to where the font files are located on your website. For example, it might be url('../fonts/WebFontName.otf').

The preceding code only includes one font file, but you'll commonly be linking to multiple files for each font, because different operating systems support different types of font files. So, your code might look more like this:

```
@font-face {
    font-family: WebFontName;
    src: url('WebFontName.eot');
    src: url('WebFontName.eot?#iefix') format('embedded-
    opentype'),
    url('WebFontName.woff') format('woff'),
    url('WebFontName.ttf') format('truetype'),
    url('WebFontName.svg#webfont') format('svg');
    font-weight: normal;
    font-style: normal;
}
```

You're supplying the same font in multiple formats. The browser will use whichever one it supports.

For a list of which file types are supported by which browsers, check out "@font-face File Types Browser Support" (*http://www.stunningcss3. com/resources/fontface-file-types-browser-support.html*) written by Zoe Mickley Gillenwater, an excerpt from *Stunning CSS3: A Project- Based Guide to the Latest in CSS* (New Riders).

CREATING THE FONT STACK

To set the typeface for any HTML element, you'll use the font-family property. The CSS declaration should include more than one font, as you need to have a backup in case the font is not loaded for some rea- son (such as if your font file is linked to incorrectly, or if wherever it is hosted is down temporarily).

The browser will go through the list in order and use the first font that is available, so start with your selected font, and follow it with any back- ups. This list of font options is informally called a *font stack*.

The last item on the list should be a generic font family, usually either serif or sans-serif, which will produce the default font of that type on the device. That's an absolute backup that is very rarely used by the browser, but it's a best practice to have it there just in case.

Font names must match exactly the @font-face declaration. If they are more than one word, they need to be surrounded by single quotation marks.

In the following example, we've selected Helvetica Neue as our font. If for some reason the font is not available, the browser will next try to find Helvetica, and then Arial (both of which are commonly available as installed fonts on devices). If none of these are available, the browser will display its default sans-serif font:

```
body { font-family: 'Helvetica Neue', Helvetica, Arial,
sans-serif; }
```

When choosing what element to apply font-family to, generally, you'll have one font that is applied to most of the elements on your site. Apply that font to your <body>, and then you can use different fonts for other elements as necessary.

Typically, your backup fonts should be similar in scale to your primary font, so that the design will not look radically different if a backup font is used. Test your website using each of the fonts in your font stack, so you know that the design will still look decent regardless of which one is used. For example, if one of the fonts has much wider characters, that could throw off the line length of text elements on the page, or make headings wrap onto multiple lines.

When creating a font stack, the fonts you will be able to include are:

- Any web font you have linked to using font-face, either via a service or self-hosted on your website.

- Any font that is installed on the user's device. See "Default Fonts" (*http://www.granneman.com/webdev/coding/css/fonts-and-for-matting/default-fonts/*) from Scott Granneman for lists for each operating system.

- The browser's generic font families, which you specify by using serif or sans-serif.

Some older browsers don't support font-face for linking to font files, so you need to include system fonts as options.

Sizing Text

Even if you don't style your text at all, you need to pay attention to the size of the text and make sure it's appropriate for the design and it's readable for the user. One of the benefits of responsive design is that you can give all of your text proportional sizes, rather than absolute sizes. That way, the size of type can respond to the size of the viewport.

FORGET ABOUT PIXELS

You may be used to sizing text in pixels. Until recently, this was an appropriate way to size text, as pixels were a consistent unit no matter what monitor you had your computer hooked up to.

But no longer. Now technology allows pixels to be much smaller. High-density screens have a much greater number of pixels in a given space, so that the display can look much crisper. Additionally, the number of pixels can vary depending on the type of screen.

So, pixels are no longer a form of measurement that is consistent across devices. If you use pixels for measurements, your design will still look good on most devices—for now. But as we move to an increasing variety of devices in the future, including types of devices that haven't even been invented yet, we can't trust that pixel measurements will continue to work the way that we expect.

If you want your site to be responsive and look good on all screen sizes and device types, therefore, you need to move away from pixels and rely on relative units of measurement.

SCREEN DISTANCE

Another thing to consider is that even when you think pixels are consistent across devices, it turns out they aren't, because the device manufacturers take into consideration how far a screen is likely to be from the user's face. The closer the text is to your eyes, the larger it looks.

For example, if you hold up an iPhone, which has a screen that's 320 pixels wide, next to your computer screen with a browser window sized to 320 pixels wide, you might be surprised to see that they aren't the same size. You can see the difference in Figure 9-2.

Figure 9-2. The same site at 320 pixels wide on different devices isn't the same physical size.

If you hold them up right next to each other, the computer text is larger—it has to be, because the computer monitor is further away from your eyes.

For the most part, you don't need to worry about this, because the device manufacturers have already made all the adjustments. But still, sometimes things don't come out the way you think they will, so you need to test on a variety of devices and screen sizes so you can make sure the text is a good, readable size regardless of the screen size.

Read "Relative Readability" (*http://wm4.wilsonminer.com/posts/2008/ oct/20/relative-readability/*) by Wilson Minor for more information on font sizes and reading distances.

ABSOLUTE VERSUS RELATIVE

Pixels are an *absolute* measurement—that means that the units of measurement have a set definition that is supposed to always be the same. *Relative* measurements, on the other hand, are in relation to each other, once you've defined a starting point.

If you've designed web pages using pixels—or if you've sized text in anything, such as a word processor document—you're used to using absolute measurements. Text gets a numbered measurement to determine how big it is, whether it's 14 pixels on your web page, 12 points in your word processor, or 3 feet if you're designing a billboard.

When you're using a fixed canvas such as paper, where the size of the canvas will never change, that makes sense. But for a website, the size of the canvas changes depending on the size of the screen, so you need to make sure the text is flexible so it can change along with the screen size when appropriate.

Thus, instead of an *absolute* unit like pixels, responsive design uses *relative* units such as ems and rems. Relative measurements simply mean that the numbers we use in the measurements will show the size relative to the size of something else. We'll get into that in detail shortly.

If you've been working on responsive sites, you've probably learned that you can just use a formula to convert all your font size pixel measurements to a responsive unit such as ems.

While this can be handy if you are converting an existing pixel-based site to a responsive design, it's not a sustainable method of working with websites. Pixels are no longer a measurement we can trust, so we need to entirely stop thinking of our text being sized in pixels.

In this book, we'll focus on starting out with relative units in our design, rather than converting from pixels. (If you do need to convert an existing site, I'll tell you how to do that later in the chapter.)

SETTING A DEFAULT FONT SIZE

When you're styling the text on your website, the first thing you need to do is set the default font size for the website. Remember that all of your measurements are relative—this is what they will be relative to.

But where to start? Well, it's pretty easy, actually. Each browser can set its own default font size, and each will choose an appropriate default size that is large enough to be easy to read for most users. To start out with your text this size, all you need to do is set the <body> font size to 100%. You've likely already done this in your reset CSS:

```
body { font-size: 100%; }
```

Setting the default font size for the document is the only time we'll use a percentage for **font-size**. Everything else will be in ems or rems to be relative to this base size.

If you're wondering how big 100% is—well, create a test page and check it out in your browser. For most devices, the default font size works out to 16 pixels (although I did just say to stop thinking in pixels, you probably have an idea in your head of what 16 pixels looks like, if you don't want to fire up your browser at the moment).

There are a few devices that have a different default font size. For example, the Kindle Touch browser has a default font size of 26 pixels, because it has a higher pixel density. But 26-pixel text on the Kindle Touch will look similar to 16-pixel text on other devices.

The great thing about using relative sizes for fonts is that if you decide you want all of the text on your website to be a different size, you can just change the base font size: all the text will change size, but it will still have the same relative scale.

WHY 100%?

Although I told you in the last section to use 100% as the `font-size` on your `<body>`, you can use any percentage you wish. But 100% is a great place to start. As I mentioned, the browser makers have already determined how large the text on a website needs to be to make it easy to read for most users, and that size is what you get at 100%.

However, if you give a website that default of 100%, it might look to you like it's *too big*. That's because you're used to looking at much smaller text on websites. Until recently, very few sites set their main body text that big. But over the last few years, many websites have been moving to larger type.

Surprisingly, this has been controversial, especially for sites like web design blogs. It's unbelievable how many web designers feel the need to complain about the text on sites being too big—like it's a personal insult or something.

For a lot of users, yes, it doesn't *need* to be that big. However, for many other people, the big text is a huge relief. If you don't have perfect vision, small text on a web page can be very difficult to read. Statistically, people's eyesight deteriorates after around 40, making it increasingly difficult to read small type. I'm not quite 40, but I find a lot of website text too small to read comfortably.

There's a neat keyboard trick, Command-+, that increases the size of all the text on a web page. I use it fairly frequently on websites with small text, because I'd rather be able to read comfortably than have to squint at small letters.

Some web designers will argue that because users do have the option to make text bigger themselves, it's not necessary to design the text large enough to be easy to read. But guess what? Not everybody knows that Command-+ trick.

And even if they did, it's not the *user's* responsibility to make a website usable; it's the *designer's* responsibility.

So go ahead and set your base font size to 100%, so that most users can comfortably read the text on the page. That doesn't mean *everything* has to be that big. You can use the relative measurements we're going to talk about next to make some components of the text, such as a footer, slightly smaller. But the main body text on your website should be at least 100% of the browser's default font size.

If you still feel like 100% text looks too big, it may simply be a factor of not having other parts of the design, such as whitespace or images, at a similar scale. And if you're not sure, when it comes to type, bigger is always better.

UNITS OF MEASUREMENT

There are a few different units of measurement that are used for type.

You might be used to using *points* when editing text in word processor. Regular text might be set at around 10 or 12 points. A point has a physical measurement of 1/72 of an inch. Thus, your 12-point text is 1/6" tall. Picas are a related term; a *pica* is simply 12 points.

If you've worked on websites, you're probably used to using pixels. A pixel is in theory 1/96 of an inch. Thus, your 16-pixel text is 1/6" tall on most—but not all—displays.

For responsive websites, we're going to use a unit of measurement you may not be so familiar with, the *em*, which will allow you to tailor the font size to the display.

Ems

An em is equal to the current font size of an element. For a more detailed explanation of ems, see "Ems" in Chapter 4.

In the code example here, the value of 1 em means the <p> font size will be equal to the page's default font size, which appears as 16 pixels on most devices. The value of 1.5 ems means the font size of the <h1> will be one and a half times the default, or 22 pixels, as you see in Figure 9-3:

```
body { font-size: 100%; }
p { font-size: 1em; }
h1 { font-size: 1.5em; }
```

This is the heading

This is the paragraph.

Figure 9-3. The heading is 1.5 times as large as the paragraph text.

If you're working with an existing website and need to convert pixels to ems, you can simply divide by 16; so, 16-pixel text is 1 em, and 32-pixel text is 2 ems. If you don't want to bother with a calculator, designer Jon Tan has a "Pixels to Ems Conversion Table for CSS" (*http://v1.jontan-gerine.com/silo/css/pixels-to-ems/*) that lists em equivalents for a wide range of font sizes, assuming you're using 100% as your default size.

Nested ems

There is something a little confusing about ems that you need to be aware of—their relative size is based on the font size of the parent element, not the default font size of the page. So, for example, suppose you have this code:

```
body { font-size: 100%; }
p { font-size: 2em; }
span { font-size: 1.5em; }

<div>This is 1 em.</div>
<p>This is 2 ems <span>(and 1.5 ems)</span>.</p>
```

The <div> doesn't have a font-size applied to it, so it will inherit the page's default size of 1 em.

The <p> has a font-size of 2 ems, so it will be twice as big as the text in the <div>.

The <span> has a font-size of 1.5 ems, but that's not based on the base font size; it's based on the font size of the containing element, the <p>, in which the text is already 2 ems. So the font size of the span, then, is 1.5 times 2, which works out to 3 ems. You can see the result in Figure 9-4.

This is 1 em.

This is 2 ems (and 1.5 ems).

Figure 9-4. The text in the span is much larger, because its font-size multiplies against the font-size of the containing element.

Although this can cause some unexpected results for elements that are nested inside other elements, if you put a little thought into your CSS, it won't often be a problem. Assign font-size values only when they're needed, not to every element.

Rems

Another unit of measurement that can be used to size text is the *rem*.

A rem is the same size as an em, but it's based on the root element's font size (<html>), not on the size of the parent element. This is handy because you don't have the issue with font sizes multiplying against each other like you do with ems.

When using rems, you need to set the document's font-size to 100% on the <html> element, instead of the <body> element as you would if you were just using ems:

```
html { font-size: 100%; }
```

However, there's a downside to using rems—not all the browsers support them. Specifically, IE 8 and earlier and Opera Mini won't see your font-size numbers at all if you're using rems.

There are two options for how to deal with this.

Using fallback values

The first option, if you want to make sure those older browsers are displaying the font size you intended, is to declare a fallback value in pixels.

Keep in mind that if you have two declarations for the same property on an element, the browser will use the *last* one. So you need to put the fallback first, and the rem value last. If the browser understands rems, it will use the second declaration, which is in rems. If it doesn't understand rems, it will ignore the second declaration and use the first, which is in pixels:

```
p { font-size: 18px; font-size: 1.1rem; }
```

To get the equivalent font-size in pixels—assuming your base font size is 100%—you just need to multiply by 16.

However, having to include pixels for everything is a lot of extra work. There's another, easier option.

Using browser defaults

The second option is not very precise, but is very easy. You'll probably only want to do this if you aren't actively supporting users with IE 8 and earlier. But even though you're not supporting those browsers, you should still use this easy fix, because it will make a big difference in the usability of the site.

If you don't want to bother with declaring fallback font sizes, you can let the browser use its chosen default values for each element (i.e., <h1> very large, <h2> slightly smaller, down to <p> at the default font size).

The browser *would* do this automatically, except that when we added a reset CSS to our site in Chapter 4, we set all the elements on the site to use a default font-size of 100%, which makes them all *exactly the same size*.

Go back into the reset CSS on your site and remove the font-size: 100%; that is applied to a list of several dozen different elements. Instead, make sure font-size: 100%; is *only* applied to the <html> element.

This may cause some issues with font sizes on your site, if something that was previously set to 100% is now a different size because you didn't apply a font-size to it in rems. But if you remember to remove the unwanted font-size from your reset before you start setting font sizes, you won't even notice.

As I mentioned, this option is not very precise. Fonts are not going to be the sizes you chose for them. In fact, nearly everything will be in your base font size of 100% (big enough to read), except for headings <h1> through <h6>, which will be a range of sizes. But having headings in appropriate sizes will make the page far more usable than if everything was the same size.

Deciding between ems and rems

So how do you decide between ems and rems? Each has disadvantages. Ems may cause weird things to happen if you nest elements with **font-size** applied, and rems require you to do extra work of adding fallback code (unless you don't support older browsers).

For most of your styles, ems should work all right, and you shouldn't frequently run into the nesting issue. And if you do have issues, you can often solve them by changing which particular elements you're applying **font-size** to.

Using ems also gives you the benefit of being able to change the **font-size** of entire sections of the site all at once—such as making everything in the **<header>** slightly larger.

You can also use both ems and rems on the same site, if you wish.

RELATIONSHIP BETWEEN SIZES

Once you've decided to start with 16 pixels for your content, where do you go from there? You know your headings need to be bigger, but how much?

Many websites make the **<h1>**s twice as big as the paragraph text, and that's a pretty good place to start:

```
p { font-size: 1em }
h1 { font-size: 2em }
```

There needs to be enough differentiation between your body text and the headings that the user can easily tell where the headings are when scanning the page.

But you won't only use the font size to differentiate heading levels. You can also use bold or different colors to make them stand out.

If you're using all the heading levels from **<h1>** to **<h6>**, you'll need to plan ahead so you have enough differentiation between them:

```
p { font-size: 1em }
h1 { font-size: 2em }
h2 { font-size: 1.8em }
h3 { font-size: 1.6em }
h4 { font-size: 1.4em }
h5 { font-size: 1.3em }
h6 { font-size: 1.1em }
```

On most sites you won't use all the heading levels, so you can try different sizes to see what works.

The font size you choose for headings can also be influenced by how long your headings are. If they are usually only a couple of words long, the type can be bigger so they fill the width of the line. If they are several words long, you may want to make the font size a bit smaller to minimize wrapping, or use a narrower typeface.

Want to go even fancier with the numbers? Use the "golden ratio" to determine the ratio of the sizes of your headings to other page elements. For more information, see "More Meaningful Typography" (*http://alistapart.com/article/more-meaningful-typography*) by Tim Brown on *A List Apart*.

LINE HEIGHT

The height of each line of text is important for legibility. This is also called *leading* in typographic terms, because it originally referred to adding bars of lead underneath the letters on a printing press, to add space between the lines.

On a web page, any text is rendered in a box (as we saw in Chapter 3), and the line height is the height of the box. Visually, a greater `line-height` will mean more space between lines of text.

`font-size` should be set using a unitless number so that the line height is always proportional to the text. You don't even need percentage or ems—it's just a number:

```
p { font-size: 1em; line-height: 1; }
```

A `line-height` of 1 means that the box is exactly as tall as the type, no matter what the font size is (i.e., from the top of the ascenders on the tallest letters to the bottom of the descenders on the lowercase letters). The text on the first line in Figure 9-5 has a `line-height` of 1, while the second line has a `line-height` of 2, which means the line height is twice as tall as the font size. You can see the extra space.

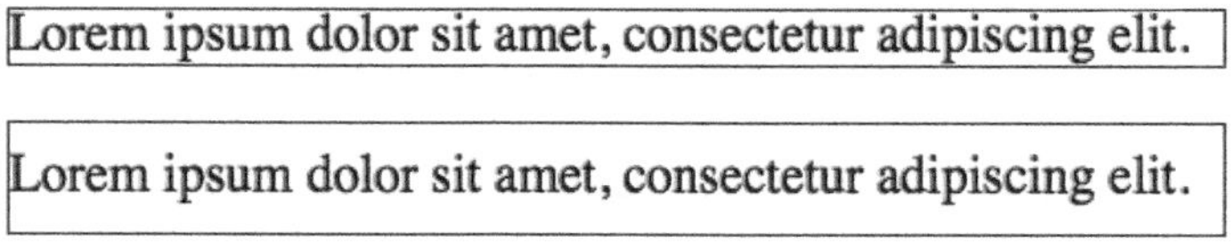

| Lorem ipsum dolor sit amet, consectetur adipiscing elit. |

| Lorem ipsum dolor sit amet, consectetur adipiscing elit. |

Figure 9-5. Comparing text with a `line-height` of 1 and text with a `line-height` of 2.

This unitless number you're using for `line-height` is measured against the `font-size` of the element, so the line height will adjust according to the font size.

The text is always vertically centered in the box created by the `line-height`, as you see in Figure 9-5.

A good benchmark for line height is 1.4, but it can vary a bit according to which typeface you use, or other factors.

If lines are too close together, it's difficult for the user to focus on only one line at once. You can see in Figure 9-6 that the text looks cramped and is hard to read.

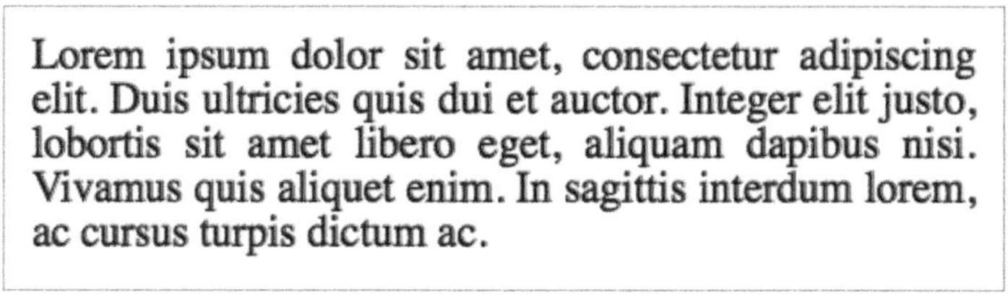

Lorem ipsum dolor sit amet, consectetur adipiscing elit. Duis ultricies quis dui et auctor. Integer elit justo, lobortis sit amet libero eget, aliquam dapibus nisi. Vivamus quis aliquet enim. In sagittis interdum lorem, ac cursus turpis dictum ac.

Figure 9-6. Text with a `line-height` of 1.

Lines that are too far apart are also troublesome. If they are too far apart, it's difficult for the user's eyes to get from the end of one line to the beginning of the next line.

A line height of 2 will create too much space between the lines for easy reading, as shown in Figure 9-7. Using such a tall line height on large blocks of text will make it difficult to read, but this effect could be used sparingly on small blocks of text like quotations.

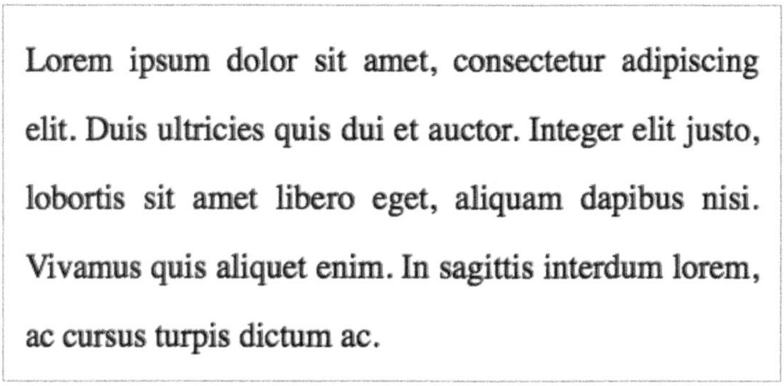

Lorem ipsum dolor sit amet, consectetur adipiscing

elit. Duis ultricies quis dui et auctor. Integer elit justo,

lobortis sit amet libero eget, aliquam dapibus nisi.

Vivamus quis aliquet enim. In sagittis interdum lorem,

ac cursus turpis dictum ac.

Figure 9-7. Text with a `line-height` of 2.

As you see in Figure 9-8, a line height of 1.4 makes the text very easy to read and allows for breathing space.

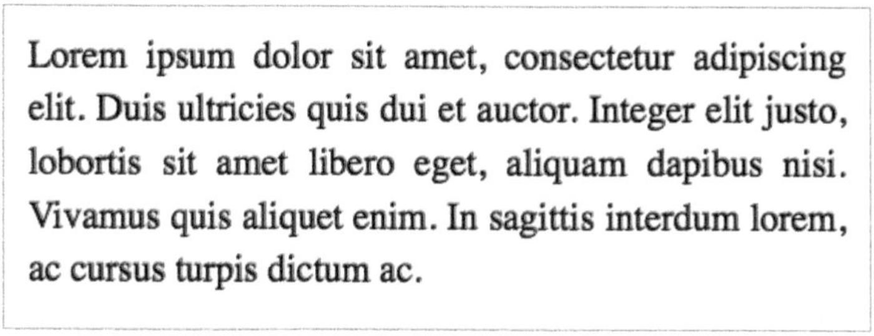

> Lorem ipsum dolor sit amet, consectetur adipiscing elit. Duis ultricies quis dui et auctor. Integer elit justo, lobortis sit amet libero eget, aliquam dapibus nisi. Vivamus quis aliquet enim. In sagittis interdum lorem, ac cursus turpis dictum ac.

Figure 9-8. Text with a line-height of 1.4.

The width of the text also influences which line height will look appropriate on the page. The wider the lines of text are, the more space you need between the lines. You can use media queries to make this adjustment.

Additionally, heavier text (think: thicker lines in the letters) will need a greater line height than would lighter text.

Line Length

For legibility, the optimum line length (the technical term is the *measure*) for large blocks of text is 45–75 characters, including spaces.

In responsive sites, you especially need to pay attention to this, because the width of your content will vary according to viewport width.

Super-long lines, as in Figure 9-9, are difficult to read, because it's hard for your eyes to move from one line to the next.

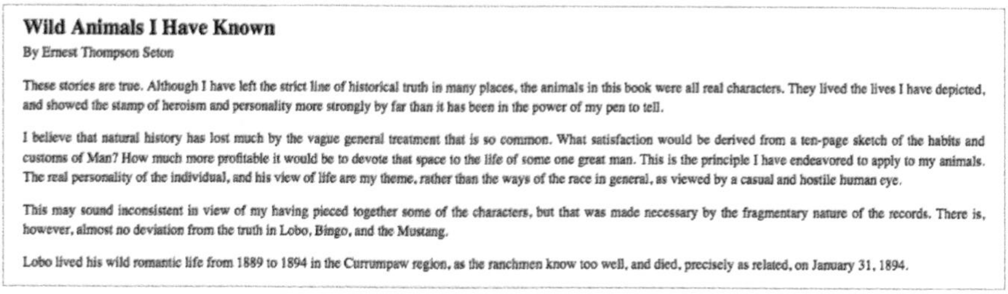

> **Wild Animals I Have Known**
> By Ernest Thompson Seton
>
> These stories are true. Although I have left the strict line of historical truth in many places, the animals in this book were all real characters. They lived the lives I have depicted, and showed the stamp of heroism and personality more strongly by far than it has been in the power of my pen to tell.
>
> I believe that natural history has lost much by the vague general treatment that is so common. What satisfaction would be derived from a ten-page sketch of the habits and customs of Man? How much more profitable it would be to devote that space to the life of some one great man. This is the principle I have endeavored to apply to my animals. The real personality of the individual, and his view of life are my theme, rather than the ways of the race in general, as viewed by a casual and hostile human eye.
>
> This may sound inconsistent in view of my having pieced together some of the characters, but that was made necessary by the fragmentary nature of the records. There is, however, almost no deviation from the truth in Lobo, Bingo, and the Mustang.
>
> Lobo lived his wild romantic life from 1889 to 1894 in the Currumpaw region, as the ranchmen know too well, and died, precisely as related, on January 31, 1894.

Figure 9-9. Very long lines of text are difficult to read.

Very short lines, as in Figure 9-10, are tiring to read because your eyes have to move back and forth too often.

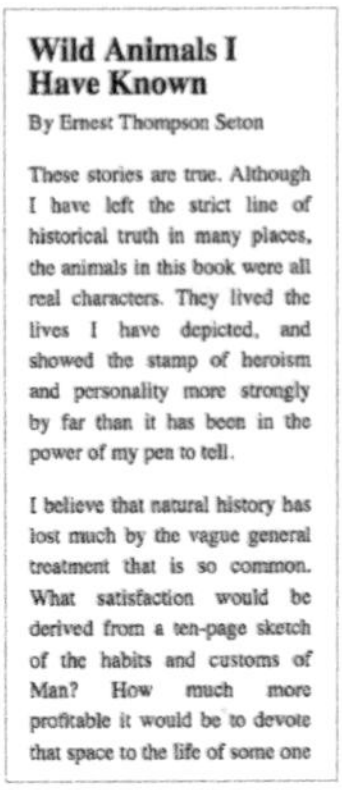

Figure 9-10. Your eyes will tire quickly when you're reading very short lines of text.

Remember that these numbers are a guideline, not set in stone. You'll need to try them out on your page and think about what looks good.

TESTING LINE LENGTH

To make sure your line length always falls in an acceptable range, you need to be able to test it without counting characters every time. One easy way is to put a `<span>` around the 45th to 75th characters and use CSS to highlight the text, as in Figure 9-11. You could give the text a background color, like in this example, or make the text a color like red that stands out on the page:

```
<p>These stories are true. Although I have left <span
class="testing">the strict line of historical</span>
truth in many places, the animals in this book were all
real characters.</p>

.testing { background-color: #aaa; }
```

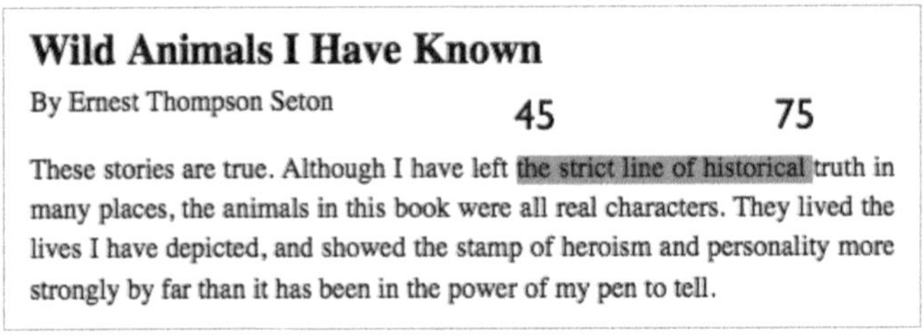

Figure 9-11. Count out the characters from 45 to 75 and use CSS to highlight them.

If you want to do a quick check of any site, there's a bookmarklet (*http://codepen.io/chriscoyier/pen/atebf*) by Chris Coyier that does the same thing—it colors the 45th–75th characters red in any text element on any page. You just need to click the bookmarklet, then click to select any element on the page; there's no need to touch the HTML or CSS.

If you're testing your own site and refreshing the same page over and over again, though, you'll probably find it easier to add a `<span>` rather than having to use the bookmarklet each time you refresh.

ADJUSTING MARGINS AND FONT SIZE

So, you're probably wondering how you get your text to always be the optimal number of characters per line, when the website can be any width. This is actually pretty easy.

As an example, we'll use a one-column site, but you can do the same thing within individual columns in a multi-column layout as well.

When you begin designing a website you start from the smallest screen, the size of a mobile phone (resize your browser window to 320 pixels wide). Designing at that size, try to get the number of characters per line to be in the range of 45–75, although it might be slightly less. You'll want to make your horizontal margins pretty narrow, although the margins shouldn't be zero—if your text is touching the edge of the screen, it's harder to read.

By giving the element a width of 94% and left/right margins of `auto`, you're telling the browser to split the remaining 6% into margins of 3% on each side:

```
article {
    margin: 15px auto;
    width: 94%;
}
```

Next, slowly make your browser window wider until the highlighted text goes all the way to the end of the line, as in Figure 9-12. This means you have 75 characters on the first line—if you make the window any wider, you'll be over the maximum. This is where you need to add a media query.

If you have a tool like MQTest.io (*http://mqtest.io*) open in a separate tab of the same browser window, you can easily see the width of the window. In this example, it's 31 ems, so that's where we'll add the media query.

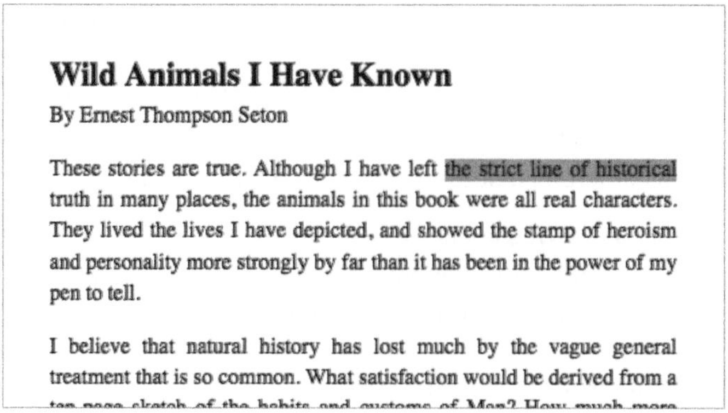

Wild Animals I Have Known

By Ernest Thompson Seton

These stories are true. Although I have left the strict line of historical truth in many places, the animals in this book were all real characters. They lived the lives I have depicted, and showed the stamp of heroism and personality more strongly by far than it has been in the power of my pen to tell.

I believe that natural history has lost much by the vague general treatment that is so common. What satisfaction would be derived from a

Figure 9-12. Make the browser window wider until your highlighted text goes to the end of the first line.

To make the text stay within the 45–75 character range, we'll increase the margins:

```
@media screen and (min-width: 31em) {
    article { width: 70% }
}
```

In Figure 9-13, you'll see that when the browser window is slightly wider than 31 ems, the page has wider margins, and now the text is right in the middle of the 45–75 character range.

Again, make the browser window wider until the highlighted text goes to the end of the line, as in Figure 9-14.

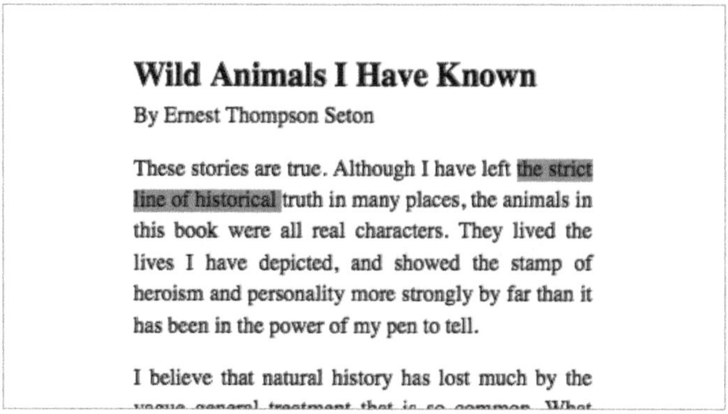

Wild Animals I Have Known

By Ernest Thompson Seton

These stories are true. Although I have left the strict line of historical truth in many places, the animals in this book were all real characters. They lived the lives I have depicted, and showed the stamp of heroism and personality more strongly by far than it has been in the power of my pen to tell.

I believe that natural history has lost much by the vague general treatment that is so common. What

Figure 9-13. After increasing the margins, the first line is in the middle of the ideal range of 45–75 characters.

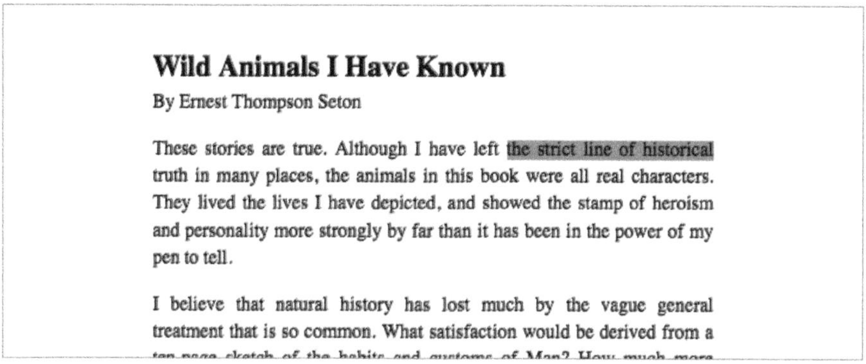

Figure 9-14. Again, make the browser window wider until your highlighted text goes to the end of the first line.

Now we're at a viewport width of 40 ems. This time, instead of increasing the margins, we're going to increase the font size, which will reduce the number of characters per line:

```
@media screen and (min-width: 40em) {
    article { font-size: 1.1em }
}
```

The result is what you see in Figure 9-15.

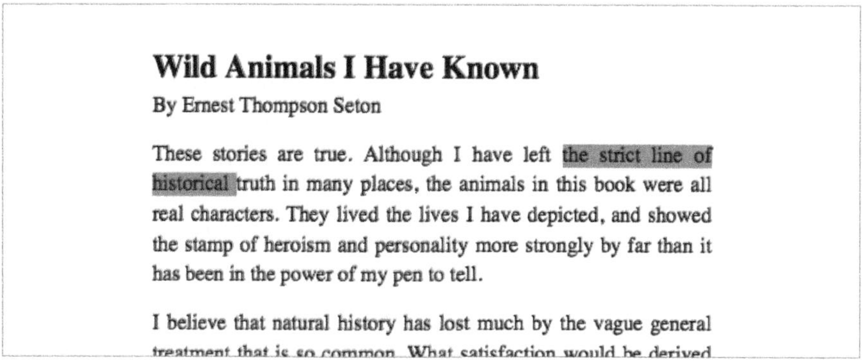

Figure 9-15. With an increased font size, the first line is again in the middle of the 45–75 character range.

You'll notice we changed the font size on the `<article>` element, which will increase the size of everything inside that element—the heading as well as the paragraph text—so that everything will continue to be proportional.

You can keep going by making your browser window wider, increasing the margins and/or the font size. If the site had additional content, you could split it into multiple columns at some point, as we learned in Chapter 5.

But at some point, you aren't going to want to make your site any wider.

You can make this one-column layout look good on narrow phones all the way up to regular desktop monitors, by increasing the margins and font size. But aiming toward even wider screens, there's a point at which it won't make sense to increase the font size anymore. At that point, you can just tell the layout to stop getting wider using `max-width`, as we learned in "Setting a Maximum Width" in Chapter 5.

HYPHENATION

Hyphenation is a useful part of web typography, as it allows more consistent line lengths. This makes reading easier, and makes your design look more polished. Hyphenation makes it possible to fit more characters on a line, which can mean less scrolling.

On the Web, the hyphenation property is new in CSS3. It's not supported in all browsers and requires prefixes in the browsers that do support it. But it's handy when available. If you use `hyphens`, browsers that don't support it will simply not hyphenate the text. It will still look fine. The following code will make all the text on your website hyphenated:

```
body {
    -webkit-hyphens: auto;
    -moz-hyphens: auto;
    -ms-hyphens: auto;
    -o-hyphens: auto;
    hyphens: auto;
}
```

However, there are some cases where you won't want certain text to be hyphenated, so you can exclude those elements.

For example, code samples shouldn't be hyphenated, because including hyphens in code would be confusing:

```
code {
    -webkit-hyphens: none;
    -moz-hyphens: none;
    -ms-hyphens: none;
    -o-hyphens: none;
    hyphens: none;
}
```

Depending on your design, you may want to turn off hyphens for certain levels of headings, blockquotes, or other elements.

Note that you must have `<html lang=en>` in your `<head>`, as described in Chapter 3, because hyphenation is language-dependent.

OVERFLOW WRAP

Occasionally you'll come across really long words or character strings that don't fit in the line of text and don't get automatic hyphenation. This might be the case for a made-up word like supercalifragilisticexpialidocious, or a URL that has long pieces without slashes or other characters that automatically break.

By adding the style `overflow-wrap: break-word`, you'll allow all those extra-long words to wrap.

`overflow-wrap` is part of CSS3 and doesn't yet work in all browsers. However, it's simply replacing a previous property from CSS2, `word-wrap`, so by including both in your CSS you'll cover pretty much all of the browsers:

```
body { word-wrap: break-word; overflow-wrap: breakword; }
```

[NOTE]

By the way, underscores in URLs won't automatically break, but dashes will: this is one reason it's better to use dashes instead of underscores in directory names or filenames on your website.

Whitespace

Whitespace, as a design concept, refers to the empty parts of your layout—the margins, the space between lines of text, the space around elements on the page, and the space between columns. It's not necessarily white, but the background color of the area.

There needs to be whitespace around text. If your text runs right up to the edges of the page or touches other elements on the page, it will be difficult to read.

Whitespace increases legibility by making it easier for the eyes to focus on the text.

A lot of websites try to cram in as much information as possible at once, as in Figure 9-16. This makes it hard to focus on individual items on the page, and just looking at the page increases your stress level. Adding whitespace, through line height, padding, and margins, will create a more balanced and open layout.

For more information on using whitespace in web design, check out:

- Paul Boag's "Why whitespace matters" (*http://boagworld.com/ design/why-whitespace-matters/*) on *Boagworld*

- Mark Boulton's "Whitespace" (*http://alistapart.com/article/white-space*) on *A List Apart*

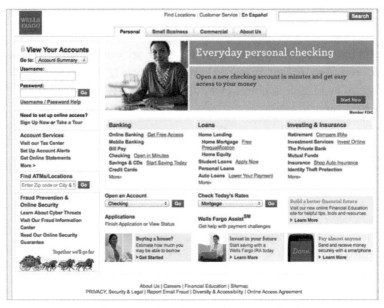

Figure 9-16. This website has a lot of text without enough whitespace.

Margins and Padding

If you're starting your CSS with reset styles, all of your content elements will have been reset to margins of zero, allowing you to choose your own. To start, you need to set margins for `<p>` and all the headings (`<h1>` to `<h6>`) so that there's vertical space between each of them.

None of these elements need left or right margins (although you may add them for stylistic purposes). Top and bottom margins should be set in ems, so that they increase and decrease in proportion to the **font-size**. This is in contrast to the left and right margins and padding, which are in percentages so they change in proportion to the width of the containing element.

The margins you choose will vary based on the **font-size** and typeface of each element. A larger typeface may need relatively smaller margins. Don't forget that the **line-height** will also add to the visible space between elements.

Often you'll give headings a smaller **margin-bottom** so they are closer to the text below them, and a larger **margin-top** to separate them from the previous section.

A good place to start is to set the top and bottom margins for each of these elements to 1 em, and then adjust each individually to what looks visually appropriate after you've set the **font-family**, **font-size**, and **line-height**:

```
h1, h2, h3, h4, h5, h6, p { margin: 1em 0; }
```

[NOTE]

Earlier we discussed using rems instead of ems to size fonts. When dealing with margins, you should use ems, not rems, because the margins should be relative to the current element, not to the root document.

Changing Typeface for Screen Size

Using fancy decorative typefaces can look really good on a larger screen, where's there's plenty of space. But sometimes that typeface doesn't work as well on a smaller screen, such as in Figure 9-17.

Figure 9-17. A decorative typeface may not look as good on a small screen.

Although the intro text still looks decent on a small screen, it takes up the whole screen—and you can't even see the whole section of text. Normally you could just make the font size smaller, but with this particular typeface—especially because it's in all capitals—it would be difficult to read at a smaller size, so it's only slightly smaller than on the wide screen.

Although the typeface is part of this site's branding, sometimes a trade-off is necessary. In this case, it would be better to use a different typeface for smaller screens, and not use all capital letters.

This is simple to accomplish using a media query. For example, a media query at 30 ems could make the type for the narrow screen size smaller, change it from all capitals to normal text, and change the font family from the current typeface, Populaire, to something simple like Helvetica. The entire intro paragraph would then fit on the screen at once, and would be much easier to read:

```
#intro { font-size: 1.2em; text-transform: uppercase;
font-family: Populaire, sans-serif; }

@media screen and (max-width:30em) {
    #intro { font-size: 1em; text-transform: none;
    font-family: Helvetica, sans-serif; }
}
```

Summary

The text on your website is key to communicating your message, so it needs to be both easy to read and visually appealing.

The first choice you'll make is the typeface. There are thousands available for you to use, many for free. Make sure to pick a well-designed typeface that's appropriate for your message.

Fonts are the digital files that are needed to display the characters on the screen. You will embed the fonts you plan to use on your website, either hosting your own files or using a font service. You need to also specify backup fonts that can be substituted if the font file isn't available or if it can't be used by the browser.

When sizing the text on your site, set a default font size for the entire page using a percentage, then size elements relatively using ems or rems. Body text should be at least 1 em, so it will be easy to read for most users. Setting an appropriate line height is also important for readability.

Setting a good line length makes the text easier to read. Use media queries to make sure your line length stays in the optimal range no matter what size viewport the page is being displayed in. Use whitespace to make the text on the page look better.

Keep in mind that with responsive websites, you'll lose control over the exact appearance of the text. Embrace the flexibility, and make your content look good across all devices.

Next, in Chapter 10, we'll look at how to create responsive navigation and header layouts.

[10]

Navigation and Header Layout

Making your navigation and other elements in the page header responsive is one of the most challenging parts of designing a responsive website.

The *header* of a web page consists of the section at the top of the page that contains the site's branding, and usually contains the site's main navigation as well as supplemental items like form fields or links for search and site login. The header is generally consistent throughout the website.

The components in the header perform two very important functions: they tell the user what site he is on, and they allow the user to navigate through the site.

In this chapter, we'll go back to our example site and add in some simple navigation styles. Then we'll look at examples of some common patterns for how navigation can be displayed on mobile-sized screens, and how those navigation layouts will adapt across screen widths.

We'll also look at how to incorporate site branding, search, and other components into a unified header.

Responsive Navigation

No matter what your responsive navigation looks like, the key is to start with straightforward HTML and then use media queries to change the CSS that styles the navigation, so it looks the way you want it to at different viewport widths.

Using our example site, we're going to add some basic styles to make our <nav> look like a real navigation, then add a media query to change the navigation style for wider viewports.

START SMALL

We're going to go back to our narrowest view of the example site and start there. The navigation is an unordered list, as you see in Figure 10-1. Here's the code:

```
<nav role="navigation">
<ul>
<li><a href="/">Home</a></li>
<li><a href="/about/">About</a></li>
<li><a href="/links/">Links</a></li>
<li><a href="/contact/">Contact</a></li>
</ul>
</nav>
```

Figure 10-1. Going back to the narrowest view of the site, the navigation is in an unordered list.

STYLING YOUR LIST

A bulleted list of links is usable, but doesn't look very good.

First, we're going to add some code to get rid of the bullets, and remove the margins and padding so the list items aren't indented (this is what you see in Figure 10-2):

```
nav ul { list-style-type: none; padding: 0; margin: 0; }
nav li { margin: 0; padding: 0; }
```

Next, we're going to make the links into boxes, which will look a bit nicer. We'll add a border around each list item, give them a little background color, and add some padding and margins to give them a good touch target size, as you see in Figure 10-3:

```
nav ul { list-style-type: none; padding: 0; margin: 25px
0 0; }
nav li { border: 1px solid #666; background-color: #eee;
padding: 10px 1em; margin: 3px 0 0; }
```

Figure 10-2. We've styled the unordered list to remove the bullets, margins, and padding.

Figure 10-3. The plain links have now turned into gray boxes.

Next, we'll make the text a little bigger, center the text in each box, and remove the underlines (you can see the result in Figure 10-4):

```
nav ul { list-style-type: none; padding: 0; margin: 25px
0 0; }
nav li { border: 1px solid #666; background-color: #eee;
padding: 10px 1em; margin: 3px 0 0; text-align: center; }
nav li a { text-decoration: none; font-size: 1.2em; }
```

Figure 10-4. Centering the text in each box and removing the underlines makes it look a bit nicer.

At this point, we're still pretty much worrying about the layout and not the visual design of the site, so we're only adding basics. Your finished site would definitely be more designed than this!

But as far as layout, we have a navigation for the narrowest viewports that looks pretty decent. So let's move on to a wider viewport.

HORIZONTAL NAVIGATION

Like I did before, I'm going to start with my browser window at the narrowest viewport width, and slowly make it wider until the design "breaks," or starts to not look good. That's where I need a breakpoint.

There's no requirement that I use the same breakpoint as I did when I made layout variations, so I'm not going to worry about those numbers—I'll just focus on the navigation and figure out where it starts to look bad.

At a viewport width of around 30 ems (480 pixels), the navigation items start to look too wide, as you see in Figure 10-5.

I'm going to adjust the navigation style at this point so all four items are in a horizontal line, but only when the viewport is wider than 30 ems.

Figure 10-5. At this viewport width, the navigation links no longer look good.

To do that, I'm going to give each list item a style of **display: block** so they act like boxes instead of list items, and then float them to the left so they appear one after another in a horizontal row, as you will see in Figure 10-6:

```
@media only screen and (min-width: 30em) {
    nav li { display: block; float: left; }
}
```

Figure 10-6. For wider viewport widths, we're making the vertical navigation into a horizontal navigation—but it doesn't look quite right.

After doing that, I have two problems. First, the navigation overlaps the top of the article element. Second, each navigation item is only as big as it needs to be to contain the text, but it would be nicer if each were the same size.

Let's tackle the second problem first. I simply give li a width of 25% (you'll see the result in Figure 10-7):

```
@media only screen and (min-width: 30em) {
    nav li { display: block; float: left; width: 25%; }
}
```

Figure 10-7. Now the navigation buttons are equal width.

The other problem is a little trickier. Normally, I would just clear the next element after the floating element, but because the <nav> is the last thing in the <header> element, doing this wouldn't move the bottom edge of the <header> element downward.

The solution is to add padding to the bottom of the <nav> element to make space for the navigation. I'll use ems for the padding so that it can change if the text size changes (you'll see how this makes it look in Figure 10-8):

```
@media only screen and (min-width: 30em) {
    nav li { display: block; float: left; width: 25%; }
    nav { padding-bottom: 3em; }
}
```

Figure 10-8. We've fixed the navigation buttons so they don't overlap the following element.

That navigation style continues to look good at even wider viewport widths, as you see in Figure 10-9, so there's no need to add another breakpoint. Navigation done!

Figure 10-9. At a wider viewport width, the layout still looks good.

Branding

Generally, the first thing your users see when they visit any page of your website is your branding. Users who have clicked a link from somewhere else need to verify that they've arrived on the correct site, and users who are navigating from another page on your site need to be reassured they're still on the same site.

It doesn't take a lot. The site or company logo, or even just the site title, is generally all that is needed. Often you'll include a tagline, so new site visitors will know exactly what your company does.

For a responsive site, it's often as simple as changing the size of the logo or title text to fit well on the screen, but sometimes you have to get a little creative.

In Figure 10-10, instead of using the full logo on the small-screen design, the designers separated the swirly bits and moved them off to the side of the "Dorigati" text, making a horizontal branding that takes up less space than the full logo would have. The company's tagline, "Fine wines since 1858," is at the top of the small- and medium-screen designs but is further down the page on the wide-screen design, although it still appears on the screen without scrolling.

Making the branding fit well on different viewport widths can be challenging when working with a brand that has an existing logo that's *always* displayed the same way. Established brands often have very specific style rules for how their logos are to be displayed. You'll need to get stakeholders on board with the idea of responsive design so that hopefully they'll be open to being flexible with the company's branding.

It's a big challenge to fit a bunch of important stuff in a small space. The more flexible everyone is, the better able you'll be to rise to that challenge.

Another option might be using the company logo on wider versions of the design, but only using the text of the company name in the small-screen version, as you see in Figure 10-11. If you're not using the logo on the smaller-screen versions of the design, you still need to be consistent with other design elements, so that cross-platform users will have the sense that it's the same website. In this example, the consistent colors carry the brand across screen widths.

Figure 10-10. The size and placement of the logo and company name change depending on the width of the screen.

Figure 10-11. On the Sprungmarker website, the narrow-width design only displays the company name and not the logo.

Navigation Links

The navigation is one of the most important parts of a website. If it's not designed well, your users will have trouble getting from one section of the website to another.

MAKE IT FLEXIBLE

Before thinking about what your navigation should *look* like in the site design, you need to decide what links are in the navigation. Don't try to design a navigation using generic link text, like "Nav Item #1" or similar. Invariably, the text in your generic links will be of much different lengths than the actual navigation items, and what seemed to fit perfectly will end up being a big mess.

At the same time, even if you know what the navigation items are going to be, remember they aren't set in stone forever. The needs of the site or organization may change, and you may need to add or remove links in the future. Is your navigation flexible enough to accommodate changes?

This is especially relevant if you'll be handing off a finished site to a client or a team that may not have the web skills to make significant design changes later. It should be relatively easy for them to make changes without breaking the design.

WHAT DO USERS WANT TO DO?

When designing a responsive navigation, just as with the layout, you'll start with the small screen first.

The great thing about designing navigation for a small screen is it forces you to analyze what you're including in your navigation, and make choices as to which items are really important.

In the past, a common way to design a website navigation went like this: 1) make a list of every section you're going to have on your website; 2) get the stakeholders together to do a card sort to divide the links into categories; 3) make a multi-level navigation based on those categories.

Don't do that.

Remember, first of all, that your navigation is for your users, not your stakeholders. Design the navigation around how users will be able to successfully navigate the site. Don't just make it an inventory of the site's content, or worse, a reflection of the company's organizational chart. Refer to the "Information architecture" section in Chapter 7 for more about creating an information architecture for the site.

Hopefully you've already sorted out what content actually needs to go on the site, and gotten rid of some dead weight. Now think about how your users will want to use that content. Use analytics from your current site, if applicable, to see which pages users actually visit frequently.

I love the responsive site from the city council in Manchester, England shown in Figure 10-12. On most city websites, the most prominent elements are news and information about elected officials. Not so in Manchester. The council has clearly focused on what people are asking for—bins (a fancy British word for trash and recycling cans) may not be the most glamorous part of city government, but it's likely one of the topics that users most often seek information on.

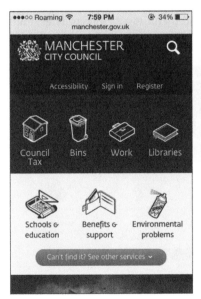 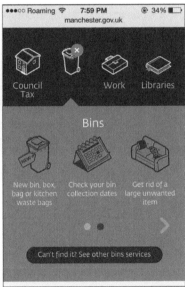

Figure 10-12. The Manchester City Council website focuses on the things that users will actually be looking for.

The site's designers didn't take up valuable space on the tiny screen with press releases or photos of the council members—they focused on the information that people are visiting the website to get.

Icons do take up space on the screen where more options could be fit in, but because the initial screen is only for the navigation, using icons keeps it from appearing too dense, and also makes each touch target a size that's easy to tap. A lot of sites use icons that don't actually add anything to the site, but in this case, the designers did a great job of using icons that are straightforward and obvious.

Additionally, they used language that's clear for the users, rather than the "official" names of departments and such. Everybody knows what "bins" refers to (at least in the United Kingdom), and this makes it much easier for the user than trying to wade through phrases like "Refuse Collection," "Collection Services," or "Solid Waste & Recycling" (all of which I found as navigation items on other cities' websites).

On the wider version of the site, as shown in Figure 10-13, the site's designers had space to add a supplemental description below the main icons, and some additional frequently accessed links below the second row of icons (e.g., "Schools & education Including... Holiday dates, Find a school").

Figure 10-13. On the wider-screen layout, there's room for additional icons, and supplemental descriptions below the icons.

Note that even though there are more icons visible on the wide-screen design, the small-screen users aren't missing anything. All the links to services are available no matter what device you are using, via a button at the bottom that says, "Can't find it? See other services."

GOAL-BASED NAVIGATION

When designing for a desktop screen, there's plenty of room to add a lot of navigation options—and many sites take advantage of that. After all, you want to make it as easy as possible for users to get to what they need.

In fact, there's been a long-standing, unofficial "three-click" rule in web design: every page on your site must be no more than three clicks away from anywhere else on the site. Having detailed, multi-layered navigation menus was often the way to make that happen.

It sounds good in theory—the fewer clicks, the better—but if it's difficult for the users to figure out what to click on, it doesn't matter how many times they click.

Studies have shown that users don't mind additional clicks, as long as they have confidence they are going down the correct path toward their goal, and as long as each click makes them feel like they are moving forward.

It's the frustrating clicks that they mind, where they feel like they're getting sent in the wrong direction, or that they're no closer to their destination.

In Figure 10-14, you'll see what the navigation on the GoDaddy website looked like a couple of years ago. The menu had multiple options on each tab—and each of those options had its own submenu on hover.

Sure, you could get to any part of the site with very few clicks, but you needed to know exactly what you were looking for, and be able to figure out how it was categorized.

For someone with a technical background, this is probably not a big deal, but for potential customers without that background, such as small business owners who want to set up their first websites, it's incredibly confusing. If it's too difficult to get started, customers might give up and look for a different website that will meet their needs with less effort.

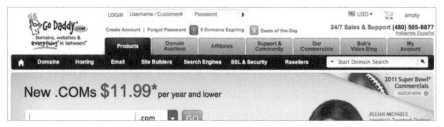

Figure 10-14. The old GoDaddy website had a lot of options, and new customers might not have known what they all meant.

After a redesign, as you see in Figure 10-15, the site's navigation appears much simpler. It's clear that GoDaddy is trying to hook in new customers. The four most visible menu items are based on goals, rather than products. For those who are not familiar with website terminology, "Build your Website" will give them a very clear path to follow.

And for those users who know exactly what they want, all the other options are still there, under "All Products." It takes an additional click to get to them, but that's all right.

Figure 10-15. The new GoDaddy website has clear paths for new users to take.

Although this isn't a responsive site, it's a good example of goal-based website navigation. GoDaddy has similar navigation options on its separate mobile site.

KEEP IT CONSISTENT

Whatever changes you make to the navigation of your responsive website for different viewport widths, remember that to your users, it's still the same site. If the navigation they see on a mobile phone is vastly different from what they see on a desktop screen, your users will get confused.

Users might access the navigation differently depending on the width of the screen, but the same primary navigation items should be there, in the same order. If the desktop-width design has prominent links on top for frequently accessed functions such as login, your users will expect to find those on the small-screen version of the site too.

It's more common for the navigation to be different on a website with separate mobile and desktop sites, but it also can be an issue on responsive sites.

As an example, look at the Ikea website—desktop and mobile versions—in Figure 10-16. The desktop site has a list of "Departments," and the mobile site has a list of "Products."

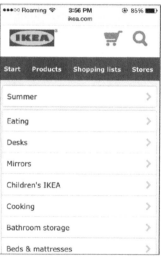

Figure 10-16. The desktop and mobile versions of the Ikea website have slightly different categories in their navigation.

The two lists are very similar. For example, they both have "Cooking" and "Decoration," but while the desktop site has "Dining," the mobile site has "Eating." Those two links actually lead to the same items.

And while the desktop site has "Bedroom," encompassing beds, mattresses, textiles, and bedroom furniture like nightstands, the mobile site has simply "Beds & mattresses." There's a separate textiles link, but none of the options seem to cover nightstands.

Now, while I'm sure there could be many arguments over which navigation is better, the real problem is that they are *different*.

If you're browsing the site during your lunch hour on your work computer to pick out a nightstand, you'll remember that the "Bedroom" link got you to the nightstand section. Then suppose that later that evening you're watching TV and want to take another look at nightstands, so you pull out your mobile phone. You probably won't notice the navigation is different—you'll just click on "Products." The options look similar, so you'll click on "Beds & mattresses," assuming it's the same link you clicked on from the desktop site. And you won't have any idea why the nightstands are now missing.

This is one of the drawbacks of having separate desktop and mobile sites—you're a lot more likely to end up having a different user interface, which confuses people. But it can still be a problem on a responsive site.

It's common for designers to assume that mobile device users want or need different options, and hide things on the small-screen version of a responsive site.

Keep in mind, though, that often they are the exact same users, just using a different device, and they expect the same website.

KEEP IT SIMPLE

You've already learned that you need to make sure your responsive site will work on all devices, regardless of capability or screen size. This is especially important for your navigation, because if your navigation doesn't function for some users, the site is essentially unusable for them.

Keep in mind that just like the layout, your navigation needs to start with basic HTML, for users whose devices don't support media queries or JavaScript.

Although some of the more complicated types of responsive navigation rely on JavaScript, you need to make sure the navigation works (i.e., the navigation items are visible and clickable) at any screen size and on any device type. Users without JavaScript will likely be a very small percentage of your users, so you don't have to make it look great for them; you just have to make it work.

Keep in mind, also, that the more complicated your code is, the harder it will be to maintain, and the more likely it is that something will break if you make changes to the site. Think about whether you really need that fancy flying navigation, or if a simple row of links will suffice. Is it worth the trade-off?

Navigation Patterns

Most nonresponsive sites that are designed for desktop monitors follow the same general pattern for their main navigation: a horizontal bar across the top, as you see in Figure 10-17.

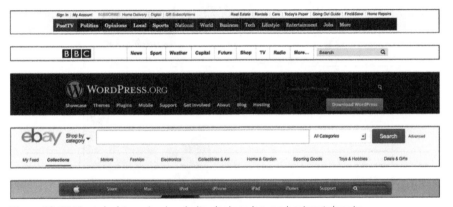

Figure 10-17. Most desktop-sized website designs have a horizontal main navigation bar across the top.

Although left navigation was popular several years ago, as the Web has matured this has gone out of fashion, as well it should: studies have shown that left navigation is far less effective than top navigation.

You sometimes still see a left navigation on major sites, such as in Figure 10-18, but it's generally used as a list of topics, while the main functional navigation is still at the top of the page.

For the most part, responsive navigation that works across all viewport widths—from mobile to wide-screen monitors—is going to follow this existing pattern for the wide-screen design, because it's already familiar to everybody who uses the Web.

When working with responsive websites for the first time, many design-ers find that their biggest challenge is the navigation. But the problem isn't really making a *responsive* navigation; it's making a good *small-screen* navigation. Once you get that down, adding media queries to change or move it at wider viewport widths is a piece of cake.

Figure 10-18. Left navigation is sometimes used for lists of topics or categories, although primary navigation items remain at the top.

There are a lot of great small-screen navigation designs out there, and they generally follow one of several *patterns*—that is, they can be grouped according to shared characteristics.

We're going to look at a few basic patterns for responsive navigation, providing explanations of how they work and showing examples on real websites.

Beyond the patterns we look at in this book, there are many others out there. A good resource is Brad Frost's website Responsive Patterns (*http://bradfrost.github.io/this-is-responsive/patterns.html*). There, you'll find not only navigation patterns, including examples with HTML and CSS you can dissect, but also patterns for responsive layouts, forms, and other modules.

Keep in mind that you should use the <nav> element, and the corresponding WAI-ARIA role, to code the navigation, as we discussed in Chapter 3:

```
<nav role="navigation">
  ...
</nav>
```

[NOTE]

To find more user interface patterns for mobile devices, check out Theresa Neil's *Mobile Design Pattern Gallery: UI Patterns for iOS, Android and More* (*http://www.mobiledesignpatterngallery.com*).

TOP NAVIGATION

The easiest pattern for dealing with your navigation on a responsive site is having all your navigation items at the top of the page regardless of screen width, and using media queries and CSS layout styles to rearrange them depending on the width of the screen.

You saw the code for a simple version of this in the example website we worked on earlier in the chapter, but here we'll look at a couple of examples on real websites.

You might want to start by having the navigation items vertically stacked on the small screen and then move them to a horizontal bar at a wider viewport width, like on the Enoch's Fish & Chips website in Figure 10-19.

Figure 10-19. The items in a top navigation will rearrange as the viewport width changes.

In this example, the HTML elements are very simple:

```
<ul class="nav">
    <li><a href="#food">Food</a></li>
    <li><a href="#fish">Fish</a></li>
    <li><a href="#news">News</a></li>
    <li><a href="#contact">Contact</a></li>
</ul>
```

Media queries are then used to link to separate stylesheets, which use absolute positioning to change the location of the navigation items depending on the width of the screen.

If you've heard that responsive websites always look boring and blocky, the Enoch's site certainly proves that they don't have to.

The Food Sense website also rearranges its navigation items at the top of the page. In Figure 10-20, you can see how the navigation items and site logo stay at the top of the page (or left, before the content), no matter the viewport width.

Figure 10-20. Media queries and basic layout styles can be used to rearrange the navigation and site branding at the top of the page depending on viewport width.

The elements at the top of the page are in a <header> element—the navigation is an unordered list inside a <nav> element, and the logo is an <h1>. Similarly, the site uses basic layout styles like float and margins inside media queries to rearrange the navigation at the different viewport widths.

The wider layouts have icons next to each navigation item, which are simply background images that are removed at the narrower widths with background-image: none.

But if you have a lot of navigation items, this just isn't going to work. On small screens, the navigation will end up taking up the whole phone screen, like in Figure 10-21.

Figure 10-21. If you have too many navigation items, they'll end up taking up the whole screen on a mobile device.

Your navigation solution must leave space on the small screen for the content. You want to make sure that a visitor to your site, even on a mobile phone, sees something interesting without having to scroll.

FOOTER NAVIGATION

One of the easiest things you can do to get your navigation out of the way on the narrow-width version of your site is to move it to the bottom of the page and then link to it with an anchor link (a link that takes you to a different point on the same page). This is often called *footer navigation* or *footer anchor navigation*.

The *Contents Magazine* website uses this type of navigation. In Figure 10-22, you see an "Explore" link at the top of the page, with a downward-pointing arrow. Clicking that link brings you to the place near the bottom of the page where the search box and navigation links appear.

Figure 10-22. The *Contents Magazine* website uses a footer navigation.

Although this site only has four navigation links, those links plus the search box take up nearly half of the available space on the small screen, so moving them away from the top of the page gives more space for the branding and the start of the page content.

The code to do footer navigation is pretty simple—just start with an anchor link at the top of the page, like this code from the *Contents* website:

```
<p class="go-nav">
    <a href="#site-nav"><b>Explore</b></a>
</p>
```

The code for the search box and links will go near the bottom of the HTML document, to correspond with the actual location on the narrow-width design. In this case the site's designers used one <div> to contain the search box and navigation links, with the navigation as a <ul> inside a <nav>.

At wider screen widths, there's plenty of room for the navigation and search box at the top, as you see in Figure 10-23.

Figure 10-23. At wider viewport widths, the navigation is moved to the top of the screen.

Using a media query, the entire `<div>` containing the navigation items is moved to the top of the page using absolute positioning:

```
@media screen and (min-width: 48em) {
    #site-nav { position: absolute; top: -5em; width:
    100%; z-index: 5; }
}
```

That bar with the "Explore" link is no longer needed, so it's hidden from the screen by giving it a negative position that will always be outside the viewport's dimensions:

```
.go-nav { left: -1000em; }
```

Footer navigation is a good solution if you only have a few links, but a downside is that it can be disorienting to users to click a link and suddenly be at the *bottom* of a page.

TOGGLE PUSH NAVIGATION

The Starbucks site uses a common type of navigation for the narrow-width view, often called a *toggle menu* because you click to toggle it from hidden to visible and back.

At the left of Figure 10-24 you see the narrow-width design for the Starbucks website. The icon with three horizontal bars at the top right is a common icon for navigation. Just click it and the navigation shows up, pushing the content below it down the page. You can see that the navigation is either one or two columns, depending on how much space is available in the width of the screen.

Once the navigation is visible, you can just click the X to make it disappear again.

At wider screen widths, as in Figure 10-25, there's room for the entire navigation at the top of the page, in a horizontal row, and additional media queries further rearrange the components as space allows.

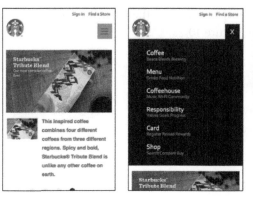

Figure 10-24. Clicking the three-line icon at the top of the screen makes the navigation appear, pushing the page's content down the screen.

Figure 10-25. When viewed on a wider screen, the navigation appears as a horizontal bar.

The caveat on this is that it's kind of complicated, and it uses JavaScript. If you don't know JavaScript, don't worry; there are plenty of examples out there that you can copy and paste into your code.

You can find code to implement this type of navigation in Brad Frost's Responsive Patterns collection: Toggle Navigation (*http://codepen.io/ bradfrost/full/sHvaz*).

In Frost's example (as in Figure 10-24), the way the small-screen version of the navigation \works is that when the icon is clicked, it triggers a JavaScript action (**toggleClass** in jQuery) that adds the **active** class to the <nav> element.

When the page first loads, the icon does not have the **active** class, and the <nav> element has these styles applied to it:

```
nav { max-height: 0; overflow: hidden; }
```

The **max-height** of zero means the element is given no space on the screen, and **overflow: hidden** means the content of the <nav> element doesn't show up outside of the element. All that together means the <nav> element is not visible.

When the user clicks the icon, triggering the JavaScript to add the active class to the element, this CSS is applied:

```
nav.active { max-height: 15em; }
```

The max-height of the <nav> is changed to 15 ems, which means that element can take up all the space it needs on the screen (up to 15 ems in height, which is a lot more than it actually needs). Thus, that element is visible and the content below it is pushed down the page.

The navigation items are in an unordered list, so they appear stacked vertically (and additional styles are applied to make the navigation look nice, of course).

For wider screens, as in Figure 10-25, this CSS is applied:

```
@media screen and (min-width: 48.25em) {
    nav { max-height: none; }
    nav li { display: inline-block; }
    a.menu-link { display: none; }
}
```

The max-height of the <nav> is set to none, which means that the navigation will appear at full size. The list items are styled with display: inline-block so they will appear in a horizontal row. The "Menu" link is given a style of display: none so it's no longer visible—we don't need to display the option to toggle the menu on, because the menu is already visible.

Don't forget to make sure your navigation works for users with JavaScript disabled. If you load the Starbucks site with JavaScript disabled, at the narrow width the menu is already expanded by default, and it stays expanded throughout your visit to your site. Unfortunately, the Starbucks website's front page design relies on JavaScript, as you see in Figure 10-26.

> [NOTE]
>
> With menus that open and close, you can use CSS *transitions* to make their movement smoother. To learn more about how transitions work, read "transition" (*http://css-tricks.com/almanac/properties/t/transition/*) on the CSS-Tricks website.

Figure 10-26. When JavaScript is disabled, the small-screen menu is expanded by default, although not all of the content is visible.

With a toggle menu, you can also have the menu appear at the very top of the screen, above rather than below the icon bar. The example in Figure 10-27 is from Responsive Nav (*http://www.responsive-nav.com*), a site made to demonstrate this navigation, which is a very lightweight JavaScript plug-in (free and open source).

Figure 10-27. A toggle menu can also make the navigation appear above the icon, rather than below it.

If the browser doesn't have JavaScript, it just displays the navigation menu by default, without the button (unlike the previous example in Figure 10-26, which still had the button, although it didn't do anything).

If you download the demo ZIP file, there are seven different examples to choose from, including unstyled versions with the menu opening above or below the icon bar; a heavier version of the plug-in that provides support for older versions of IE; a version with the wide-screen menu on the side instead of the top, as in Figure 10-28; and a version that combines two separate navigations, as you see in Figure 10-29.

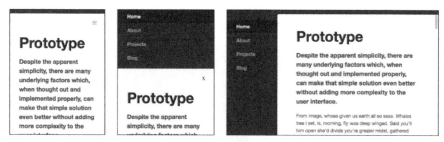

Figure 10-28. With a toggle navigation, the wide-screen design could use a left navigation instead of a top navigation.

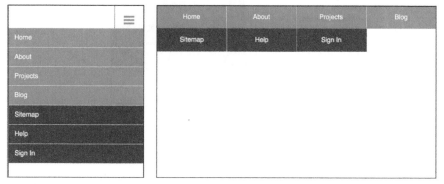

Figure 10-29. This example combines two separate sets of navigation links into the same toggle navigation.

As with any plug-in, you can modify it to suit your needs, using the code as a starting place for something more complicated. Change the style as you wish, including the typography, transitions, and layout. You can also add more media queries to have additional navigation designs for mid-width screens.

TOGGLE OVERLAY NAVIGATION

If you want to implement a toggle menu without using JavaScript, there are ways, but they have disadvantages.

For example, in Figure 10-30 you see a microsite that allows potential Nichols College students to request information. The user clicks an icon at the top to get the navigation to appear, but unlike in the previous examples, instead of pushing the content down and out of its way, the navigation overlays the content.

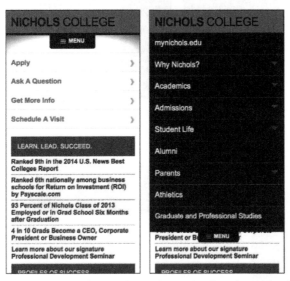

Figure 10-30. In the toggle overlay navigation, the navigation appears on top of the content instead of pushing it out of the way.

Aaron Gustafson wrote about his approach to creating the navigation for this site in "Build a CSS dropdown menu" (*http://www.creativebloq.com/css3/build-smart-mobile-navigation-without-hacks-6122800*), in *.net Magazine*. He used the :target attribute to make the navigation element open and close.

Because the content is hidden when the menu is open, it needs to be easy to make the menu get out of the way. So, Gustafson created an "extra" link to close the menu, which essentially covers the entire rest of the page—meaning that anywhere the user clicks on the page will close the navigation. Unfortunately, this has the side effect that if you leave the navigation open and scroll down to fill out the form, as soon as you click anywhere, you'll jump all the way back up to the top of the page.

PRIORITY NAVIGATION

Sometimes on the mid-width version of a responsive design, you have room for some of the navigation items, but not all of them.

In Figure 10-31, you can see an example of this. At the narrowest screen width, there's only room for a "Menu" button; in the widest version of the layout, there's a horizontal menu of nine navigation items. At the in-between widths, where there's not room for all nine, instead of going right to that Menu button, the four most important links in the navigation (the first four from the full navigation bar) are displayed, followed by an additional link at the right for "More," which is a drop-down that displays the other navigation items.

Figure 10-31. In the mid-width design, there's room to display some but not all navigation items in the top navigation bar.

Developer Michael Scharngal coined the term "priority navigation" for this technique. It's a good way to take the best advantage of space in the in-between screen widths.

In the preceding example, JavaScript was used to produce the navigation design you see on the mid-width screen, but you could produce a similar effect using media queries and CSS.

SELECT MENU NAVIGATION

This mortgage company website from the UK uses a <select> menu to display the main navigation at the narrowest screen widths, as you see in Figure 10-32.

Figure 10-32. On a mobile device, a select menu will display according to the device default: iOS in the center, and Android on the right.

At wider screen widths, as in Figure 10-33, the website has a regular horizontal menu with drop-down subnavigation items.

On touch devices, the form field will display a touch-friendly selector, with the default style for the OS. In Figure 10-32, you can see that the selector is different for iOS and Android.

One advantage of this type of navigation is it uses very little space on the screen.

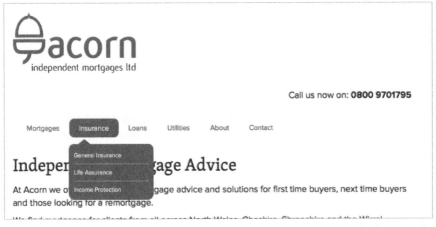

Figure 10-33. At a wider viewport width, the navigation is a regular horizontal menu with drop-down subnavigation.

However, many designers question the usability of this type of navigation. Although it seems like an easy way to compress a list of navigation items, it can be a bit confusing to users, because it uses a form element, which users would usually only see in a form. Personally I don't recommend it, but a lot of sites are using this type of navigation.

To code this select menu navigation, you create two separate sets of HTML for the website's navigation menu—a `<select>` element that creates a drop-down menu, and a `<ul>` for the horizontal navigation on wider screens. The site uses media queries to hide one or the other depending on the width of the screen.

A downside of doing it this way is you will have two separate sets of HTML for the navigation. In addition to adding to the weight of the page, this means that you have to always make sure that any changes are made in both pieces of code, so that the menu is the same no matter which type of navigation the user sees.

Another way of switching between a select menu and a regular navigation is to use JavaScript. The jQuery Responsive Menu Plugin (*https://github.com/mattkersley/Responsive-Menu*) and SelectNav.js (*http://lukaszfiszer.github.io/selectnav.js/*) are plug-ins that use jQuery to change a `<ul>` or `<ol>` into a `<select>`.

FLYOUT NAVIGATION

The website for Emeril's Restaurants (that's Emeril Lagasse of "Bam!" fame) has a complicated navigation, but the designers did a great job with it.

This website has what's called a *flyout navigation* or an *off-canvas navigation*, which you can see in Figure 10-34. When you click the navigation icon at the top, the navigation flies out on the left side of the screen, and pushes the content to the right. This flyout navigation even includes subnavigation items, which you get to by clicking the arrows. The subitems push the other navigation items down to make space. Clicking the arrow a second time closes the subnavigation items but keeps you on the main navigation.

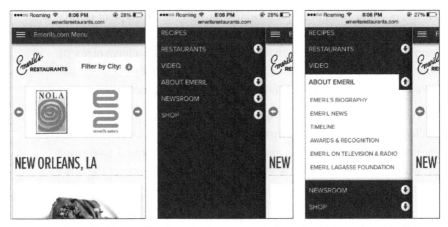

Figure 10-34. The flyout navigation comes in from the side, and pushes the page content to the right.

When the menu is on the screen, you only see the very edge of the actual page content. Although it would certainly be easier to *only* display the navigation on the screen, keeping that bit of the page visible gives the users a sense of where they are on the site. The page didn't disappear—it's still there—and they only need to click the icon again to bring it back.

At a wider screen width, there's space for the full horizontal navigation, as you see in Figure 10-35. The subnavigation items are there—you just click or tap each navigation item to get a traditional drop-down menu.

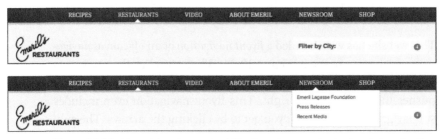

Figure 10-35. At a wider viewport width, there's a regular horizontal navigation with drop-down subnavigation.

This navigation is good for situations where you need to include a lot of navigation items. If you style it well, it can look very elegant.

The downside is that the code to do this kind of navigation is fairly complex and requires JavaScript. If you implement a navigation like this, make sure to test it on many devices and browsers, because there are a lot of things that can go wrong and make it not work.

You can find code for this type of navigation on Brad Frost's Responsive Navigation Patterns site: The Left Nav Flyout (*http://codepen.io/brad frost/full/IEBrz*).

Another option is the jPanelMenu (*http://jpanelmenu.com*) jQuery plug-in from Happy Cog's Anthony Colangelo.

BOTTOM NAVIGATION

On a narrow screen, bottom navigation is exactly the same as the footer navigation you saw earlier in this chapter. In Figure 10-36 you see that the Grey Goose website has a "Menu" button at the top, which takes you to a footer menu at the bottom of the screen.

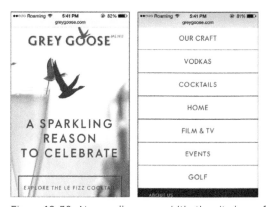

Figure 10-36. At a small screen width, the site has a footer navigation.

The difference is on the wide screen. Instead of using positioning to move the navigation to the customary location at the top of the screen, the navigation stays at the bottom, as you see in Figure 10-37.

Pages with a multi-level navigation have an extra bar perched on top of the main navigation bar, still at the bottom of the screen, as in Figure 10-38.

Figure 10-37. At a wider viewport width, the navigation remains at the bottom of the screen.

Figure 10-38. The navigation stays at the bottom of the screen, even when you scroll down; subnavigation items appear above the main navigation items.

Although at first this seems strange, it actually makes sense.

As we move toward more and more touchscreen devices—not just the tablets that are increasingly popular, but also convertible laptops and other larger devices—it will become more common for our desktop screens to be touch-enabled, allowing us to use multiple input methods on the same device.

On touchscreens of any size, having the navigation at the bottom of the screen just works better. The buttons are closer to where our fingers and thumbs are, so easier to tap. Luke Wroblewski has written a great article called "Responsive Navigation: Optimizing for Touch Across Devices" (*http://www.lukew.com/ff/entry.asp?1649*) that discusses the reasons why in detail.

But at the same time, going against one of the Web's engrained conventions—navigation is nearly always at the top of a page—should not be done lightly. Even if the top of the page might not be the best location for a navigation, the fact that users are expecting it to be there counts for a lot.

A design like this needs to be very well thought out and tested, to make sure that it's not detrimental to the user experience. So don't go changing all your sites to a bottom navigation just yet—but keep in mind that as the devices we're using to access the Web change, our design conventions may eventually need to change too.

SKIP THE SUBNAVIGATION

While it's pretty easy to find a place for navigation, it gets more difficult when you have subnavigation items—a second level of navigation in the same menu.

As we've gone through our examples of responsive navigation patterns, you'll have seen that although some include a multi-level navigation, it's very difficult to successfully implement a multi-level navigation on a small screen.

Even if you can get all the options in there, it's easy for the users to get confused if they can't see all the options at once.

In many cases, you may decide that the small-screen design only needs one level of navigation, and that the subnavigation items can be accessed on the landing page of each section. It's fine to do that and still include a drop-down subnavigation on the wider versions of the site design, if there's space for it.

One example is the Ikea website. It has separate desktop and mobile versions (i.e., it's not a responsive site) but you could combine both designs into a responsive site, using media queries to switch between the navigation layouts.

In Figure 10-39, hovering over "Departments" gets you a lengthy list of departments that roughly coincide with what you'd see in the physical store. For anyone who has been to an Ikea store, this list is very familiar and makes the site easy to navigate, especially if you know what you're looking for.

Figure 10-39. The main menu on the desktop website allows you to view a list of "Departments," corresponding to what you'd find in the physical store.

On the mobile site, as you see in Figure 10-40, instead of trying to fit such a lengthy drop-down menu onto the home page, there is instead a "Products" link that takes you to a separate page. This page only contains a long list of links, no other content. The list of "Products" is very similar to, but not exactly the same as, the list of links under "Departments" on the desktop site.

There's plenty of space, and the links are spaced out and easy to tap.

Although displaying the list of products requires an extra click, it's a click that makes users feel like they are going in the right direction, and because the page it leads to has minimal content, it should load quickly.

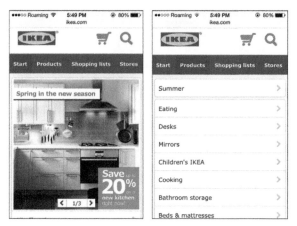

Figure 10-40. The mobile site has a "Products" menu that's on a separate page.

ABANDONED NAVIGATION

Some sites deal with the issue of navigation on the mobile-size screen by simply removing it. This is really not an appropriate option, because you're not letting the mobile users access all of the content on the site.

We discussed content parity in Chapter 2. Everyone should be able to access all the content on your site, no matter what type of device they're using.

But some sites have made the decision to remove the navigation on small screens, so it's worth discussing.

Consider the Authentic Jobs website. At the smallest screen width, as seen in Figure 10-41, you have buttons that allow you to search for remote jobs, search for jobs near to your location, search by keyword, and sign in. Below that, the "Refine" button brings up an overlay with additional search options.

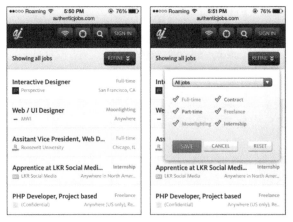

Figure 10-41. The small-screen design has buttons for several functions.

But if you view wider versions of the design, as you see in Figure 10-42, you get additional options, including the navigation bar at the top.

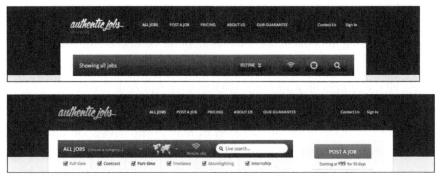

Figure 10-42. At a wider viewport width, you get additional options that aren't accessible if you're viewing the site on a small screen.

Some of the content is accessible on smaller devices. If you click on "Sign In" on the small-screen design, the sign-in page gives you a link to "Post a Job," even if you don't have an account yet. The pricing info is there also. But most new users probably wouldn't think to click "Sign In"; they would look around for an option to create an account or post a job, and not seeing those options, they would assume they aren't available on a mobile device.

"About Us," "Our Guarantee," and "Contact Us" are not available any-where on the small-screen design. At minimum, they should have been moved to the site's footer, but there isn't any footer at all on the small-screen design—the page just ends at the last job listing.

This is a situation where the designer assumed the mobile users wouldn't want to access all the site functionality on a small screen. But more and more people are relying on mobile devices as their only way to access the Internet—or just using mobile devices more often, because they're handy. If you want to maximize your potential users and cus-tomers, don't give them a small-screen version of your site that's miss-ing features.

STICKY MENUS FOR WIDER SCREENS

One additional thing you can do with navigation is make your menus *sticky*—that is, have them stay locked to the top or bottom of the screen when the user scrolls, instead of scrolling off the screen. This is also sometimes called *persistent navigation*.

Although this is not a usual pattern for websites, it's a familiar pattern for computer users. Think of apps such as Microsoft Word, or even your browser. The menu bar is always on the top, no matter what.

One site that uses sticky menus is Facebook, where the top navigation functions more as a menu of site functionality options rather than as a way to navigate between sections of the site. You see in Figure 10-43 that the navigation is at the top, even though the user isn't at the top of the page.

Figure 10-43. A sticky menu stays at the top of the screen, even as you scroll down.

This tends to not have many downsides on a wide-screen design, as there's plenty of room to have space taken up by a persistent navigation bar. On the Facebook site, the navigation is only persistent when the viewport is 1,000 pixels or wider; at narrower viewport widths, it will scroll away at the top of the screen. (By the way, this is an example of how you can use media queries to add a little bit of responsiveness to a site that's not responsive.)

On smaller screens, using a sticky menu definitely has a downside: your screen real estate is limited, and you don't want to waste any. But at the same time, it can be handy: it's easier for the user to get to the navigation from the middle of the page, without having to do a lot of scrolling.

Header

The branding and navigation fit together at the top of your website, along with other site functionality like search and login. And many sites have more than one navigation component.

You need to think about how your navigation will fit in with these other pieces.

MINIMALIST HEADER

The website for the US Senate Committee on Homeland Security & Governmental Affairs, shown in Figure 10-44, takes a minimalist approach, with a single "Menu" link that gives you a toggle overlay menu with several options, and the committee's name below it.

The wide-screen version that you see in Figure 10-45, however, offers a few more options and enhances the site name with a graphic element.

The wide-screen design also has social media icons at the top, which appear nowhere on the entire page of the small-screen design. These icons could easily have been added to the footer, so they would be available to all users.

The menu is toggled by JavaScript, which changes the height of the <ul> containing the menu from 0 pixels (before toggling, making it hidden) to a height that will accommodate all the menu items.

Figure 10-44. This minimal header has only one link, the site's title, and a search box.

Figure 10-45. On a wider screen, you get additional options and an enhanced logo.

Keeping the header section of the site simple on narrow screens means that it takes up less valuable space, but you have to make sure you're not leaving out anything important.

COMPLICATED HEADER

Many websites have additional elements at the top of the page that aren't part of the navigation but are essential to the site.

For example, The University of Vermont has a lot of options at the top of its website when it's viewed on a wide screen, as seen in Figure 10-46.

Figure 10-46. Viewing on a wide screen, this site has quite a few different components in its header.

This ends up being a bit confusing on a small screen, as you see in Figure 10-47. *Two* navigation icons appear at the top of the page. One of these, labeled "Main Menu," gives you a small, two-column toggle push menu.

Figure 10-47. On a small screen, you get two similar navigation icons, and a few other links.

The other isn't labeled, and is actually a little easy to miss, perched in the top-left corner above the university's logo. And not only is that navigation button too small to tap easily, but it gives you a toggle push menu—that appears in the *middle* of all the header pieces—in which the links are smaller type, closer together, and also difficult to tap accurately (using two columns would have solved that problem).

The menu you get from that unlabeled menu button is the *audience menu* from the top of the desktop site (Students, Faculty, etc.). This is an interesting type of navigation that generally supplements the main navigation by presenting some of the same items that can be accessed from the main navigation, but grouped into frequently accessed links per audience.

University sites are one of the few places where this is actually useful in a navigation, because the audiences they are targeting generally have very specific needs. Presumably, if you are in one of those categories, you'll access the website enough that you'll eventually figure out that button is there. If not, you'll just use the main navigation and still be able to access all of the site.

The last screenshot in Figure 10-47 shows that when you tap the search icon in the top-right corner, you get a search box that pushes down the part of the header that's below it.

This site did a fairly decent job of fitting a lot of items into a small space, but the designers perhaps could have reconsidered whether all of these items really need to be in the navigation.

NAVIGATION ICON

As you've seen in many of the navigation patterns, on the small screen there's often an icon or other image or text you need to tap to get access to the menu.

When designers were first creating navigations for mobile sites, a lot of different options were tried out, but over time one particular icon has evolved as the standard: three horizontal lines (see Figure 10-48).

Figure 10-48. The standard navigation item is three horizontal lines, as you see in this example from Bootstrap.

This is sometimes called the "hamburger icon," as it kind of resembles a flat burger between two buns... well, a little bit. It's sometimes also called a "pancake icon."

The lines do give the sense of a list, but it's not absolutely necessary that users be able to independently identify that as a navigation icon. They simply need to be able to identify it as the most likely thing to click to get to the navigation, when they're at the top of a website.

Variations include four lines instead of three; lines next to dots, to resemble a bulleted list; or adding the word "Menu" to make sure it's clear to users. Figure 10-49 shows a few alternatives.

Sometimes a word other than "Menu" is used, as seen in the examples in Figure 10-50. "Explore" is a nice action word, but it takes up more space than "Menu." The word "Nav" might be less obvious to users, because less-experienced web users don't tend to think of the thing at the top of the page as a "navigation."

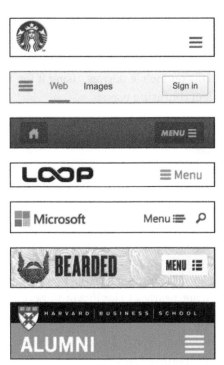

Figure 10-49. Variations on the standard navigation icon from the Starbucks, Google, dConstruct 2012, Loop Recordings, Microsoft, Bearded, and Harvard Business School Alumni websites.

Figure 10-50. Other words besides "Menu" can be used, as long as users will know what they mean; these examples are from Contents Magazine, Bond Art + Science, and United Pixelworkers.

Some sites use other symbols, such as the gear symbol in Figure 10-51. Users will probably figure out this is the navigation, because it's the only thing at the top of the page to click; but because the gear symbol is associated with settings, especially on mobile devices, using it for a different purpose will run the risk of confusing users.

Figure 10-51. This site from Nathan Sawaya uses a gear icon, which could be confusing to users as it's often used in applications for settings, not menus.

While there are a lot of options for displaying a navigation icon, just as with other images—a font icon, an SVG image, plain old CSS, or even a Unicode character—in reality, this is a very small asset on your site, and because the image can be loaded once to display on every page throughout your site, it's probably not nearly as significant to performance as other assets on your site.

If you want to learn more about different ways to display a navigation icon, check out "The Semantic, Responsive Navicon" (*http://mobile. smashingmagazine.com/2012/10/08/the-semantic-responsive-design-navicon/*) by Jordan Moore on *Smashing Magazine*.

OTHER ICONS

Because space is so limited on a small-screen design, icons are frequently used in place of text for menu options, or to display hidden components.

For example, on Skinny Ties, an ecommerce site, there are three icons at the top: a shopping cart, a head-and-shoulders profile of a person, and a magnifying glass.

Shopping cart icons are fairly universal, and clicking on it on the small screen, as you see in Figure 10-52, gives you a toggle push to see either a message that your cart is empty, or a list of the items in your cart and links to view your cart or check out. This is the same content you get when hovering over the cart button in the wide-screen version, as seen in Figure 10-53.

Because there's more space in the wide-screen version, an enhancement was added: a number in the cart button to show you how many items are in your cart. Although this adds to the user experience, the small-screen users aren't missing out on content or functionality; they can still find out how many items are in the cart by clicking to see the cart's contents.

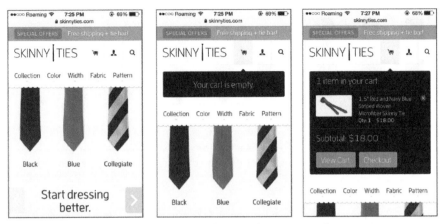

Figure 10-52. The cart icon toggles a box showing the contents of your cart.

Figure 10-53. You get the same information on the wide-screen view by hovering over the cart button.

In Figure 10-54 you can see that clicking on the center icon, showing a person's head and shoulders, gives you a toggle push to see the links for "Sign In" and "Register." Clicking the magnifying glass icon gives you a toggle push to get a search box.

Figure 10-54. Additional icons give you the Sign In/Register links, and the search box.

The magnifying glass for search is fairly universal, but the person icon may not be familiar to all users. However, in this case that's okay. If someone wants to log in or register, they will start looking for those links at the top of the page, as that is the customary location on most websites. Glancing at the top of the page, they won't find those words in links, but of what they do see the person icon will clearly seem the most likely option for finding what they need, so users will go ahead and click on it.

That's called *discoverability*—the idea that users are able to easily find and get to what they need, without necessarily having to follow a hierarchical structure to get there.

The last part of the navigation is the browsing options—"Collection," "Color," etc. Clicking on these on the small screen, as you see in Figure 10-55, gets you a toggle overlay listing choices under the selected category. For example, choosing "Pattern" allows you to browse by "Solid," "Striped," etc.

The wide-screen layout, also in Figure 10-55, gives you a similar overlay, just with a different layout that takes advantage of the additional space by making the tie images larger.

Figure 10-55. The main navigation items give you similar overlays, with a different layout depending on viewport width.

The special offers section is at the top of the page, no matter what size device you are viewing it on, but the tagline is longer when there's space for it.

This site does a great job of providing a comprehensive shopping experience, no matter what size screen the user's device has.

The header section on the small screen does take up a lot of space, but because all of the functions are so important to the site experience, that's all right.

Summary

The first thing users will see on a website is the branding, which will let them know that they're in the right place. On a responsive site, the size and composition of the logo and website title may need to change to take best advantage of available space.

Navigation needs to be designed well so that users can successfully and easily navigate through the site. Make sure to design the navigation to be flexible, in case navigation items need to be added or changed later.

A good navigation focuses on the paths that users will take through the site to get to the content they need, rather than just providing a hierarchical sort of the website's content.

Think about the navigation layout for small screens first, streamlining and including only the items that are actually needed.

You don't have to design a responsive navigation from scratch. There are many common responsive navigation patterns that you can base your own navigation on. Which one you use depends on how many items you have in your navigation, whether you need a subnavigation, and whether it's necessary for your site to support non-JavaScript users.

When designing a header around the navigation, you'll start with the small-screen design. You can keep it minimal, as long as everything is still accessible through the navigation or other links.

There are a variety of options you can use to signify that a navigation is available. Many sites use the three-line "hamburger" icon, but you can use other icons or words like "Menu" or "Explore."

Just make sure to keep the navigation consistent across screen widths, so that you don't confuse cross-platform users.

In the next chapter, Chapter 11, we'll talk about how to improve the performance of your site.

[11]

Performance

One often-heard criticism of responsive design is that responsive websites tend to have poor performance—that is, they take longer to load and render.

For many responsive websites out there, that's true, but it's not because responsive sites are inherently slow; it's because those sites were not developed with performance as a goal. There are a lot of techniques to make websites lighter and faster.

In this chapter, we'll first talk a bit about why performance matters, and why performance should be a consideration as you're designing a website.

Then we'll go through, step by step, what happens as a web page is loaded and rendered in a browser, so you'll have a better understanding of all the things that are going on and what can go wrong.

Next, we'll look at how to test the performance of your site, to figure out what the areas are.

Finally, we'll go into detail about what you can do to improve the performance of your website. Some of the areas we'll look at are cleaning up your code, minimizing HTTP requests, compressing files, enabling browser caching, and removing JavaScript that blocks loading.

> **[NOTE]**
>
> One of the best resources for addressing performance on your website is Google's PageSpeed Tools (*https://developers.google.com/speed/ pagespeed/*). Some of the suggestions in this chapter are based on Google's PageSpeed Insights Rules, and used according to terms described in the Creative Commons 3.0 Attribution License (*http://creativecommons. org/licenses/by/3.0/*).

Why Performance Matters

Studies have shown that users judge the visual appeal of a website in less than a fraction of a second, which is why first impressions are important. But what if a user's first impression is 5–10 seconds of a blank screen, before she sees anything?

A 2012 study by Strangeloop of Alexa's top 100 retail sites[1] discovered that the median load time for first time visits to those sites was 7.14 seconds.

Seven seconds doesn't seem like a lot, but when you're staring at a blank screen, it can seem like forever. Try counting to seven seconds right now to see how long it feels. Even if users bother to wait, the first impression they'll have of the website is that it *wasted their time*. No matter how good it looks, that first impression will always remain in their minds.

But more likely than not, they won't wait. Users expect a site to load in a couple of seconds. In a 2012 study by Econsultancy, 74% of mobile users abandoned a site after waiting five seconds for it to load.[2]

However, the most important metric isn't how fast your website actually is, it's how fast the user *perceives* it to be. Metrics can tell you how long it takes to load and render every part of a web page, but if users see things on their screens before the whole page is done loading, it's going to seem faster.

Besides what your users experience on the website, there's a less obvious—but just as important—reason to optimize the performance of your site: it will give you better placement in search results.

In 2010, Google announced that site speed would be a factor in its search engine ranking algorithms, for both desktop and mobile: slow sites would be penalized in search rankings. The reasoning was that site speed affects the user experience, and a faster site means a better-quality site—one that users will prefer over a slower site.

---

1 Strangeloop's Fall 2012 "State of the Union: Ecommerce Page Speed & Web Performance" (*http://www.strangeloopnetworks.com/resources/research/fall-2012-state-of-the-union/success/*).

2 David Moth, "Mobile Websites and Apps Optimization Best Practice Guide," Econsultancy, October 23, 2012 (*https://econsultancy.com/blog/10936-site-speed-case-studies-tips-and-tools-for-improving-your-conversion-rate*).

Performance as Design

Because performance is so essential to the user experience of a site, it needs to be considered a design element, rather than just a technical specification.

That means that from the start of a project, performance should be part of the project documentation, such as proposals, statements of work, and deliverables.

Designers and developers need to work together throughout the process. Otherwise you have designers coming up with great ideas but having no idea of the performance cost, and developers blindly implementing those ideas because that's what they were provided with. Often, small tweaks to the design can dramatically change performance, but there needs to be room in the process to make those tweaks.

It's easier to include the client in decisions involving performance if they've been told all along how important it is.

CONNECTIONS

It's easy to blame responsive design, but the truth is, we've just gotten into the habit of building bloated websites.

In the two decades since the Web came along, computers have swiftly been getting faster and more powerful. And our Internet connections, in our homes and offices, have just as swiftly increased in speed (many times over).

Our computers can do all sorts of magic things, so we want our websites to do magic things too.

As we're designing or developing sites, we're generally sitting in front of computers with pretty speedy connections in our offices or homes. It's easy to forget that not everybody is using such a fast connection.

Remember dial-up? It seems archaic to even think about it. That screechy noise we had to listen to every time we connected to the Internet... It took a little while for everything to load, but we didn't mind too much, because that was the only option. And it wasn't even *that* slow, because websites were so much lighter a decade ago.

Today, only about 3% of Americans still have dial-up Internet access at home. That's hardly anybody, right? Well, there are 300 million people in the United States, so 3% is only... 9 million. Hmmm. Well, perhaps that's a few people we need to worry about. But forget about them for a moment, because the real issue we want to talk about is mobile Internet access.

While devices of all sizes have gotten more powerful, our connections—at least some of them—have gotten slower. So now what?

BALANCE

The issue is striking a balance. There are all sorts of amazing things you can do with HTML, CSS, and JavaScript to make your website look incredible and do incredible things.

But the goal of a website isn't to look good, it's to provide information and interactivity. And if your visual effects are slowing down your site so much that they're getting in the way of the main goal, then you need to reexamine what you're doing.

THE BLOATED WEB

The first thing that needs to be pointed out is that slow performance isn't an issue that's unique to responsive design—it just tends to get noticed more on responsive sites because we're paying attention to how they perform on mobile devices, which generally have slower connections.

Over time, websites have gotten more and more bloated.

According to the HTTP Archive, which compiles statistics based on thousands of the most popular websites, in the past two years the average page weight has increased from 807 KB to 1,492 KB.[3] That's nearly a megabyte and a half of data being downloaded to view just *one* page on a website!

Of course, that includes everything that's needed to render the web page: HTML, CSS, JavaScript, images, web fonts, Flash, and so on.

Whether or not your website is responsive, there are many things that you can do to make it faster, and most of what we'll discuss in this chapter is applicable to all websites, not just responsive websites. Even if your site isn't responsive, there will likely be people visiting it using mobile devices and slow connections, so do your best to make it as fast as is feasible.

---

3   For more information, see "Interesting stats" (*http://httparchive.org/interesting. php?a=All&l=Jul%2015%202011*) from the HTTP Archive.

It's not that simple, though. Responsive design is just a tool, and whether or not using responsive design produces a good website is up to the designers and developers who work on the site.

Simply taking a desktop design and adding responsiveness to it will frequently result in bloated code. That's why you're often better off starting at the beginning and designing carefully and thoughtfully.

> **[NOTE]**
>
> To learn more about improving the performance of responsive websites, read Tim Kadlec's article "Responsive Responsive Design" (*http://24ways. org/2012/responsive-responsive-design/*).

How Web Pages Are Loaded and Rendered

To understand all the things that affect the performance of a web page, we must look at everything that happens when a web page is *rendered*. Rendering is the process by which the browser reads the HTML, CSS, and other resources, and then displays a web page in the browser window.

This explanation is a bit simplified so that you can understand it without being an IT expert, but it covers all the major bits that have an impact on performance. It's long, but bear with me.

Later in the chapter, we will go into how each part of the process affects performance, and what you can do to improve performance, but to start out, it's necessary to understand how all the different parts of the process fit together and what order everything happens in.

LATENCY

First, you're at your browser, either on your desktop/laptop computer or a mobile device. You type in a URL, or click on a link.

Latency is the amount of time it takes to connect to the Internet provider.

If you're on a stationary connection (such as a broadband connection at your home or office), you don't have to worry about this because you're continuously connected to the provider.

But if you're on a mobile network, there is a limited amount of bandwidth at any given point in time, so you don't have a continuous connection; you're only connected when you're actively requesting or sending information to the Internet.

So, your mobile device needs to connect to the network in order to load a web page. To do this, the device contacts a local cellular tower and says it wants to start a connection.

Under ideal circumstances, the tower will reply right away and set up the connection. But circumstances aren't always ideal, so this process could end up taking several seconds—and we haven't even started loading the web page yet! Unfortunately, you (the website owner/developer) can't do anything to speed up this part of the process for users, but you need to know that these delays can exist.

The speed of the original connection (latency) depends on how many devices are trying to get a connection at the same time. For example, if you're at a major sporting event, or in a large city, it may take longer to connect because so many other people are trying to connect at the same time.

Speed of Connection

After you've established a connection, how quickly everything happens can depend on a few factors, which are also out of your control.

One is the technical quality of the network—different carriers use different frequencies, so the connection might be quicker on one mobile carrier than another. A 4G connection will be faster than a 3G connection, but this also depends on whether the mobile device being used is 4G capable or not.

It also matters how close the device is to a cellular tower, and whether it is on its home network or roaming. Additionally, if the mobile device has other apps running in the background that are accessing the Internet, such as maps, those can slow down what's happening in the web browser.

All of these things can add delay to the loading of a page. You don't have control over any of them, but the user doesn't necessarily know that—he just wants his page to load quickly. So you need to make the parts you can control as fast as possible.

DNS REQUEST

Once the connection is established, the browser sends out a request to the DNS provider, which is usually the Internet provider.

DNS (the Domain Name System) is what translates the URL into an IP address so the browser knows where to find the website. The DNS provider sends back the correct IP address, and then the browser knows where the website is hosted.

The browser is looking for the site located at a particular URL, such as *http://www.example.com*. However, websites are actually identified by the numerical IP address, such as *192.0.2.0*, of the server they are hosted on.

REDIRECTIONS

A URL doesn't necessarily go directly to an IP address, though. Sometimes you have a URL that redirects to a different URL. For example, if you type *www.washpost.com* in your browser's address bar, the text will actually change to *www.washingtonpost.com* as it loads the site.

The redirection happens as part of the DNS process before the browser is told the IP address of the actual website.

This is relevant to performance, because any redirects can add time to the loading process. This applies not only when you redirect from one domain to another, but if you redirect to a different subdomain on the same site, such as if you have it set up to add *www* to a URL (so *example.com* would change to *www.example.com*).

Having one redirect in the process, such as for the *www*, isn't a big deal, but sometimes URLs are set up in a convoluted way so that there are multiple redirects to get to the actual site. This can increase the loading time of your pages.

HTTP REQUEST

Once the browser finds out the IP address of the server where the website is located, the browser sends an HTTP request to the server, requesting that the server send the page located at the URL.

The HTTP request also contains additional information in the HTTP header (think of this as the metadata of the request). One of the key parts is the *user agent*, which identifies the requester's operating system and browser.

In some cases, the website is set up so that the server will send back a different website based on the information contained in the user-agent string.

For example, if the website's server knows that it's a mobile browser making the request, it may send the mobile version of the website (an m-dot site) instead of the regular website. Unfortunately, the user agent cannot always be relied on as always correct, although it's fairly accurate.

SENDING THE HTML FILE

When the server receives an HTTP request, it sends a response, which consists of an HTTP header along with the file requested (in this case, the HTML file).

In the response, the HTTP header may contain additional information to be used by the browser. One important bit is whether the browser is permitted to cache the resource, and how long it can be cached. This is information provided by the website's server (you can adjust these settings on your site's server), not information that is part of the HTML file.

You can see HTTP headers using the Developer Tools in Google Chrome, as in Figure 11-1. Go to the Network tab, and click on any resource in the first column. On the right panel, you'll see the HTTP headers for the request and the response.

DECOMPRESSION

Often, files such as HTML, CSS, or JavaScript will be compressed using *gzip* so that the file size is smaller and they will download faster.

When the browser sends its request, one of the HTTP headers tells the server whether the browser can accept compressed files (most modern browsers can). If the browser can accept a compressed file, that's what the server will send. Otherwise, it will send an uncompressed file, which can take a bit longer.

Once the browser receives the compressed file, it will unzip the entire file right away.

Figure 11-1. The HTTP headers for The Washington Post website, viewed using the Google Chrome Developer Tools.

DOM

The next thing that happens is that the browser parses the HTML, creating a Document Object Model (DOM). Essentially, the DOM is a representation of the web page as it will be displayed. The DOM starts out being the same as the HTML for the page. But if you have JavaScript events that change the content of the page, the changes will be made to the DOM, not to the HTML.

For example, you might have a script that allows you to click a "more" link to view additional text directly on the page. The HTML for the page doesn't contain the additional text, and when you first load the page, neither does the DOM. But after you click the "more" link, activating the script, the additional text will be added to the appropriate place in the DOM and will be displayed on the page.

You can find a more detailed explanation of the DOM in Chris Coyier's "What Is the DOM?" (*http://css-tricks.com/dom/*) on CSS-Tricks.

RENDERING THE <HEAD>

Once the DOM is ready to go, the browser starts to render the HTML document. It goes one element at a time, starting with the very first element in the <head>.

External resources

Each time the browser gets to an element that's a link to an external file (e.g., a CSS or JavaScript file), it loads the file.

Parallel loading

Each external CSS or JavaScript file requires a separate HTTP request (i.e., a request to the server).

Although older browsers can only load one file at a time, newer browsers can download more than one resource at the same time. This makes the process go a bit faster, but it can only do a few files at once, not all of them if you have a lot.

If the browser has cached the resources, they may not need to be loaded at all. Most of the time, when you load a web page, the browser will *cache* (or save locally) resources such as images, CSS files, and JavaScript files, so they don't have to be downloaded again as you browse to other pages on the same site, or if you return to the site within a set period of time. This means the first page a user visits on a site will generally take longer to load than any subsequent pages, as nothing has been cached yet.

The amount of time particular files are allowed to be cached for is set on the website's server, and can range from 24 hours up to a year.

Single-threaded execution

JavaScript is *single-threaded*, which means the browser can only execute (run) one file at a time.

Each <script>, starting with any that are in the <head>, is executed as it's encountered. This includes both inline scripts and external scripts, which cannot be executed until they're done being loaded.

At this point, as scripts are being executed in the <head>, the user is still looking at a blank page, because the browser has not gotten to the <body> HTML yet.

RENDERING THE <BODY>

Only after the browser has finished with the <head> can it start rendering the <body>.

It starts at the top and renders one element at a time. The browser needs to know what each element should look like, and where it will go on the page, so it looks at the CSS to figure out what to do.

Loading HTML images

When the browser gets to an `<img>` element, it starts loading the image file. For a large file, this might take a while, so the user may see an empty spot in the design until the image finishes loading.

It used to be common practice to specify the `height` and `width` attributes of each image in the HTML tag, to "reserve" a blank space of the correct size where the image is supposed to go. But in responsive design, your image may be different sizes depending on viewport width, so it's no longer appropriate to do this.

The trade-off is that once the image finishes loading, the browser will only then know the dimensions of the image, and may have to reflow some of the page (move things around in the layout) to make a space for the image.

Loading background images

When the browser gets to an element that has a background image applied via CSS, it will start loading that image.

More JavaScript

You might also have JavaScript in the `<body>`, either as an external file or an inline script. The browser cannot render the page and execute a script at the same time. So, if it encounters a `<script>` within the `<body>` element, it will stop rendering while it executes the script, and then continue on with the rendering.

ONLOAD EVENTS

After everything in the page has been loaded and rendered, the document executes any `onload` JavaScript events. `onload` simply means that the event will be triggered as soon as the page is finished loading.

Measuring Performance

You can test the performance of your website with some online tools that will give you an estimate of how long it will take your pages to download.

Mobitest (*http://mobitest.akamai.com/m/index.cgi*), from Akamai, is a great tool that can help you figure out how fast your website is. You enter the URL of your page, choose from a few different mobile devices, and request a test run. Everything goes through a queue, so you'll have to wait a little bit, but when it's done you'll find out the average load time of the page in seconds and the average page size in KB, as you see in Figure 11-2.

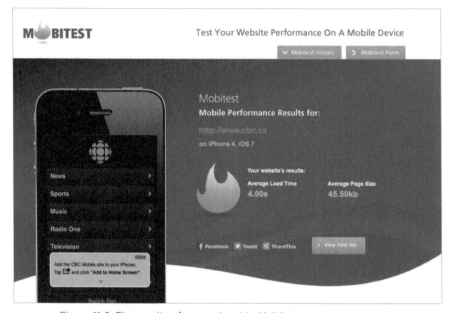

Figure 11-2. The results of a speed test in Mobitest.

For example, a test of Yahoo.com on an iPhone 4 had a load time of 5.41 seconds, and an average page size of 853.49 KB. Testing Google.com on the same phone showed a load time of 2.9 seconds and a page size of 359.47 KB.

You can also click on "View HAR file" to see a waterfall chart that shows the order the page assets load in, and how long it takes each asset to load. This will let you know if there are particular page assets causing a problem—for example, if a third-party add-on is significantly slowing down your site. Mobitest works like a proxy server, testing your site using a real phone, so it should give you pretty accurate results.

YSlow (*http://developer.yahoo.com/yslow/*) is another tool for analyzing page performance, as you can see in Figure 11-3. It is a browser add-on, or a bookmarklet for desktop or mobile browsers. When it analyzes a site, it will grade specific areas where problems commonly arise, and offer you suggestions for optimizing your site. For example, it might point out if you are making too many HTTP requests, or if you could save some KB by minimizing your CSS.

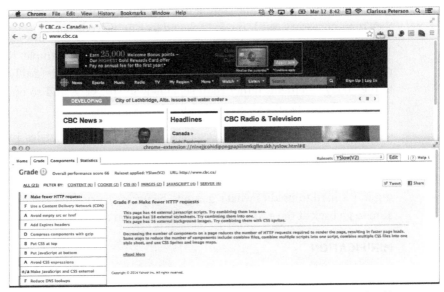

Figure 11-3. YSlow shows the grades for specific performance areas you should address.

Other tools include WebPagetest (*http://www.webpagetest.org*) and Pingdom Website Speed Test (*http://tools.pingdom.com/fpt/*).

Cleaning Up Your Code

The first few things we'll look at to improve your site's performance are ways to clean up your code and make it take up less space.

USE STRAIGHTFORWARD CODE

This seems obvious, but write your code as straightforward as possible.

Don't add a class or ID name in order to apply a style to an element if you can apply the style without it. For example, don't do this:

```
<header>
<ul id="navigation">
...
</ul>
</header>
```

If there's only one `<ul>` in your `<header>`, you don't need an ID, and you can apply styles like this:

```
header ul { ... }
```

That one is pretty obvious, but extra classes/IDs have a tendency to work their way in during the coding process, and you many not realize they're unnecessary until you go back and look at the code later.

Take advantage of the cascade to avoid repeating CSS. For example, if most of the text on your site uses a certain font, apply the `font-family` to the `<body>` element, rather than separately to `<p>`, `<li>`, and so on. Then you'll only need additional CSS for the exceptions.

Go back and clean up your stylesheets. You probably have styles in there that apply to something on your site that no longer exists.

Although it's best to keep your code straightforward while you're writing it, it's hard to predict what's going to be necessary or not, so make sure to go back at the end to look for any pieces you can take out.

MINIFICATION

We add a lot of empty space as we write code, because it makes it much easier to read, but the browser doesn't need all those extra spaces, line breaks, and indentions.

Minification is the process of removing these unnecessary characters from your files. For example, instead of:

```
p {
    font-family: Georgia, serif;
    font-size: 1.1em;
}
li {
    font-family: Helvetica, sans-serif;
    font-size: 1.2em;
}
```

the browser only needs to see this:

```
p{font-family:Georgia,serif;font-size:1.1em;}li{font-
family:Helvetica,sans-serif;font-size:1.2em;}
```

In this example, I was able to remove 10 spaces, 2 tabs, and 7 line breaks—nearly 15% of the characters!

Of course it would be incredibly difficult to have to write your CSS like this, with no spaces. And you can't simply search for and replace all the spaces and line breaks in a document—some of them actually do need to be there (e.g., applying a style to nav li wouldn't work if the browser saw navli).

Thus, there are tools called "minifiers" that you can use to minify your CSS, JavaScript, or HTML files before uploading them to your web server, removing comments (unnecessary for the browser) as well as whitespace.

There are a few ways to make this happen.

First, for a very small site with infrequent edits, you could minify each file individually before uploading it to your web server. If you want to minify one page at a time, there are several websites that can do this via a simple form—try CSS Minifier (*http://cssminifier.com*) or YUI Compressor (*http://refresh-sf.com/yui/*), or search online for a "CSS minifier" or "JavaScript minifier." But for many sites, minifying the files manually would be too much extra work.

If only one person is working on a site, it's easy—if all your files are saved on your own computer, you can use a preprocessor or an app such as LiveReload (*http://livereload.com*) or Mixture (*http://mixture.io*) to minify your files before uploading them to a server, allowing you to always edit the original file with spacing and comments intact.

If you collaborate on files, it's a little trickier, as everyone will have to work from the same original files, rather than downloading the files from the server to get the latest versions.

You could set up your server to automatically minify files on the fly, by using a tool like Minify, which works on PHP, but the extra processing time tends to offset the benefit of sending a smaller file, so it's not recommended.

Minimizing HTTP Requests

An *HTTP request* is what happens each time the browser needs to request that the server provide a file.

Each file, such as an image, stylesheet, or web font, requires a separate HTTP request. For each one, the "round trip" from the browser to the server and back may take a small fraction of a second on broadband, or up to a full second on a mobile connection.

One of the most effective ways to improve the performance of your website is to minimize the number of HTTP requests that are made to the server. You can do this by combining your CSS, JavaScript, or image files.

You also need to make sure any third-party code embedded on your site (e.g., social media widgets, ads, or analytics) isn't requesting a large number of files.

CONCATENATION

One easy way to reduce HTTP requests is to call fewer CSS and JavaScript files by using *concatenation* to combine them.

Again, it might be more convenient for the developer to separate everything out into separate files that serve different purposes, but because each file requires a separate HTTP request, this can increase the load time of the page.

If you decide to have multiple files for development purposes, you can combine the multiple files into one or two files before uploading them to the server. Many of the same apps that you use for minification will also do concatenation, such as YUI Compressor (*http://yui.github.io/yuicompressor/*) or Minify (*https://code.google.com/p/minify/*). You can also use something like QuickConcat (*https://github.com/fila-mentgroup/quickconcat*), which works sever-side if you're using PHP.

And obviously, some files can't be combined—for example, if you're using media queries in stylesheet links to target different stylesheets to different screen sizes, or if some stylesheets are only called on certain sections of the site.

And of course it would be easier to simply decrease the number of stylesheets by combining the code in a few files rather than many. You can use comments to separate sections for easier reference, and use a minifier to strip out the comments for the live version.

However, don't go overboard. Browsers do have the ability to download a few files at once in parallel, so having a couple of CSS files may be better than one very long one.

THIRD-PARTY CODE

Anything that's being downloaded from another domain can cause a delay. This might include embedded videos, maps, ads, or analytics.

The main issue is that every additional domain adds another DNS lookup during the process of loading the page. This is avoided if all the content is coming from the same domain.

A secondary issue is that you're relying on someone else's site to provide the content. If that site is slow—or not available—your site can get held up or stuck while trying to load the assets.

One of the most common culprits here are social media widgets—you know, those little icons for Facebook, Twitter, and other sites, with a "Share This" link.

These are often implemented on the page using third-party software that allows you to track how many users click on each action, on any given page. The problem is that usually they are made up of a ton of code.

Figure 11-4 shows what the social media widget looks like on *The Washington Post* website.

Figure 11-4. The social media widget from *The Washington Post* website.

It looks simple enough, but part of the problem is the "More" link at the bottom, which includes links to several other social media sites. The code is not optimized—each option is a <div> and a <span> inside a <li>, along with several classes and an onClick event.

That's not to mention all the icons, which at least are in only one image sprite, although it's a whopping 22 KB.

Think about whether you really need such a complex widget. Users will still be able to share your content without it. Oliver Reichenstein wrote a great blog post called "Sweep the Sleaze" (*http://ia.net/blog/sweep-the-sleaze/*) on the Information Architects Inc. website that details the reasons why social media widgets don't add value to your website.

But if you do need to keep widgets like this, which are usually made of JavaScript, definitely think about whether their loading can be deferred to after the page has rendered (later in this chapter we'll talk more about deferring JavaScript). Sure, it will pop up on the page a second later, but users generally will at least have started reading the page before they make a decision to share.

IMAGE SPRITES

Image sprites, as we looked at in detail in "Image Sprites" in Chapter 6, are a way to reduce the number of files to download by combining several small images into one large image.

This is most effective when the images are related to each other (e.g., a set of icons that are displayed together).

Server Stuff

The next few things we'll look at have to do with server settings, so if you're a designer, they may not be areas that are directly under your control—and whoever does have control may not realize they're important to the performance of your website. But that doesn't mean you can ignore them. It's definitely worth figuring out who you need to talk to so that these changes can be made.

AVOID REDIRECTS

An *HTTP redirect* is when a user loads a page from a URL that is different from the actual URL of the page, and the browser is redirected to the correct URL. This is something that would be configured on your web server, such as by using *.htaccess* in Apache, or by using functionality in your content management system (CMS).

The most familiar kind of redirect is when a website can be accessed from alternate domains. For example, if you type *www.newyorktimes.com* into your browser, once the page loads, you'll see in the address bar that you're actually viewing *www.nytimes.com*.

You may also use redirects when the URL of a page has changed and you want to make sure users who go to the old URL will still get to the correct page, or if you want users directed to a particular subdomain of the site.

On sites with separate mobile and desktop versions, it's common to use redirects to get users to the correct version of the page for their device—for example, a redirect from *www.example.com/pagename* to *m.example.com/pagename*. (One of the advantages of responsive design is that you don't have to worry about this type of redirect.)

Obviously, there are many occasions when you need to use HTTP redirects. But keep in mind that they do have a performance cost.

Especially make sure that any files used by your website, including images or stylesheets, are being called using the correct URLs. As a start, use relative links (*/images/file.jpg*) rather than absolute links (*http://www.example.com/images/file.jpg*) when linking to files on the same domain.

If URLs on your site change during a redesign, change the actual links on the site whenever possible, rather than using redirects to get users to the right place.

Avoid having more than one redirect chained together.

FILE COMPRESSION

Compression can be used to reduce the size of all the files being sent.

Most web servers are able to use the *gzip* format to compress files before sending them to the user's computer. When a browser requests a page, it will tell the server whether it can process compressed files. The server will send compressed files to browsers that can handle them.

You can use GIDZIPTest (*http://www.gidnetwork.com/tools/gzip-test.php*) to check whether a web page is compressed and, if so, to compare the file sizes. For example, if I test the front page of *The Washington Post* website, I see that it is gzipped, with a savings of 69.5% (300 KB to 92 KB).

You can enable server compression as a configuration on your web server. For example, Apache sites use `mod_deflate` (*http://httpd.apache.org/docs/current/mod/mod_deflate.html*). Your web hosting provider may offer this as a setting on your control panel, and it may be enabled by default. If you're on a shared host, you may not have the ability to turn compression on and off.

All of your HTML, CSS, and JavaScript files should be compressed.

BROWSER CACHING

A lot of the files that are downloaded to display a web page will be reused as the user browses to other pages on the site. This includes stylesheets, images, JavaScript files, and fonts.

Browser caching means that the browser can temporarily store these files on the user's computer for a specified period of time, so that as the user visits other pages on the site, or if she comes back to the site another day, the browser doesn't have to reload those files.

Not only can this decrease the load time of a page by reducing the amount of data that needs to be downloaded, but it also decreases the bandwidth required to download the page, which is helpful to mobile users who have plans with limited bandwidth, or have to pay per MB.

Browser caching doesn't necessarily happen automatically. The browser doesn't decide what to cache; rather, your web server has a set of rules that tell the browser if and when it's all right to cache certain files.

How you set up browser caching depends on the type of web server you have. For example, in Apache you would edit the *.htaccess* file.

Your hosting may have browser caching turned on by default. If you aren't sure, you can use Google's PageSpeed Insights (*http://develop-ers.google.com/speed/pagespeed/insights/*) to check.

You can set different expiration times for different types of files. For example, you could specify that *.jpg* files expire after one month. The browser would then save any *.jpg* files, and not try to reload them until a month after the first time they were downloaded.

Choosing how long to allow files to be cached depends on the types of the files, and how frequently you update those file types on your site. For example, you probably don't change image files on your site often, so it would be safe to allow them to be cached for a long time. If you do need to change an image file, such as changing to a new version of the site logo, you could simply give the replacement image a different file-name, so the browser would be forced to download it.

If you change your stylesheets very frequently, you may want to give them an expiration of one day. That would allow the user the benefit of not having those files redownloaded as he browses the site, but changes would show up for the user within 24 hours after you make them.

Keep in mind that the browser's cache is likely limited in size, so if a user visits a lot of websites, not all assets with long expiration times will actually be stored for that long. This is especially an issue on older mobile devices, which have very limited caches. But even with minimal cache storage, files will be kept in the cache during the user's current visit to the site, decreasing the load times of every page except the first one visited.

Generally, static resources should have an expiration of at least a week, and longer if possible. The maximum allowed is one year. Only assets that change many times a day, such as the front page of a news web-site, should be set with no caching at all. Even allowing a few hours of browser caching on frequently changing resources can decrease the load times of a website.

JavaScript

If you aren't familiar with JavaScript, you need to understand a bit about how it works. The first sections here, "What JavaScript Does" and "How It Works," give a little background. If you're already familiar with JavaScript, feel free to skip to the following section, "Blocking JavaScript."

WHAT JAVASCRIPT DOES

You already know that your website is built in layers, starting with HTML for the content, and then a second layer, CSS, for presentation.

The third layer is JavaScript, which is for interaction, or behavior. It's an optional layer—you can create a perfectly good website without any JavaScript at all, as long as you are only building something for users to read and look at, and perhaps have only basic interactions with.

Some of the common things that JavaScript is used for are validating form field entries, allowing the page to load new content without reloading the whole page, and the animation of page elements.

JavaScript is a client-side programming language. That means that all the JavaScript code has to be loaded by the browser (the client), and the browser does all the work of making things happen. This is in contrast to a server-side language like PHP, which does things to the page on the server before it is even sent to the browser.

HOW JAVASCRIPT WORKS

JavaScript can be included in either your HTML page, or as a separate file with the *.js* extension (linked from a `<script>` element in either the `<head>` or the `<body>`).

After the browser loads an HTML document, it starts at the very top of the `<head>` and loads/renders/executes each element as it encounters it. So, if the first element in the `<head>` is a link to a CSS file, it loads the file before moving on to the next element.

When the browser encounters JavaScript—either a link or an inline script—it loads and then executes the script before moving on to the next element.

So, if you have scripts in your <head>—either inline or links to separate JavaScript files—the browser will execute these scripts before it even gets to the <body>, and before it starts putting content on the screen! That means your users will be looking at a blank screen while the scripts run.

However, that doesn't mean that when this JavaScript executes, it's actually making anything happen.

Most JavaScript is triggered by an *event*. For example, you might see onclick—that means that whatever that bit of JavaScript does, it's not going to happen until the user clicks on a specified element. onload means that the JavaScript does its thing when the page is done loading. Another example is having a script that validates form fields when the user clicks the submit button.

Much of the JavaScript in a web page is simply getting everything set up for something that will happen later, via an event like onclick.

Unfortunately, these scripts can cause a lot of problems, because depending on *where* on your page you add or link to JavaScript, it can block the rendering of the page, slowing it down considerably.

Additionally, the way that browsers work means that the browser can't be rendering the page *and* executing a script at the same time. So although a browser can kind of do more than one thing at once (it's complicated...), if it encounters a script, it has to stop any rendering while it's executing the script.

BLOCKING JAVASCRIPT

JavaScript that blocks the loading of page is sometimes called *blocking JavaScript*.

Because the browser has to run the JavaScript as it encounters it, the browser may be forced to run all the JavaScript before it renders the HTML and CSS, even if doesn't need most of the JavaScript until after the page has finished loading.

If you aren't sure whether any of your JavaScript is blocking rendering, try Google's PageSpeed Insights (*http://developers.google.com/speed/pagespeed/insights/*), which will tell you if your site has any blocking elements. See Figure 11-5 for an example.

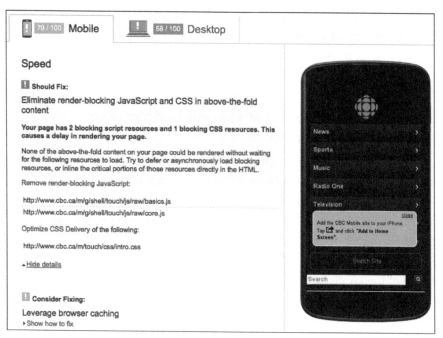

Figure 11-5. PageSpeed Insights will tell if you if any of your JavaScript is blocking the rendering of the page.

To keep your JavaScript from blocking the rendering of the page, you should make sure that as the browser loads and renders the page, it's only loading the JavaScript that's necessary to display what the user will first see on the page. All other JavaScript should be loaded after the page is rendered.

Load above-the-fold code first

If JavaScript is needed to display the section of the page that is "above the fold" (i.e., visible on the screen before the user scrolls down), that script should be loaded right away, as the page is loading.

Other JavaScript can be deferred, as we will address in the next section. This would include any scripts that are only needed after the page loads (such as for onclick events) or scripts that apply to content that's far down the page.

Think carefully about whether each script is actually needed right away, and whether deferring it is an option.

With responsive sites, you may have JavaScript polyfills or feature tests that make your site work on older browsers (i.e., making media queries work in older versions of IE). These scripts need to be in the <head> because they're necessary to render the pages in those browsers.

Inline scripts

If you have small scripts, they can be included inline in your HTML, so that the browser will not have to load additional resources.

The trade-off here is the lack of caching. If you include the script inline, it will need to be loaded every time the page is loaded. So this might not be a good idea for large scripts, or for scripts that are needed on every page of your site, but if you have something special just on the front page of your site that needs JavaScript, including the script inline may be a good idea:

```
<head>
    <script type="text/javascript">
        . . .
    </script>
    . . .
</head>
```

If your site only has a little bit of JavaScript, it's generally best to include it inline instead of adding a file that needs to be downloaded.

Delay loading

For all the other scripts that the page won't need until later, you can delay loading until after the page is rendered by moving them to the end of the page, right before the </body> tag.

These scripts will no longer be blocking the page rendering. Only after the last HTML on the page is rendered will these scripts start to load and then execute.

Defer execution

Something a little trickier is using the defer attribute on your <script> element. If you use this on a JavaScript link in your <head>, the browser will still load the file when it first encounters it, but will defer executing the file until after the page is rendered.

This is a Boolean attribute, which means if the attribute defer is present it's turned on, and if the attribute is not present, it's turned off:

```
<script type="text/javascript" defer>
    ...
</script>
```

This will work in all current browsers except Opera Mini. See "Can I use defer attribute for external scripts?" (*http://caniuse.com/script-defer*) for more details.

Note that this only works on external scripts (links to JavaScript files), not on inline code.

Generally, you're better off just moving your JavaScript to the end of the HTML document. There's no point in having the JavaScript load before the page is rendered if you aren't planning to have it execute until after the page is rendered.

Asynchronous loading

Something new in HTML5 is the async (asynchronous) attribute.

When you add this as an attribute to your <script> element, the browser will go ahead and start loading the JavaScript file when it first encounters it in the <head> or <body>, but the difference is that the browser will *not* put all the other loading and rendering on hold while it waits for that particular script to load and execute.

Instead, it will load the script at the same time it is loading other resources (if appropriate), and then will execute it at the first chance it gets (i.e., when it's done loading).

Note that this only works on external scripts (links to JavaScript files), not on inline code.

This is also a Boolean attribute, so if the attribute async is present it's turned on, and if the attribute is not present, it's turned off:

```
<script async src="example.js">
    ...
</script>
```

This is supported in the most recent versions of all browsers except Opera Mini.

Generally, if you are putting a script in the <head> because it's needed to render the page, you should consider including the async attribute, with one exception: don't use async if you have multiple scripts that need to execute in a particular order, such as if one is dependent on another. Each one will render as soon as it's loaded, but they may not *finish* loading in the same order as you placed them in the <head>, and therefore they may not execute in that order.

One scenario where you would particularly want to use async is when you're loading JavaScript files from a third-party source (such as when you have embedded content like a map or ads). That way, if there is an issue with loading files from the other website, it won't keep everything else on your site from loading.

Loading only necessary code on each page

Additionally, you should make sure you're not having every page load all the JavaScript for the site if it's not needed on that page.

This is pretty common—the <head> will link to all the script files used on the site, even if certain ones are only used on the front page, or in particular sections of the site like ecommerce pages.

Although caching means that the script files won't be loaded over and over, the first page the user visits on the site will be much slower because *all* the script files will have to be downloaded.

Using HTML/CSS instead of JavaScript

Something that you might not be aware of: with HTML5 and CSS3, you can do a lot of things with plain HTML/CSS that you used to need JavaScript to do.

For example, if you have a form with a date field, you used to need JavaScript to create a little pop-up calendar where the user can pick a date. In HTML5, there's a new date input type that automatically creates a calendar based on browser default styles, without the need for any JavaScript (although it's not supported in all browsers yet).

You can also use CSS to do things like make an image change to a different image when you hover over it.

In most cases, using HTML or CSS instead of JavaScript will help your performance. It can save loading a lot of code—creating and styling a calendar pop up is pretty involved, but if the browser already knows how to make the calendar, you only need <input type="date">.

However, HTML and CSS are not always a better choice. For example, you can do some pretty detailed animations using purely CSS— but sometimes the same effect can be created in JavaScript with less impact on performance. You need to look at each situation individually to decide the best approach.

And sometimes, using JavaScript for some fancy effect might be not worth the performance trade-off at all. Remember that performance is part of your design, too.

JAVASCRIPT LIBRARIES

Using JavaScript libraries or frameworks can be another cause of bloat on your site.

A *JavaScript library* is a collection of prewritten JavaScript that makes it easy to write scripts for your website. Basically, it sets up a bunch of common functions that you can use on your site, so you only have to write a single line of JavaScript, rather than having to write all the JavaScript from scratch.

There are many different JavaScript libraries, with the best known being JQuery (*http://jquery.com*). A *JavaScript framework* is similar to a library, only with more capabilities.

The problem with adding a JavaScript library to your website is that you may only be using a small part of its functionality—but you're stuck with all the other code in the library that you don't need.

If you're using a JavaScript library on your website, look at whether you really need a whole library. You can now find a lot of micro-libraries or micro-frameworks, which are much smaller (generally 5 KB and under) and only contain the code to do one particular task. Visit the Microjs (*http://microjs.com*) site, which has collected a list of hundreds of them, and allows you to search for exactly what you need.

Another option, of course, is to just write the JavaScript you need, instead of relying on someone else's prewritten code.

CSS

As mentioned earlier, the first step with CSS is to minimize the amount of CSS you need. Use straightforward code and don't repeat things unnecessarily.

CSS can also block rendering of the page. The browser will wait until all the CSS files are loaded before it starts rendering the page. It needs the CSS to know how and where to render each element.

One thing that you can do to speed up the loading of stylesheets is to use `<link>`, which will allow stylesheets to load at the same time, rather than `@import`, which will make them load sequentially.

Another thing you can do is delay the loading of CSS that isn't needed for the initial page load (above the fold) by moving it to the end of the page, right before the `</body>` tag, just as you can do with JavaScript.

And if you have a lot of style rules that are only applicable to certain sections of the site, put those styles in a separate stylesheet that is only loaded on those pages.

CSS FRAMEWORKS

Using a CSS framework can cause a similar problem to using JavaScript libraries—you end up with a lot of code that you don't actually need. Frameworks take into account all the possible things that a site might need to do, and they include code for all of that. As such, they're far more complex than is needed for most websites that use them.

If you use a framework, such as Bootstrap or Foundation, to build your site, be aware that this is an issue.

The CSS in frameworks is generally easy to follow, so you should be able to go through and pull out broad sections of CSS that you know you won't be using.

For example, if your website doesn't contain any data tables, you can remove all the CSS referring to tables. Of course, you can always add this CSS back in later if you decide to add tables to your site.

You can save some more code, although with a bit more of a time investment, by going through and removing any specific classes you aren't using on the site.

Additionally, make sure you aren't duplicating CSS rules. The framework will provide values for pretty much everything. If you need to change something, such as the **font-size** for <h1>, don't just add that CSS on the end. Instead, find the <h1> in the framework stylesheets and replace the value. Adding a separate declaration at the end not only adds unnecessary code, but it also can create confusion for developers who are trying to edit the stylesheet later.

Finally, although frameworks can come in very handy if you need to get a site up quickly, or if you need to create a website using staff that aren't experienced developers (e.g., for nonprofits, small businesses, or hobby projects), you're never going to get a site that's as lean as one that is created from scratch.

Hosting

Where you host your website can certainly affect the loading time of your site.

If you only spend a few dollars a month for budget hosting on a shared server, your site is likely to be slower than if you are paying big bucks for a dedicated server and a better data connection. But more expensive doesn't always mean better. Shop around, and look at customer satisfaction ratings for the various hosting companies.

Additionally, if your hosting plan has a bandwidth limit, the provider may throttle the speed of your site after you pass the limit (or disable your site entirely).

CONTENT DELIVERY NETWORKS (CDN)

You can use a *content delivery network* (CDN) as part of your web hosting solution. When using a CDN, instead of having all of your website files hosted on one web server, copies are hosted on servers at data centers in various geographic locations. When content is requested from your website, the requests are routed to the most optimal servers, based on physical location, current web traffic patterns, and so on.

This can increase the performance of any site, although it is most particularly useful for live, streaming content, or for sites with a high volume of traffic.

A site may choose to host only part of its content on a CDN. For example, a high-traffic ecommerce site may host all of its images on a CDN, because the site is very image-heavy, but host the rest of its content on regular hosting.

You can purchase CDN service either as an add-on from your web host, or from a separate company, typically an Internet service provider (ISP). Prices can start as low as $10/month for very small websites, up to thousands of dollars each month for very large sites.

CONTENT MANAGEMENT SYSTEM

Your content management system (CMS) might also be slowing down your site. This is more of an issue with enterprise CMSs than with basic CMSs like WordPress or Drupal.

Unlike just sending a plain HTML page when requested, a lot more has to happen for a CMS to send a requested page to a browser. Your entire website is contained in a database. A bunch of queries will run to piece together all the separate elements of the page on the fly—navigation, content, plug-ins.

Ideally it will happen very quickly, but a lot of things can go wrong and add delay.

Studies have shown definite performance differences among CMSs, so you should research performance when choosing a CMS.

If you already have a CMS, check all the settings to make sure you've done everything you can to improve performance.

Always make sure you have the most recent version of your CMS and any plug-ins—outdated software is likely to run slower, and may cause conflicts that add delay.

Conditionally Loading Content

You know that you need to make the same content available to all users, no matter what devices they're using. But that doesn't mean all the content needs to be available on the same page at the same time.

For example, you may have supplemental content that in a wide-screen view would easily fit in a sidebar. However, on the narrow-screen view, you don't want to take up a big chunk of screen space displaying the content—but you still want to give the user the option to view it.

That's where *conditional loading* comes in. This technique uses JavaScript to query the width of the browser window, similar to a CSS media query, and then only run a function to display the content if the screen is a minimum size.

> **[NOTE]**
>
> It's acceptable for users to see different content depending on the size of their screen, as long as they can access the content in another way—in this case, the small-screen users just need to click a link to see the headlines.

Jeremy Keith described this technique in "Conditional Loading for Responsive Designs" (*http://24ways.org/2011/conditional-loading-for-responsive-designs/*) on 24 Ways.

Using the example in Keith's article, let's say you want to provide links to current Google News stories about your topic, which is cats.

On the small screen, you don't want to include all the news stories, so you can start with a simple link to the Google News search results for your topic:

```
<div id="newsresults">
    <a href="http://www.google.com/
    search?q=cats&tbm=nws">Search Google News for Cats
    </a>
</div>
```

You would then add a JavaScript function at the end of the page that would replace the contents of that **<div>** with the Google Search results (check out Keith's article if you want to see the code to do that), but only if the page is wide enough:

```
<script>
if (document.documentElement.clientWidth > 640) {
    searchNews('cats');
}
</script>
```

If the viewport is wider than 640 pixels, the searchNews function will run and will change the newsresults <div> to display totally different HTML, with titles, links, and descriptions for several news articles, as you see in Figure 11-6.

Figure 11-6. Example of conditional loading.

One thing you need to keep in mind is that this only works if the browser can run JavaScript. But that's not a huge deal, because those users who don't have JavaScript will just get the default (small-screen) content—i.e., the link instead of the list of stories. They won't actually be missing anything.

Another thing to be aware of is that unlike CSS, which will continually re-render the page if conditions change, your JavaScript function will only run once. So if the width of the viewport changes, such as if the device is turned from portrait to landscape view, this part of the layout will not adapt to fit the new viewport size, in the way that CSS would via media queries.

And of course, using this functionality means that the small-screen users are loading a bunch of JavaScript that they don't need. But if that saves them from loading a larger amount of content that doesn't need to be on the page, it may be a good trade-off.

Reflows and Repaints

Once the browser is totally done rendering the page, there's still more that can happen.

Sometimes the visual appearance of an element will change after the page is loaded. A simple example is when the color of a link changes on hover. When the browser needs to make a change like this, it's called a *repaint*.

Other times, the layout of the page will change. For example, when the user changes the size of the browser window (or rotates the device from portrait to landscape), flexible elements will change size, and their contents, like text, will move around to accommodate the change. A layout change is called a *reflow*.

When we talk about "performance" in the context of responsive design or mobile websites, we're generally referring to the amount of time that it takes the page to load. But changes to the appearance of the page after it's loaded can also go slowly or quickly, depending on how the code is written.

These examples are pretty simple, and the user will likely feel like the changes happened immediately. But there are many other things that cause repaints and reflows, such as when you have complicated CSS animations on the page, or when you are manipulating the page with JavaScript, and there may be a noticeable delay before such changes are completed.

This isn't specific to responsive websites, and it's fairly technical in nature and beyond the scope of this book. But in the context of designing for mobile devices, you need to be aware that mobile devices tend to have less processing power than desktop computers, so repaints and reflows may be significantly slower and can cause issues that you didn't encounter while developing the site on your desktop computer.

To learn more about this topic, check out Nicole Sullivan's blog post, "Reflows & Repaints: CSS Performance Making Your JavaScript Slow?" (*http://www.stubbornella.org/content/2009/03/27/reflows-repaints-css-performance-making-your-javascript-slow/*).

RESS

RESS stands for *responsive design + server-side components*, and it's a bit controversial. This is the idea that you can make a site that uses responsive design, but also uses server-side solutions to only send the code and files that are needed by any particular device.

So, although you only have one set of code for a site, and that code will allow the site to respond to all viewport sizes, certain parts of the site may be implemented differently depending on the device used to view it. Luke Wroblewski describes RESS in detail in his 2011 article, "RESS: Responsive Design + Server-Side Components" (*http://www.lukew.com/ff/entry.asp?1392*).

To understand how this might work, imagine a responsive site that has a drop-down navigation on small screens, and a horizontal nav on wide screens. The HTML is the same for both, but media queries allow you to apply different CSS depending on screen size, to make it look different on the screen.

With RESS, the server would check whether the device is mobile or not, and send a different snippet of HTML and/or CSS for the navigation to mobile and nonmobile devices. So, each device would only get the code that it needs, compared to responsive design, where every device has to download all the code, whether it's needed or not.

RESS requires using backend programming (such as PHP), not just HTML/CSS/JavaScript, so it's more difficult than basic responsive design.

Besides detecting whether or not a mobile device is requesting the page, a server can also detect features, and send different code based on that. You can also do feature detection with JavaScript using Modernizr (*http://modernizr.com*).

EXAMPLE OF RESS

The University of Notre Dame website uses RESS, in addition to responsive design, to serve different content to desktop and mobile users.

The desktop version of the site has each of the main sections all on one page—About, Academics, Admissions, and so on. You can see on the left of Figure 11-7 the top of the page for the desktop site, with the Admissions section just below the main section. If you resize your desktop browser to 320 pixels and load the site, as in the center image, you still get all that content, although media queries have rearranged everything into one column. The image on the right shows what you get when the site is loaded on a smartphone—that's all of it.

Figure 11-7. Mobile phones are served an entirely different version of the University of Notre Dame's website.

On the mobile phone, you still get access to the main sections, such as Admissions, but now each is on a separate page instead of further down the main page. And you don't have content parity, because much of the desktop site is missing on the smartphone version.

I personally don't like sites where all the content is on one page and accessed by anchor links, making it seem like there are separate pages when there really aren't. It's easy to get lost on the page, and if you want to share particular content, you can't simply copy the URL from the address bar of your browser, because it's the URL of the home page. (This page doesn't even use real anchor links, which would give you an add-on at the end of the URL that would allow you to link to a particular section of the page, such as *#admissions*.)

I'm glad they aren't giving all that content on one page to mobile users, because it would be impossible to navigate through the page on a small screen. But I don't think they need to give desktop and laptop users all that content on one page either. Not only is it confusing, but it means a heavy page weight, and not everyone with a laptop has a fast connection—especially students who are toting their laptops around campus and may or may not be getting a good WiFi signal.

Summary

Website performance needs to be thought of as part of a website's design, because it has a big effect on the site's user experience. You'll do a better job of optimizing performance if you are thinking of it from the start of a project, rather than trying to fix performance issues at the end.

There are many tools you can use to measure performance, which will show you specifically what is slowing down your site and tell you what you need to fix.

To start off, write good code—HTML, CSS, and JavaScript. Your code should be straightforward and not repetitive. You can use minification to decrease the size of your files, removing extra unnecessary space.

One of the most effective ways to improve the performance of your website is to minimize the number of HTTP requests that are made to the server. You can do this by combining CSS, JavaScript, or image files. Third-party code may also be making excessive numbers of HTTP requests, so double-check any plug-ins or other code you've added to your site.

Looking at server settings, start by setting up your site in a way that avoids unnecessary redirects. You can also check your server settings to make sure you're compressing files and allowing for browser caching.

JavaScript can have an impact on your site's performance, especially if your JavaScript is blocking site loading. You can fix blocking issues by inlining scripts, or delaying loading or execution of JavaScript.

Make sure to only load the JavaScript and CSS you need on any particular page, and replace scripts with HTML/CSS where possible.

Your hosting can also affect performance. Make sure the company and plan you choose for your hosting has a good reputation for performance. You can use content delivery networks to speed up your site, and make sure your content management system isn't slowing it down.

Conditionally loading content can help with performance, as can using RESS (responsive design + server-side components).

Good performance comes from putting a lot of thought into how your site is put together.

[*Index*]

Symbols

<!-- --> (angle bracket, exclamation), enclosing HTML comments, 60, 114

{ } (curly braces)
  enclosing CSS declarations, 64
  enclosing CSS for media queries, 107

( ) (parentheses), enclosing media query expressions, 107

% (percent), unit of measurement, 83

; (semicolon), separating CSS declarations, 64

/* */ (slash, asterisk), enclosing CSS comments, 81

A

abandoned navigation, 331–333
absolute positioning, CSS, 93–95
absolute units of measurement, 82
Accessibility Handbook (Cunningham), 245
accessibility (universal design), 244–251
  audio issues, 249
  cognitive issues, 251
  input methods
    keyboard-only navigation, 250
    speech recognition software, 250
  visual issues
    color blindness, 248–249
    color contrast, 246–248
    screen readers, 51–52, 245–246, 258
    text size, 246
  WCAG (Web Content Accessibility Guidelines), 247
adaptive content, 30–33

Adaptive Images polyfill, 172–173
Adobe Dreamweaver, 209
Adobe Edge Reflow, 208–209
Adobe InDesign, 207–208
Adobe Photoshop, 207
alignment of images, 166–168
alt attribute, <img> element, 138, 140–144
and operator (in media query), 106
Android phones. *See also* mobile devices
  aspect ratios, 112
  browsers for, 256–257
  operating systems for, 256–257
  screen size for, 242
  SVG images, 147
angle bracket, exclamation (<!-- -->), enclosing HTML comments, 60, 114
animated graphics, 251
<article> element, 53
<aside> element, 53, 55
aspect-ratio media feature, 112
assistive technology. *See also* accessibility
  screen readers, 51–52, 245–246, 258
  speech recognition software, 250
  testing, 258
async attribute, <script> element, 370–371
attributes. *See* specific attributes
audio, accessibility of, 249
auditing content, 24

B

background-image property, CSS, 138, 164–168
background-position property, CSS, 166
Ball, David, 246

classes, 50
  avoiding, 357–358
  CSS styles for, 64–65, 75, 80
clear property, CSS, 96–98
clients
  deliverables for, 215–217
  expectations of, 215
  presentations to, 217–218
  selling responsive design
    to, 211–215
CMS (content management
    system), 375
cm, unit of measurement, 83
code. *See also* CSS; HTML;
    JavaScript
  compressing, 363–364
  concatenating, 360
  minifying, 358–359
  simplifying, 357–358
  third-party code,
    minimizing, 361–362
cognitive disabilities, 251
color blindness, 248–249
color contrast, 246–248
Color Contrast Checker tool, 247
Color Contrast Check tool, 247
color-index media feature, 113
color keyword media feature, 113
columns, designing with, 121–122,
    124–130
Command-+ keystroke, 275
comments
  in CSS, 81
  in HTML, 60
Communicating Design: Developing
    Web Site Documentation
    for Design and Planning,
    Second Edition
    (Brown), 184
compression
  of code files, 363–364
  of images, 150–151
concatenating code files, 360
conditional comments, HTML, 60,
    114–115
conditionally loading content,
    376–377
contact information for this
    book, xiii
content
  adaptive, 30–33
  auditing, 24

conditionally loading, 376–377
headings for, 26–27
hierarchy of, 190
internationalization of, 43
maintaining, 29–30
managing, 21–24
metadata for, 32–33
outline for, 186–187
plain language for, 27–28
reducing, 22–23
reflows and repaints of, 377–378
separating from presentation,
    59–60
strategy for, 19–21
structuring, 24–27, 50–58,
    185–191
timeless, 29–30
Content Delivery Network
    (CDN), 374–375
content governance, 21, 29–30
content images, 137–138, 153–164
content management system
    (CMS), 375
content marketing, 21
content parity, 28–29
Content Strategy for Mobile
    (McGrane), 20
Content Strategy for the Web,
    Second Edition (Halvorson;
    Rach), 20
cost, 214–215
Coyier, Chris, bookmarklet for testing
    line length, 285
Cross Browser Testing tool, 258
CSS2, 11, 104, 108, 289
CSS3, 66, 100
  browser prefixes, 69–71
  embedding fonts, 266
  media queries, 11–12, 104
  performance improvements
    using, 371
  properties, 88, 288–289
CSS (Cascading Style Sheets), 64–65
  blocking, 373
  box model, 82–90
    border property, 87–88
    box-sizing property, 88–90
    height property, 84–85
    margin property, 85–87
    padding property, 85–87
    positioning elements, 95–96

src attribute, 138, 155
srcset attribute, 169
!important rule, 74
@import rule, 72, 110
InDesign, 207–208
information architecture
    (IA), 185. *See also* content:
    structuring
inherited style rules, 75, 78
initial-scale attribute, viewport, 49
inline elements, 90–91
inline scripts, JavaScript, 369
inline styles, 72–73, 75
input methods
    accessibility issues regarding, 250
    touch screens. *See* touch screens
Instapaper service, 31
internationalization, 43
Internationalization Techniques:
    Authoring HTML & CSS
    (W3C), 43
Internet connection, 349–350
Introduction to HTML (Mozilla
    Developer Network), 38
in, unit of measurement, 83
inverted pyramid technique, 25–26
iPad. *See also* mobile devices
    browsers for, 256–257
    history of, 11, 232
    operating systems for, 256–257
    Paper app, 191
    screen size for, 242
iPhone, 231. *See also* mobile devices
    aspect ratios, 112
    browsers for, 256–257
    history of, 8, 10, 235
    operating systems for, 256–257
    resolution, 148–149, 272

J

Jankord, Brett (author)
    Style Guide Boilerplate, 206
JavaScript, 366–368
    asynchronous loading of,
        370–371
    blocking, 367–372
    compressing, 363–364
    concatenating files, 360
    deferring execution of, 369–370
    delaying loading of, 369

events
    hover events, 236–237
    onclick events, 237, 367
    onload events, 355
    touch events, 236–237
    execution of, 354–355
    flyout navigation using, 327
    HTML and CSS as alternative
        to, 371–372
    inline scripts, 369
    libraries and frameworks, 372
    minifying, 358–359
    select menu navigation
        using, 325
    toggle push navigation
        using, 318–321
Jehl, Scott (developer)
    Picturefill polyfill, 171
jPanelMenu plug-in, 327
JPEG files, 145
jQuery library, 372
jQuery Responsive Menu
    Plugin, 325
Just Ask: Integrating Accessibility
    Throughout Design
    (Henry), 245

K

Kadlec, Tim, 349
Keith, Jeremy, 376
Kellum, Scott, 149
keyboard-only navigation, 250
Krantz, Peter (developer)
    Fangs Screen Reader
        Emulator, 245

L

language, plain, 27–28
laptop computers, 234
    aspect ratios, 112
    browsers for, 257
    operating systems for, 257
    screen size for, 242
latency, 349–350
layout, 191–194
    prototypes for, 194–201
    sketches for, 191–192
    wireframes for, 195
left navigation, 311
libraries, JavaScript, 372
linear design, 190

line-height property, CSS, 281–283
line length, 283–289
<link> element, 72, 108–109
liquid layout, 8, 207–208
literacy, 27
LiveReload tool, 359
logos, 302–303

M

Marcotte, Ethan, ix, 14, 164
margin property, CSS, 85–87
margins, 85–87, 285–288, 291
max-height property, CSS, 318–319
maximum-scale attribute,
    viewport, 50
max-width property, CSS, 131,
    159–163, 179
McGrane, Karen (author)
    Content Strategy for Mobile, 20
m-dot websites, 9, 14, 15
measurements, 82–90
    for borders, 87–88
    for box-sizing, 88–90
    for margins and padding, 85–87
    for positioning elements, 95–96
    for text, 276–280
    units of measurement for, 82–84
media attribute, <style> element, 109
media features, querying, 110–113
@media rule, 105
media queries, 11–13, 103–105
    for aspect ratio, 112
    breakpoints for, 116–117,
        123–124, 129–130, 132
    browser support for, 113–116
    changing typefaces using, 292
    for color characteristics of
        screen, 113
    design ranges for, 117–118
    for images, 158–161
    in <link> element, 108–109
    for navigation layout, 298–301
    for orientation of screen, 111
    for resolution of screen, 112
    for screen dimensions, 111
    structure of, 105–108
    in <style> element, 109
    in stylesheet import, 110
    in stylesheets, 104–105
    testing, 115–116
    uses for, 104–105, 110–113

    for viewport dimensions,
        110–111, 117
Media Types (W3C), 106
metadata, 32–33
<meta> element
    charset attribute, 44–45
    viewport attribute, 45–50
        initial-scale attribute, 49
        maximum-scale attribute, 50
        user-scalable attribute, 49–50
        width attribute, 13, 48–49
Meyer, Eric (developer)
    reset stylesheet by, 78
minification of code, 358–359
Minify tool, 360
min- properties, CSS. See specific
    properties
min-width property, CSS, 160–161,
    170–171
Mixture tool, 359
mm, unit of measurement, 83
mobile content strategy, 21. See
    also content: strategy for
Mobile Design Pattern Gallery: UI
    Patterns for iOS, Android
    and More (Neil), 313
mobile devices. See also specific
    devices
    browsers for, 8–9, 256–257
    content parity for, 28–29
    emulators and simulators
        for, 257–258
    ereaders, 233
    feature phones, 231–232
    game consoles, 233
    media queries for, 11–13
    operating systems for, 256–257
    screen size of, 242
    separate website for, 4–5, 9–10
    smartphones, 231–232, 242, 257
    tablets, 232–233
    testing on, 253–254
    touch screens for. See touch
        screens
    which to support, 251–252
mobile first design, 228
mobile-only users, 224–226
mobile-primary users, 226
Mobitest tool, 356
Modernizr tool, 54, 379
monochrome media feature, 113
Moore, Jordan, 340

Respond.js polyfill, 115
responsive design + server-side
        components (RESS),
        378–381
Responsive Design Workflow
        (Hay), 191
responsive images, 168–178
Responsive Images Community
        Group (W3C), 169–171
Responsive.io service, 174
responsive navigation, 295–301
Responsive Patterns website
        (Frost), 312, 318
responsive prototypes, 195–196
responsive web design (RWD), x–xi,
        3–6
    benefits of, 14–17, 211–215
    coding. *See* CSS; HTML;
        JavaScript
    cost of, 214–215
    design elements
        columns, 121–122, 124–130
        content components,
            187–188. *See also* content
        grids, 119–120, 127–129
        images. *See* images
        maximum page width,
            130–131
        navigation. *See* navigation
        performance as, 347–349
        typography. *See* fonts; text
    design process, 118–123
        content hierarchy, 190
        device-agnostic design, 227
        layout, 191–194
        linear design, 190
        mobile first, 193–194, 228
        progressive
            enhancement, 118–119
        prototypes, 194–201
        sketches, 191–192
        small screen first, 123,
            192–193
        style guide for, 204–206
        tools for, 207–211
        visual design, 201–206
        wireframes, 195
    flexible content. *See* flexible units
        of measurement
    history of, ix–x, 14
    media queries. *See* media queries
    partial responsiveness, 228–230

search engine optimization, 17,
        346
    user experience. *See* user
        experience
    when not to use, 214
ReSRC service, 174
RESS (responsive design + server-
        side components), 378–381
retina display. *See* high-density
        screen
role attribute
    <aside> element, 53
    <footer> element, 53
    <header> element, 52
    <nav> element, 52, 313
Rose, Dan, 207
rotation of screen, 243–244
RSS reader, 31
rules. *See* style rules, CSS
Rutter, Richard, 265
RWD. *See* responsive web design
        (RWD)

S

Safari browser. *See also* browsers
    Resize extension, 255
    resolution media feature, 112
    WebKit rendering engine for, 69
Salminen, Viljami (developer)
    MQtest.io website, 115–116
Santa Maria, Jason, 265
Scala, Giovanni (developer)
    Check My Colors tool, 247
scaling. *See* zooming
scan media feature, 113
Schmitt, Christopher (author)
    Designing Web & Mobile
        Graphics: Fundamental
        Concepts for Web and
        Interactive Projects, 151
    HiSRC plug-in, 173–174
screen. *See also* viewport
    aspect ratio of, 112
    color characteristics of, 113
    dimensions of, 111
    high-density, 148–150
    orientation of, 111
    resolution of, 112, 147–148
    rotation of, allowing for, 243–244
    size of, 242
    touch screen. *See* touch screens

Vinh, Khoi (author)
  Ordering Disorder: Grid
      Principles for Web
      Design, 120–121
visual accessibility issues
  color blindness, 248–249
  color contrast, 246–248
  screen readers, 51–52, 245–246,
      258
  text size, 246
visual design, 201–206
  style guide for, 204–206
  style tiles for, 202–204
  tools for, 207–211
Voiceover for OS X, 258

W

W3C (World Wide Web
      Consortium), 39–40
  CSS Validation Service, 255
  Markup Validation Service, 255
  Responsive Images Community
      Group, 169–171
WAI-ARIA (Web Accessibility
      Initiative - Accessible Rich
      Internet Applications),
      51–52. See also role
      attribute
Warren, Samantha (designer)
  Style Tiles, 202
Way, Jeffrey, 78
WCAG (Web Content Accessibility
      Guidelines), 247
Web Accessibility Initiative -
      Accessible Rich Internet
      Applications (WAI-
      ARIA), 51–52. See also role
      attribute
Web Content Accessibility Guidelines
      (WCAG), 247
Web Ink service, 268
WebKit rendering engine, 69
WebPagetest tool, 357
websites
  content of. See content
  design of
    fixed-width design, 7–8
    history of, 6–14
    responsive. See responsive
        web design (RWD)

separate mobile website, 4–5,
      9–10
  goals of, 183–184
  page weight of, 348–349
  rendering process for, 349–355
  user research for, 184–185
Webtype service, 268
What & Why of Usability, 185
whitespace, 289–290
width attribute, viewport, 13, 48–49
width media feature, 110–111, 117
width property, CSS, 84–85,
      130–131, 157–163
Wilson, Drew, 140
wireframes, 195
word-wrap property, CSS, 289
workflow
  content, structuring, 185–191
  goals of website, 183–184
  prototypes, 194–201
  sketches, 191–192
  small screen first, 192–193
  tools for, 207–211
  user research, 184–185
  visual design, 201–206
World Wide Web
      Consortium. See W3C
      (World Wide Web
      Consortium)
Wroblewski, Luke, 242, 329, 379

Y

YSlow tool, 356
YUI Compressor tool, 359–360

Z

zooming, 49–50

Get even more for your money.

Join the O'Reilly Community, and register the O'Reilly books you own. It's free, and you'll get:

- $4.99 ebook upgrade offer
- 40% upgrade offer on O'Reilly print books
- Membership discounts on books and events
- Free lifetime updates to ebooks and videos
- Multiple ebook formats, DRM FREE
- Participation in the O'Reilly community
- Newsletters
- Account management
- 100% Satisfaction Guarantee

Signing up is easy:

1. Go to: oreilly.com/go/register
2. Create an O'Reilly login.
3. Provide your address.
4. Register your books.

Note: English-language books only

To order books online:
oreilly.com/store

For questions about products or an order:
orders@oreilly.com

To sign up to get topic-specific email announcements and/or news about upcoming books, conferences, special offers, and new technologies:
elists@oreilly.com

For technical questions about book content:
booktech@oreilly.com

To submit new book proposals to our editors:
proposals@oreilly.com

O'Reilly books are available in multiple DRM-free ebook formats. For more information:
oreilly.com/ebooks

CPSIA information can be obtained at www.ICGtesting.com
Printed in the USA
BVOW10s1718040315

390333BV00008B/24/P